Personality and Milieu: The Shaping of Social Science Culture

by
Don Martindale

Cap and Gown Press, Inc.
Houston, Texas

Cap and Gown Press, Inc.
Box 58825
Houston, Texas 77258
U.S.A.

Printed in the United States of America

ISBN 0-88105-001-6

Library of Congress Catalog Card Number: 82-72535

CONTENTS

Preface

The theories and methods of social science are cultural products, invented by some, adopted by others. They form developing traditions, transmitted from generation to generation. Such traditions are modified, amplified, and adapted to changing needs and, over time, integrated on the basis of their inner logic. It is often convenient to separate the history of a cultural tradition into two phases: innovation and extension: consolidation and synthesis. Sometimes a given cultural tradition experiences a series of such phases.

While in the long run a scientific tradition, like any cultural tradition, is the product of both innovation and integration, activities which may be carried out by a single individual, talent and genius for both is rarely equally present in the same person. Individuals that one spontaneously describes as theorists are most efficient at response to external pressures on a cultural tradition; they display genius in moving into the unknown, pioneering and colonizing new areas. Individuals that one spontaneously describes as researchers are most efficient at working out the inner logic of a cultural tradition; they display talent in empirically testing theoretical suggestions, deciding whether they can be added to the growing body of validated theory.

Just as the development of a scientific tradition requires both innovators and integrators, theorists and researchers. understanding of it requires examination of the tradition both as (1) a changing development through time, and (2) as an achieved integration of ideas. These two approaches have been described both as historical or diachronic analysis, on the one hand, and as analytical or synchronic analysis on the other. Full understanding of a given tradition requires both types of analysis. The present monograph is an exploration of some of the major factors in the first, the historical or diachronic, type of analysis.

Whenever the origin of a tradition or major changes in its orientation or applications is at issue, personality and milieu or as it is sometimes phrased, character and social structure, are relevant.

Culture cannot invent itself. It is something men invent or learn from others. It can arise in the first place in only one way; individual men invented it in response to their needs. Their needs, in turn, are anchored in part in the natural and social environment, the milieu.

PREFACE

When one man's ideas about and responses to the milieu in which he finds himself are adopted by many others, they may make him their spokesman and leader. This normally occurs because the followers see the ideas and responses of their representative man as a paradigm for their own. Since no two people's experience is quite identical, to some extent some abstraction and generalization must occur, when the ideas and responses of one man supply a model for many. Moreover, since neither personality or milieu guarantee the truth of ideas nor the adequacy of a response, there are pressures from the beginning on an incipient tradition to make it empirically accurate and pragmatically effective. In such manner a tradition that originates as an invention of one man to meet his needs in response to his milieu is transformed into a collective possession, seeming to obey an inner logic of its own.

Whenever one is interested in the dynamics of a tradition, how it arose in the first place and major transformations in it, personality and milieu studies are useful. Such studies often reveal idiosyncratic features of a tradition which otherwise seem quite anomalous. The fact that a tradition is seen as arising to meet special needs at a particular time does not mean that it adequately meets these needs. But whether it did or not may provide insight into why it was accepted in its time and transformed. Moreover, the adaptation of a tradition does not guarantee its truth or logical coherence, but may reveal why it persists despite a lack of logical coherence and empirical adequacy. In the nature of the case, the historical or diachronic analysis of a tradition is incomplete and must be supplemented by a synchronic or systematic analysis in which the tradition is analyzed as a cultural product in terms of the problems it purports to solve and its internal logic. However, synchronic analysis, alone, tends to treat cultural traditions statically, as if they were complete in themselves. Much is lost unless such approach is supplemented by diachronic analysis.

In the present monograph, following an overview of the problem of personality and milieu, some of the more dramatic personalities who dominated sociological culture in America after World War Two are reviewed: Max Weber, who died in 1920, but through translators and disciples was a man whose time had come; Talcott Parsons who epitomized the sociological establishment from the war into the 1970s; C. Wright Mills who epitomized the anti-establishment point of view, coming into his own as a major popular figure in the 1960s and 1970s; Pitirim Sorokin who can best be viewed as the last of the founders of sociology and who epitomized in his person the status of the first school of classical sociology in the post-war period.

In addition to such central figures in post-war American sociology, two persons outside the mainstream, Joseph Roucek and Panos Bardis, are also examined. They illustrate the role of chance in social science careers, and some of the possibilities and limits to what can be accomplished by persons of high ability outside the professional establishment and in response to peripheral concerns of the sociological tradition.

Grateful acknowledgment is made to the Intercontinental Press for permission to reprint the essay, "King of the Hoboes: Portrait of an International Cultural Workman," pp. 222-242.

I

Personality and Milieu
As Dimensions of Diachronic Analysis

Individuality, the uniqueness of a living form, and community, the inclination of living forms to combine, are complementary principles operating throughout the biological world. The only living units lacking, as Lewis Thomas phrases it, a "sense of privacy" permitting them to unite indiscriminately with one another, are nucleated cells detached from their parent organisms and isolated in laboratory dishes. There a yeast cell and a chicken erythrocyte, for example, may fuse and their nuclei divide into strange hybrid offspring. "Naked cells," Thomas observes, "lacking self-respect, do not seem to have any sense of self."[1] Were it not for mechanisms that permit the units of life to maintain themselves against others, all living forms would flow into one another like the nuclear cells in laboratory dishes. It requires little imagination to realize that the monstrous hybrid cells that result would usually have little capacity to survive for long outside the protective environment of the laboratory dish.

It is conceivable that something like uninhibited fusion of living units did occur in the early stages of the evolution of life. Of the endlessly bizarre combinations that occurred, only those able to survive in the natural environment and, at the same time, preserve some autonomy with respect to other living cells survived. At the level of the smallest units of life something equivalent to the principles of individuality and community had to be established for the evolution of more complicated forms of life to appear. We are accustomed in thinking about individuality and community among humans to consider individuality as an innovating principle, community as a conservative one. However, at the level of the lowest living units the opposite is the case: individuality is a conservative principle, securing survival, for a time, of the unit; community is an innovating principle, rearranging and casting up new combinations.

Even microorganisms are so individualized that, under the microscope, they can be easily identified by their particular style of movement. Reproduction by cell division permits the microorganism to clone itself, transmitting its peculiar form of selfness to succeeding generations. Moreover, it is clear that this kind of selfness prepares the ground for a specific otherness relation with other organisms.

Beans possess glycoproteins special to each legume line which give them affinities for particular nitrogen-fixing bacteria which colonize them. Coral polyps of the same genetic line fuse into single polyps when they touch, while resisting fusion with other genetic lines. Fish, like mice, tell each other apart by smell, employing these as convenient street signs to regulate traffic with others. As Thomas, from whom these examples have been taken, sums up the matter:

> The self-marking of invertebrate animals in the sea, who must have perfected the business long before evolution got around to us, was set up in order to permit creatures of one kind to locate others, not for predation but to set up symbiotic households. The anemones who live on the shells of crabs are precisely finicky; so are the crabs. Only a single species of anemone will find its way to only a single species of crab. They sense each other exquisitely, and live together as though made for each other.[2]

The individualizing properties of living units have not lost significance for self-preservation when they make possible exclusive partnerships—the "little snoberies of which nature is pieced together" in Thomas's felicitious phrasing—Symbiotic relationships normally preserve the partners to the relation more effectively than each could manage alone. And one characteristic of the individuality of each is a readiness, even necessity, to enter into an enduring association with the other. Nor does the collectivity disappear because individualizing principles are also operating. Rather, this only means that the community acquires a more differentiated and organized form. And in the evolution of biological forms a dialectic of individuality and community is discernible. Sometimes, as in a colony of coral polyps or ants of a single family line, the division between individuality and community is so unclear that if one views a single polyp or a single ant by itself it seems to be an autonomous individual, but when in the presence of others of the same genetic line its behavior is so transformed, so organized with respect to all others that it behaves for all the world like a cell or tissue of a single complex organism.

Individuality and Community Among Humans

Since the roots of individuality and community are as deep as life itself, it is of interest to examine their manifestation among humans from the point of view of scientists who have worked with subhuman forms.

In his book on the cat, Michael Fox observed that as a solitary animal the cat is free from pressures to belong to the social group and is not forced to be deferential and submissive to superiors. The dog, by contrast, is destined to live in groups and may be forced to reconcile himself to an undesirable position in the hierarchy of the pack. Man, according to Fox, seems to possess a cat-like nature, but is forced to live in social groups like a dog. Therein is a major source of his problems.

A basic cause of mental illness in Man is said to arise from Man's difficulties in achieving a place that satisfies him in the social hierarchies. Frustration and aggression are said to be caused by failure to achieve status. A loss of status is said to be a cause of depression. Insecurity in status has been seen as a cause of anxiety and paranoia, while high status is seen as one source of megalomania. "Only in social groups of dogs, monkeys and men do we see social outcasts (the pariahs of a community) and status rivalry and despots."[3]

For himself, Fox appears to idealize those persons with courage, conviction, and strength to walk alone, like the cat, finding happiness and fulfillment in relatively solitary lives.

> They are not dependent on the views or acceptance of others, and are not swept up in the rat race around them. To be ostracized and branded as radicals, eccentrics, social deviants...does not affect them, since they are not caught up in the mainstream of conformity or bound by the limiting conventions of a structured society.[4]

However, most persons seem unable to endure life for long in isolation without deteriorating pathetically. As if in terror at finding themselves alone they scramble to join the crowd where they behave for all the world like cats trying to accomodate themselves to a dog's life.

The observation that men have difficulty living in society without snarling displays of abrasive individuality and at the same time seem incapable of enduring existence outside society is ancient. Ideological differences appear in the attempts to comprehend this ambivalence. Thomas Hobbes (1588-1679), who was strongly influenced by the advances in the physical and mathematical sciences in the 17th century, developed a materialistic and mechanistic account of human conduct which served as a major ideological foundation for the conservative view that society is essential to curb the consequences of unrestrained individualism.[5]   John Locke (1632-1704), though also somewhat influenced by the mechanistic philosophy of the times, developed an empiricist account of human conduct which served as a major ideological source for the liberal view that society is more important for the cultivation of rather than the curbing of individualism.[6]

In Hobbes' view, human conduct was a product of the environment acting upon the drive for self-preservation which, in turn, was characterized by fear of pain and the desire for power. In a state of nature there is no justice or morality. Egotism, the drive for self-preservation, creates a war of each against all and, hence, life in a state of nature is "solitary, poor, nasty, brutish and short." Fortunately, men while driven by self-preservation are guided by reason which shows that men serve their self-interest better in the long run by yielding some of their autonomy, subordinating themselves to an authority able to control the power aspirations of each in the interests of all.

A recent example of an Hobbesian appraisal of human nature and society is supplied by the anthropologist Colin M. Turnbull in a study of the Ik, who, he claims demonstrate what men are like at the bottom as well as what we all are about to become.[7]

The Ik are a former semi-nomadic people who once hunted in the valleys of northern Uganda until forced, following the establishment of the Kidepo National Park, to settle and take up agriculture, scratching out a meager living on the mountain slopes. From Turnbull's account, a more unfriendly, uncharitable, inhospitable people are hard to imagine. They steal, lie, and misrepresent as a way of life. They mate and propagate without love, associate without civility. They defecate in bathing areas and on each other's doorsteps. They greedily gobble up their food in secret lest someone see them and expect to share it. They turn out their children to fare for themselves, often by the age of three or four. They abandon their ill and old to die. Their children snatch food from the ill and the old. They are moved to laughter only by each other's misfortunes.

Turnbull suggests that the Ik once possessed the qualities conventionally assigned to humanity. However, in the course of adjusting to a changed way of life compounded by drought, all civilized virtues quickly melted away. "The Ik," Turnbull concludes, "clearly show that society itself is not indispensable for man's survival" and "man is not the social animal he has always thought himself to be.... The Ik have successfully abandoned useless appendages...such as family, cooperative sociality, belief, love, hope...for the very good reason that in their context these militated against survival."[8]

It is a shame that an independent report on the Iks with a different set of assumptions about human nature from those of Turnbull is not available. As indicated by his observations in a footnote, Turnbull has a Hobbesian vision of human nature. "The Ik, like the rest of us, are kind and generous and light-hearted and jolly when they can afford to be. I saw the last vestiges of that in the first month or two, and I saw those vestiges replaced almost overnight, it seemed, by the basic survival instincts that lie in all of us."[9] However, some members of the tradition stemming from Locke, notably Hume[10] and Adam Smith,[11] were convinced that the moral sentiments were on the same footing in human nature as the egoistic. It is quite possible that an observer of Lockian persuasion may have seen different things in the Iks or at least have interpreted what they saw differently.

Lewis Thomas was in the Lockian tradition when he took issue with the conclusion of the anthropologist that, in the Iks, he had at last touched base with original human nature in a form that would soon be manifest in the rest of us. To Turnbull's conception of the Ik as natural man, Thomas counterposed the liberal critique of society which is sometimes seen as enchaining and corrupting the noble savage.

"I have a theory," Thomas says, that "the Iks have gone crazy." Finding himself in an unworkable society, "each Ik has become a group, a one-man tribe on its own, a constituency. "And it is this that makes the Iks seem familiar; they are behaving the way groups behave from the committee to the nation." It is, of course, this aspect of humanity that has lagged behind the rest of evolution and this is why the Ik seem so primitive. In his absolute selfishness, his incapacity to give anything away... he is a successful committee. When he stands at the door of his hut shouting insults at his neighbors in a loud harangue, he is city addressing another city... Nations are the most Ik-like of all... They bawl insults from their doorsteps, defecate into whole oceans, snatch all the food, survive by detestation, take joy in the bad luck of others, celebrate the death of others."[12]

As illustrated by Turnbull and Thomas, the Hobbesian and Lockian debate about the relation of the individual to society continues. Both arguments rest upon assumptions about human nature and hence involve a speculative element which the facts may seem to confirm. If one assumes that man is fundamentally selfish, displaying affection and compassion only as learned habits, the Iks seem to confirm it,[13] but if one assumes that affinity for others is at least as basic as selfishness in the repertoire of the individual, as did Locke, Hume, and Adam Smith and as does Thomas, Ik-like behavior is more routinely characteristic of individuals in groups than in individuals when isolated and on their own.

While there is a speculative element in the choice of a Hobbesian or Lockian approach to man and society, it is legitimate to ask which seems to have the greater weight of the evidence on its side. By and large, biological and psychological research favors the Lockian over the Hobbesian approach. In the mammals generally a biologically pre-programmed (instinctive) tendency to defend the young and to a lesser degree, the weak is present. Female moose, bear, elephants, and many other species can be formidable when their young are threatened. Not infrequently females have died protecting their young. In many creatures ranging from musk oxen to babboons the more powerful males protect the young and the weak. It does not require any great stretch of credulity to presume that in man there are at least the dim not completely erased tendencies to protect the young and the weak and there is a residual biological rootedness of his charitable and altruistic behavior.

Observation of experiments on primates other than man are of special value. Since they are man's closest relatives, the primates provide excellent opportunities for exploration of the comparative role of self- and other-orientation if not in man directly, at least in his biological kin. Experiments with the role of touch, particularly between mother and young, demonstrate that its withdrawal has serious consequences. Prolonged withdrawal of an infant, even when it can see its mother, causes increasing distress and eventually collapse in attitudes that can only be described as deep grief. All bodily functions are lowered, a lower rate of growth occurs, and increased susceptibility to disease and permanent brain damage, ultimately death results.

To convince oneself that there is a biologically based response to and need for others, also in man it is necessary only to watch the normal observer of an infant monkey suffering from the shock of prolonged withdrawal from contact with its mother. He instantly sees it as a pathetic figure displaying the effects of an unutterable tragedy, experiencing inconsolable grief. He has the impulse to take it in his arms and reassure it. He may feel a rising rage at the researchers who heartlessly in the name of science inflict such punishment on an innocent creature. He would restore it to its mother if he could. Empathy, it seems, as well as selfishness is a part of man's repertoire.

The lines of everyman's individuality seem most basically laid out in his immunological system. They are manifest in the pheromones, and though few persons can distinguish others reliably by smell, a bloodhound can trace the special route followed by one person wearing shoes from the path of thousands of others for up to two days. Moreover, men appear to be designed or biologically coded to place highest value on individuals even though it may mean disability for the group, or perhaps one should say group business is usually permitted only after the individualities of its constituent members have been asserted and accomodated to one another.

This is most visible when committees are formed. The first order of business, though not on the agenda, consists in the display of self, the tryouts, as if each member were taking part in the casting of the parts they are expected eventually to play. Much time is spent in each committee member's acting out the part of himself, asserting his identity. No person who has spent time in an academic environment is without examples of Thomas's generalization: "Many committees have been appointed in one year and gone on working well into the next decade, with nothing much happening beyond these extended, uninterruptable displays by each member of his special behavioral marks."[14] Quite possibly the omnipresence of such self-displays lies at the bottom of the assumption that egoistic self-interest is the sole primary motivation of the human animal.

There is no question of the frequency of self-display nor is there any question that they are constantly being carried "too far" in the judgment of other members of the social group. Self-display is adjudged as being carried too far when it threatens the existence of the group. And it is noteworthy that most persons stop short of self-display that would be interpreted as strangeness, pecularity, or eccentricity, interfering with the possibility of collective achievement. As a matter of fact, the individuality of any given person turns out not to be constructed of egoistic self-interest alone, but carries within it a self-other ratio.

The old-fashioned human mother with many children was keenly aware that her offspring were different from birth: one might be choleric, easily upset and difficult to console; another might be stoic in the face of discomfort and easily consoled when eventually upset. No matter how hard she tried to treat all her children equally without playing favorites, her behavior toward her children from infancy could be as distinct as if one infant came labeled "hands off," another labeled "touch me." And there is little question that children arise out of infancy already endowed with various ratios of insistent autonomous individualism and sociability.

When he examined enduring, multibonded, interpersonal groupings such as the family, the play group, the neighborhood grouping, Cooley described them as primary groups and visualized them as cradles of human nature.[15] George Herbert Mead was in this tradition when he envisioned civilization as arising by the extension of relations in primary groups to wider circles, ultimately encompassing all mankind.

> This relationship of the individual to the community becomes striking when we get minds that be their advent make the wider society a noticeably different society. Persons of great mind and great character have strikingly changed the communities to which they have responded. We call them leaders, as such, but they are simply carrying to the nth power this change in the community by the individual who makes himself a part of it, who belongs to it. The great characters have been those who, by being what they were in the community, made that community a different one. They have enlarged and enriched the community. Such figures as great religious characters in history have, through their membership, indefinitely increased the possible size of the community itself. Jesus generalized the conception of the community in terms of the family in such a statement as that of the neighbor in the parables. Even the man outside of the community will now take generalized family attitude toward it, and he makes those that are so brought into the relationship with him members of the community to which he belongs, the community of a universal religion.[16]

While Cooley and Mead were not examining the manner in which individual self-interest and community are reconciled in the primary group, it is clear that they must be. Conflicts between men and women have long been visualized as a battle of the sexes and divorce seems to be as old as marriage. Sibling conflicts find one of their ancient folktale epitomys in the story of Cain and Abel. It is to be wondered whether there has ever been a family without its black sheep. Wherever there are in-laws it seems there will also be outlaws. However, despite such evidence of the difficulty of reconciling individuality and community, primary groups have by and large accomplished this successfully enough to be envisioned as nurseries of higher forms of selfhood, on the one hand, and as providing the model for civilization, on the other.

Once the individual finds a niche in his primary groups, the necessity for continuous displays of selfhood declines—though, to be sure, there are families that appear to be fighting all the time. Most of the time in the primary group displays of self are reduced to ritualistic gestures and seem to confirm rather than represent the jockeying for position. In time the primary group may function on the principle of all for each and each for all. Group identity (or morale) becomes almost indistinguishable from self-interest; loyalty to the group operates like a second self. Cooley and Mead seem to have had this in mind when they envisioned the primary group as the model of civilization.

Cooley and Mead were writing in the early days of the twentieth century when a large number of educated men had been raised on farms or in small towns where long-established, multi-bonded groups dominated social life. Cooley did not invent the concept of "secondary" group, though his usage of "primary" group implies it. However, in the instant non-primary groups were designated "secondary," people began to assume, almost unconsciously, that they differed not only in degree, but in kind.

The prototype of the secondary group is the committee. It is typically consciously formed either by its own members or appointed by some outside authority. In contrast to the multi-bonded, multi-purpose long-time primary group woven together by habit and shared experience over time, the committee is typically formed *ad hoc* to deal with some special problem or formed to deal with some special or general issue. When such a committee meets, its first order of business—though not on its agenda—is, as Thomas observed, the self-display of its members. Only after each member has asserted himself to his satisfaction—an activity that may never be satisfactorily completed in as much as it is accompanied by considerable pushing and shoving as identity jostles identity—can the committee settle down to business. Thereupon at least one function of identity-display may become clear, the parameters may have been fixed within the limitations of which the committee must fulfill its mission. These parameters may be such that the committee finds a solution impossible, whereupon its membership reverts to the more basic activity of individual self-display.

With special frequency men in committees accomplish their mission by finding the lowest common denominator in the self-other ratios of the members. Men in committees, as a result, frequently do things that no single member would care to defend if attributed to himself alone. When, however, it is the action of the committee he can defend it on the grounds that as a loyal member of the committee he has no other choice.

Secondary groups, again illustrated by the committee, characteristically fragment responsibility to a point where it no longer adheres to any single member, being reassigned to the committee—a fictitious individual without inconvenient sensibilities of shame and guilt. By contrast primary groups tend to fasten responsibility more tightly to individuals, often making each responsible for the actions of all.

In this conception, secondary groups are not under-developed primary groups, but social formations of a different kind. Responsibility instead of adhering to every member is conveniently reassigned to the committee. And when limited economic liability was legally extended to men undertaking group actions in the name of chartered corporations, an instrument had been created that gave some men unparalleled power both over individuals and primary groups.

When Cooley and Mead were developing their theories of the primary group as the cradle of all higher forms of personality and as the primary hope of humanity, it was still possible to conceive the secondary group as an adventitious development which would, eventually, be adapted to the patterns of the primary group. Neither Cooley nor Mead seems to have asked what would happen if such extensive growth of secondary groups should occur as to result in a reversal of influence: a turnabout making the secondary group the norm of collective life. However, such a reversal has been a major trend in the twentieth century. More and more primary groups appear transformed into committees, bureaucracies, or corporations—in spirit, if not in fact and in law.

When primary groups begin to operate like committees, bureaucracies, and corporations they become the scenes of interminable self-display. Joint responsibility begins to melt away. Their collective achievement declines; they become brittle. In view of the fact that the area of socialization has traditionally been the sphere of the greatest proliferation of primary groups and, in turn, socialization has primarily been the sphere both of cultural transmission and of conservatism, the penetration of the forms of secondary groups tends to carry through a major liquidation of culture.

However, even as the invasion of secondary group practices into the sphere of former primary groups occurs, men seem still to need primary groups. Whenever groups which originate as rational associations are transformed into teams operating on the principle of joint responsibility—all for each and each for all—the older ideal of the primary group reappears. This occurs frequently in wartime among flight and combat groups. It seems to occur—though more rarely—in academic departments. Many times in both amateur and professional sports primary groups arise.

It is clear from this review that it is a mistake to envision individuality and community only as conflicting principles. The highest development of individuality among men is only possible in a condition of society. Yet the more powerful forms of society, secondary groups, rarely make very extensive or effective use of the resource of individuality of their members. And far from being only in a condition of tension with any and all society, any given form of human individuality presupposes a type of society for its realization. In the best instance a relation of mutual enhancement occurs between personality and group; in the worst they are mutually destructive.

The Role of Culture in Personality and Society

Individual, society and culture are all treated conventionally as if they were entities. Conceptions of their nature and relation to one another lie at the bottom of rival theories of human social life. There is, for example, no more basic difference of perspective than that between elementarism and holism. Elementarism is the view that individuals are the primary subjects of social life; holism (which appears in two major forms, social holism and cultural holism) is the view that society or culture is the subject of social or cultural life with laws of their own not reducible to the properties of individuals. To the elementarist society is a purely conceptual entity, the term referring to what people do together; culture refers to the social heritage. To the social or cultural holist, individuals are simply the necessary vehicles through which society or culture manifests itself.

The importance of society (what people do together) and culture (the material and non-material social heritage—that is, the sum of the things shaped by human action and all things learned in the course of interaction with others) to the individual is beyond question. No human individual could conceivably under the best of circumstances survive purely on his own until the age of seven or eight. Moreover, since men are born with, at best, only the broadest scaffolding of biological pre-programming he could not survive without learning from others virtually all of the thousands of things that are necessary to get along with others and survive in nature. In fact, the evidence from man's physiology strongly suggests that the last phases of his biological evolution were presided over by his use of.tools and language—the two great cultural systems central to cultural accumulation. This evidence appears in the fact that the huge recent developments of the fore-brain appear in those areas associated with tool-use and language, also the centers associated with self-conscious, rationality, and logical thinking.

To treat the individual as an entity seems *prima facie* clear enough. The individual tends, at least initially, to be thought of in terms of his biological embodiment: born at a particular time and place, possessing distinctive physical characteristics, displaying a particular medical history and the like. However, if the individual is identified with his body this quickly turns out to be confusing. For most purposes it works fairly well with other persons, but when an individual thinks of himself, his body is visualized merely as one of his possessions and not necessarily even the most important. He usually places much higher value on his feelings, thoughts, and achievements, but such psychological and spiritual properties or activities are also merely something that belongs to him. The real person is usually more thought to be the actor and owner of this body, these spiritual and psychological attributes, and the ultimate author of his accomplishments. Yet this real person is not given directly in experience at all, though there is an inclination to identify it with self-consciousness. And that, too, is a source of trouble for when one searches for the self that is self-conscious, one only arrives at a consciousness of something else. Few persons ever expressed this problem more clearly than David Hume:

> There are some philosophers who imagine we are every moment intimately conscious of what we call our Self.... For my part, when I enter most intimately into what I call *myself*, I always stumble on some particular perception or other of heat or cold, light or shade, love or hatred, pain or pleasure. I never can catch myself at any time without a perception, and never can observe any thing but the perception. When my perceptions are remov'd for any time, as by sound sleep; so long am I sensible of *myself*, and may truly be said not to exist. And were all my perceptions remov'd by death, and cou'd I neither think, nor feel, nor see, nor love, nor hate after the dissolution of my body, I shou'd be entirely annihilated, nor do I conceive

what is farther requisite to make me a perfect non-entity. If any one upon serious and unprejudic'd reflexion, thinks he has a different notion of *himself*, I must confess I can reason no longer with him. All I can allow him is, that he may be in the right as well as I, and that we are essentially different in this particular. He may, perhaps, perceive something simple and continu'd, which he calls *himself;* 'tho' I am certain there is no such principle in me.[*17*]

Immanuel Kant reviewed Hume's argument and concluded that he was right. When one consults the empirical facts of experience, one covers only a stream of sensations.

The consciousness of oneself, according to the determinations of our state is, with all our internal perceptions, empirical only, and always transient. There can be no fixed or permanent self in that stream of internal phenomena.[*18*]

For his own satisfaction, Kant solved the problem of the existence of a real self by postulating it as the noumenal subject of experience lying outside, beyond and prior to experience, but as the ground or prerequisite of experience.

It must be *possible* that the *I think* should accompany all my representations: for otherwise something would be represented within me that could not be thought, in other words, the representation would either be impossible or nothing.[*19*]

In a brilliant chapter on the self in Volume I of his *Principles of Psychology,*[*20*] William James identified Kant's noumenal and empirical self, the transcendental ego and the self as experienced, with the grammatical categories of "I" - the self as subject and "me"- the self as object, the self as known or the empirical ego. He in turn divided the empirical ego into three: the material me which includes the body, the entire, the immediate family and property; the social me the various conceptions of the individual held by those who know him;[*21*] the spiritual me consisting of the person's states of consciousness and psychic attributes and capacities.

James's analysis, in turn, became the foundation for that of George Herbert Mead whose position can be summed up in the following quotations from *Mind, Self, and Society*:

We can distinguish very definitely between the self and the body. The body can be there and can operate in a very intelligent fashion without there being a self involved in the experience. The self has the characteristic that it is an

object to itself, and that characteristic distinguishes it from other objects and from the body...
This characteristic is represented in the word "self," which is reflexive, and indicates that which can be both subject and object. This type of object is essentially different from other objects... The importance of ...'communication' lies in the fact that it provides a form of behavior in which the organism or the individual may become an object to himself....
The self, as that which can be an object to itself, is essentially a social structure, and it arises in social experience.[22]

So, it seems, the individual is the biological individual after all, but the biological individual as transformed in society, particularly by means of the linguistic culture he acquires and uses also with respect to himself. The transcendental ego is a reification, a fiction standing for the continuity of experience as it develops and is transformed in interaction with others and mediated by culture.

The transcendental ego or mind or soul or self if thought of as independent and in some sense prior to the body is an obstacle to scientific analysis. It turns out to be a fiction, though it has foundation in transformations in behavior that occur in culturally mediated social experience. However, if one approaches it practically it quickly proves to have been a convenient fiction, a basis for assigning responsibility in human social exchange, treating individuals as if their experience was unitary through time and permitting them to behave toward themselves as others behave toward them. It is difficult to imagine complex forms of human social interaction arising without this convenient fiction. However, for scientific purposes the equation is best read the other way around. There is an individual and he is conveniently viewed as an entity. He is the primary subject not only in everything attributed to him, but also everything that happens in society and culture. However, he is not a transcendental ego that has a mind and body, but a body as transformed in association with others and as mediated by their shared (particularly linguistic) culture.

Just as there are practical conveniences in treating the transcendental ego (a fiction) as if it were an entity, there are advantages in treating society and culture as if they were entities though they are clearly fictions. Society can only mean the way individuals act together; culture can only refer to the social heritage, the learned patterns of interaction. In treating them as entities distinct from and separate from the individual—reifying them—means strengthening what would otherwise be minor aspects of a fluid process. Collective behavior and learned and transmitted ideas, sentiments, ideals, and ways of doing things are thereby given independent standing apart from the individual. Although they are then envisioned as separate from, prior to, and superior to the individual, in the end society and culture can have no other subject, (like the transcendental ego) other than the individual.

The primary value of holistic views of society and culture are practical, that is, ideological. They strengthen interpersonal patterns of behavior as against the individual and thrust the problem of cultural continuity, the transmission of collective experience, into central focus. And there is even some scientific utility in tentative holistic formulations so long as this is realized to be merely a convenient fiction for isolating a problem. By tentatively viewing society and culture *as if* they are independent entities it is possible to separate the *what* and *how* of interpersonal behavior for special analysis. But in the end only individuals can create and destroy them.

The Synchronic and Diachronic Analysis of Social Theory

Social theory represents contemporary man's attempt to under-- stand himself and his society. It characteristically employs the accumulating culture of science, rather than as in the case of earlier attempts based on theology or philosophy. Social theory can only arise in the activities of individuals either working alone or in groups of one sort or other. Ideas developed and tested by individuals or groups form an accumulating tradition, the culture of social science which is increasingly woven into logically coherent and empirically verified explanations.

One can study the emerging body of social science culture in one of two ways, though, in the long run, they are supplementary: one can examine it analytically or synchronically or historically and diachronically. In the first approach one examines the body of social science materials apart from the individuals who either alone or in concert with others created them, subjecting them to systematic logical and empirical examination. In the second case, one centers attention on the dynamics of how the body of social science notions came into being and how they are being transformed.

Each type of analysis has its special value. Synchronic analysis largely sets aside as irrelevant questions of origins and problems such as: What did the founders have in mind? What were their motivations? To what in their times were they responding? Do the issues they were addressing still exist? It tends to go directly to the questions: Are the arguments logically consistent? Are there holes, gaps, or contradictions in them? Are the empirical assertions valid? Has the evidence been adequately handled? Contemporary forms of theory construction basically attempt to codify synchronic analysis. Diachronic analysis places central importance on questions of origin and development. It sees every individual, social, and cultural development as always beginning somewhere, sometime, and changing as the result of activities of specific individuals. Conditions of a given time and place may account for the acceptance or rejection— quite apart from its truth or falsety—of a theory. Biases in a body of ideas determined by its origins may have a long-time influence on the cultural tradition within which they are evolving.

By and large, elementaristic social theories have had a greater interest in diachronic analyses; holistic social theories in synchronic analyses. However, in the nature of the case they are complementary. Each type of analysis tends to bring into central focus things the other tends to eclipse.

Among the major components of diachronic analysis are the role of personality and milieu. Only individuals create, and the hand of some particular individual is always present at the origin and transformations of a cultural tradition. But the cultural innovations of any given individual, no matter how relevant to problems of his time as he perceives and responds to them, will not constitute the beginning of a cultural tradition unless others take up his formulations or creations and make them their own. Unless the individual makes a record of his achievements, a record that could be interpreted and responded to by others, his cultural innovations will die with him. Cultural history is filled with examples of cultural innovators discovered only after their deaths.

There is, thus, always some value in looking at the cultural heroes or representative men and inquiring into the ratio of personality and milieu that placed them at the center of the cultural traditions of their times. As a matter of fact, there is always a complementary value in examining the problems of personality and milieu at the periphery of the same cultural developments.

Personality and Milieu in Recent American Sociological Culture

From its beginning American social theory has been primarily elementaristic, a property which it retained into the twentieth century until World War Two. Many historical circumstances contributed to this bias: the derivation of large populations from urban areas of Europe where traditions of individualism were strong; the predominant Protestantism of its early religiosity; the experience of immigrants who migrated to the new world because of opportunities to improve their economic and social status. By and large, the experiences of Americans tended to make them skeptical of government and to prefer reliance upon their individual initiative. American individualism carried with it a preference for elementaristic social theory.

In the course of the twentieth century collective experience began to call attention to possible limits of individualism and, in turn, opened the door to holistic social theory. During the Great Depression of the 1930s millions who wanted work could not find it. The various public works programs and initiation of a federal welfare system at this time began to force Americans to rethink the relation of the individual to the state. World War Two ended the depression and provided a unifying national experience. The emergence of the United States from World War Two as the most powerful nation of the world, carried with it a mood of patriotic euphoria. Meanwhile, the cold war and domestic witch-hunting, vigorously promoted by Congressman Richard Nixon, the House Un-American Activities Committee and Senator Joseph McCarthy, suppressed the tendency to restore a more individualistic point of view as is usual after the heightened collectivism of wartime. The times were ripe for new developments in social theory; they were not long in coming.

In the post-war period the traditional preference in America for an elementaristic approach to social life did not disappear, but it was ready to take a new direction.

The early American elementaristic social theorists have primarily been concerned with social psychological problems and with primary group experience. However, after a major depression, the rise of the welfare state, victory in world war, new international concerns, and more collective experience than at any time previously in American history, with problems of large-scale organization, bureaucracy, and comparative culture, a whole new series of concerns began to dominate social theory.

The post-war American milieu was ripe for the rapid rise in interest in the theories of Max Weber. Although Weber had died in 1920 and was known only to a relatively small circle, some members fled to America during the Nazi and war years where they made his ideas known. Weber was rapidly received into American social thought and became popular for the first time. Weber's elementarism made instant connection with the traditional elementarism of American social theory; at the same time Weber was perceived as offering insight into all sorts of problems that American theorists had touched only incidentally: large-scale organization, political sociology, the sociology of religion, the problems of bureaucracy, the rationalizing trends in Western culture, the rise of capitalism. In one of the stereotypes of the post-war period, Weber was a man whose time had come.

Also in the post-war American world, the times were ripe for the emergence of a native form of sociological holism. And it could be expected that there would be theorists who pressed it toward conservative and radical forms. Two individuals who had started their careers as elementarists, Talcott Parsons and C. Wright Mills, both of whom had, in part, founded their careers by translations of Max Weber, came eventually in the 1950s and 1960s to assume the role of representative men of establishment and anti-establishment holism.

Both Parsons and Mills advocated a form of social holism. It is an interesting question as to what role, if any, was played by cultural holism, such as that present in the works of the founder of sociology, August Comte, or in the absolute idealism of Hegel, in the rise of structure-functionalism promoted by Parsons and against which, at the time of his death, Mills was counterposing a radical romanticism.

During the 1930s, Pitirim Sorokin, who had been called to Harvard University to establish a department of sociology, was bringing into synthesis a version of cultural holism he had begun to develop in Russia between the two revolutions of 1905 and 1917. In the early 1920s, Sorokin got into trouble with the Bolsheviks and was exiled to the West, spending six years at the University of Minnesota before being invited, in 1930, to found the Harvard department. During the 1930s he completed his greatest work, the four-volume *Social and Cultural Dynamics,* in which he developed his own system of cultural holism.

In his formation of a department of sociology at Harvard, Sorokin reports the administration at first ''refused to approve the appointment of Talcott Parsons as the department's faculty instructor.''

However, "I did my best to convince Mr. Lowell to change his negative decision to a positive one. After two talks with Lowell I finally obtained his approval of Parsons' appointment."[23] However, during the 1930s Parsons was still an elementarist and in a major book during those years drew heavily on Max Weber.[24] Parsons, thus, was in tune with the dominant elementarism of American sociology, in fact, was playing a role in the reception of Max Weber. And despite Sorokin's role in beginning the formation of a major department of sociology at Harvard and completing his *magnum opus*, he was viewed primarily as a European theorist who merely happened to be completing his work in America.

However, changes were underway. With other Young Turks on the Harvard campus, Parsons was in process, as World War Two looked on the horizon, of making his bid for power on the Harvard campus. This eventually took the form of the formation of a Department of Social Relations which shifted control from the traditional social science departments and their chairmen to the committee. Finding himself without power, Sorokin resigned his chairmanship. In his autobiography he observes:

> So I am not responsible for whatever has happened to the department since, either for its merging with abnormal and social psychology and cultural anthropology to form a "Department of Social Relations," or for the drowning of sociology in an eclectic mass of the odds and ends of these disciplines or for any other change that has occurred in this department since 1942.[25]

Moreover, it seems that at the very time he was displacing Sorokin in power, Parsons was also abandoning his elementarism and adopting a form of sociological holism. In his last book on theory published in 1966, Sorokin traced Parsons's shift from elementarism to holism and prepared a detailed table of similarities between Parsons's theory of social systems and Sorokin's own formulations of socio-cultural holism made many years earlier.[26]

Sorokin was understandably embittered when, in the immediate post-war period, with the rise to popularity of structure-functionalism, he found Parsons, who had recently displaced him in power, heralded as the prophet of the decisive synthesis of sociology — for so structure-functionalism was viewed for a time. Ironically Sorokin had been advocating a form of socio-cultural holism for years and in his *Social and Cultural Dynamics* had achieved a massive synthesis of socio-cultural materials. To Sorokin, Parsons's work was amateurish by comparison with his own. His table of comparisons of the two systems suggested that Parsons had, if not plagiarized, at least pillaged Sorokin's writings for ideas. In the process he had not troubled himself to acknowledge any indebtedness to Sorokin's work.

When Sorokin first compiled a table of comparisons between his own earlier work and Parsons's writings, he sent it to the official sociological journals which refused to publish it. By this time Parsons had taken over the position of executive officer of the American Sociological Association from which position, in association with students and colleagues in strategic positions in the profession, he was able to prevent Sorokin's election to presidency of the society or publishing in the official journal. At the time Sorokin mimeographed his comparisons between the two systems. The normal reaction of persons not precommitted to Parsons at the time to this communication from Sorokin was that Sorokin had beyond question proven that Parsons had, if not plagiarized, at least borrowed ideas wholesale without acknowledgement. However, since the Parsonians seemingly controlled the professional society, no official response to it was forthcoming.

However, Sorokin was never one to permit a career setback to ruin his life—though he was not prepared to forget a setback either, but to remember and answer it in due time. He was soon busy in a newly founded center for research on love and altruism for which unexpected outside help became available. In 1956 he made a stand against those trends in sociology he envisioned as unprogressive.[27] And in 1963 he completed his autobiography in which he undertook to set the record straight. In his autobiography he observed that his 1956 volume, *Fads and Foibles,* had elicited a warm letter of appreciation from C. Wright Mills and that a few years later, in a somewhat simplified form, most of his criticisms had been "reiterated."[28] This suggests that Sorokin had a hand in the transformation of C. Wright Mills into an anti-establishment theorist.

In the 1960s a grass roots movement by the lay membership of the American Sociological Association forced the issuing of a new slate of candidates. Sorokin had once again been passed over by the executive committee of the society. In a fitting gesture the lay membership honored him by electing him to the presidency. The society had insisted on recognizing a man who could perhaps best be described as the last of the pioneers.

These four social theorists, Max Weber, Talcott Parsons, C. Wright Mills, and Pitirim Sorokin, epitomize mainstream sociology in the immediate post-war period: Weber illustrates the thrust in the elementaristic position, where it persists, toward macrosocial issues;

Mills and Parsons epitomized the radical and conservative orient-ations of a newly emerging holism; Sorokin illustrates the ambiguous standing of older and classical forms of cultural holism in the post-war world. The essays on these theorists originally formed the core of a monograph entitled *Prominent Sociologists Since World War II.*[29]

In the course of working up the topic of personality and milieu with respect to representative men of mainstream social science culture in the post-war period, the role of chance in human affairs repeatedly came into view. Some persons are lucky and find themselves in the right place at the right time. To be sure, their personal problems must be sufficiently similar to the problems of many that their personal responses are adopted as the solutions of man. However, this automatically raises the question of the individual who is in the wrong place at the wrong time. Are they embittered by what they experience as frustrating entrapment?

In times of change and expanding opportunities, creative individuals are often delayed in finding themselves and their places, but in times of diminishing opportunities this may not be possible. Furthermore, in 1975 at the time of the publication of *Prominent Sociologists,* it was already clear that a major recession in institutions of higher education was underway and there were strong indications that the recession could well spread to the entire society.

When faced with diminishing opportunities for jobs, graduate students cling to the nest and become more than usually dependent on their professors for access to jobs. When jobs do become available new graduates must take what they can get. Meanwhile, many colleges and universities are tempted to reduce their expenses by hiring new graduates, but letting them go before they are forced to grant them tenure. And while this is occurring at the bottom of the hierarchy of higher education, persons in tenured positions cling to them as if their very lives depend on it. And, of course, as a matter of fact, their livelihoods do.

In a guest editorial of *Newsweek,* Duncan Robertson, who appears to have been a non-tenured teacher of French at the University of California, Santa Cruz, calls for the elimination of the tenure system in higher education in the hope of clearing tenured mediocrities from the halls of higher education to make way for non-tenured persons of ability. His particular targets are professors who entered the ranks of higher education in the 1960s when funds were plentiful, teachers scarce, and administrators hired nearly all candidates and promoted them to tenured positions. Robertson argues:

These people, now in their mid-40's, have populated the senior ranks of the universities for the last ten years; they will be with us for the next twenty, without fail. In the meantime, we have seen an endless succession of budget cuts, and all expansion has stopped. No new positions are being created, whole programs and institutions are going under, yet tenure still protects the tenured—not from political interference, but from economic reality...The teaching profession in the humanities is now "tenured in," as they say—up to 100 per cent. Everybody concedes that this is a disaster. But so far, professors have refused to face the inevitable conclusion, which is that the tenure system itself is long overdue for reappraisal... At the present, difficult time, the professor's "academic freedom" from all job insecurity places an insupportable economic burden on the rest of us. There is a growing army of embittered, unemployable intellectuals in our midst.[30]

Robertson seems unaware of the fact that the 1970s and 1980s are not the first time academic positions were in short supply, and newly minted Ph.D.s were fortunate to obtain jobs. This was also true in the 1930s during the Great Depression. At that time some new Ph.D.s were forced to take undesirable teaching positions, some found work on a year-to-year basis, turning into virtual academic hoboes, some were forced out of the teaching profession. Moreover, Robertson is mistaken in assuming that tenure was sought only to secure academic freedom when he writes as if it originated in the early 1950s as a defensive strategy of heroic academics who resisted McCarthyism. Tenure was always sought primarily in the interest of job security for economic reasons—it was the professional man's seniority. And one may guess that in the instant that Robertson obtains tenure in an institution he considers worthy of his genius, he could well discover that tenure should be reinstituted as a desirable principle.

Despite such caveats, Robertson's statement dramatically calls attention to the accidents which may entrap scholars of high ability in situations remote from the mainstream. While such accidents are particularly onerous in economically stringent times, they are always present. Moreover, it calls attention to the value of personality and milieu studies on persons outside the elite institutions who may be occupied with peripheral areas of their disciplines. Such studies supplement personality and milieu studies of the giants or titans, the representative men of a cultural tradition. It sometimes appears, as illustrated by the studies of Joseph Roucek and Panos Bardis, which are included in the present monograph, that creative individuals outside the mainstream are as interesting as the representative persons.

In correspondence, on one occasion, Joseph Roucek told me that Sorokin had tried to obtain an appointment for him at Harvard University. He reported Sorokin's failure with some bitterness, making it clear that, at the time, he felt slighted by the academic establishment, cheated out of recognition which in terms of his abilities and achievements he deserved. In view of Roucek's publications (he has written thousands of book reviews, hundreds of essays, and authored, edited and contributed to more than 100 books), his editorial connections (he has been book review editor and contributing editor to numerous international journals), and his activities as a teacher and popularizer of the social sciences, an achievement that few members of the elite could match, he was well justified. However, ironically, his isolation from the mainstream of sociological culture may well have been a major factor in his extraordinary entrepreneural activity in working up areas marginal to the main drift of sociological culture of the time. It was certainly a component in Roucek's development of a popular forum for diffusion of his ideas and writings particularly on the problems of minorities from Eastern Europe.

The Rouceks (Joseph and his wife Bozena) developed a series of lecture programs which they offered to service clubs, women's clubs, teacher's institutes, high school, college, and normal school assemblies on world problems. He developed lectures on such topics as "The Balkans, The Cockpit of Europe's Destiny," "Central-Eastern Europe:The Core of World Wars," "Are We One America?","Our Minorities," "The Coming World War III." In a special lecture on "Czechoslovakia, Its Glory, Its Romance, And Its Tragedy," Bozena Roucek appeared in native costume, sang Czechoslovakian folk songs, and demostrated samples of native art and peasant costumes of the Balkans.

Not only did Roucek lecture in all parts of the United States, but under the auspices of Masonic lodges, Rotary clubs, Women's clubs, and similar organizations, he organized lecture and concert tours of Eastern Europe. He won recognition from the heads of a number of Central European governments and was made Knight of the Order of the Star of Romania and Knight of the Crown of Yugoslavia by heads of these governments.

In view of such popular and public recognition outside his professional field, it is hardly surprising that Roucek should have felt insulted to be treated as an eccentric by many members of the sociological elite. However, with typical independence and imagination, he responded by inventing his own international social science honor society, the Delta Tau Kappa, complete with an international set of offices, an official logo, and scrolls of recognition that could be suitably framed by persons receiving them.

Having been denied appropriate recognition by the American sociological establishment, Joseph Roucek transformed himself into a society in his own right. As International President of the International Social Science Honor Society, Delta Tau Kappa, Roucek extended honors to scholars he considers worthy of them. In return for the initiation fee, persons invited to join Delta Tau Kappa receive the scroll of the society with their names inscribed on it and are qualified to purchase and wear its key. A little sunshine is brought to the otherwise drab careers of lonely scholars starved for recognition and they have an item to add to their resumes. To those inclined to accuse Roucek of running a racket, he could well quote Nietzsche: it is more noble to give than to receive honors.[31]

However, Roucek has done much more than bring sunshine to the lives of many scholars of ability who found themselves outside the mainstream. In the name of Delta Tau Kappa he sponsored a number of minor national and international journals, calling them to the attention of scholars invited to become members of his honor society and, incidentally, helping maintain the supply of material to these journals.[32] Moreover, in his own academic work, which increasingly took the form of organizing symposia, he provided publishing outlets for scholars outside the mainstream. Still in 1982, in his eightieth year Roucek was looking forward to the appearance of his latest symposium and searching for publishers for new ones. When a personality-milieu study of Roucek was made, it was entitled "King of the Hoboes: Portrait of an International Cultural workman," and comprises Chapter V herein.

Joseph Roucek was isolated from the mainstream of American sociological culture in the 1930s. During these years he found himself as a semi-itinerant scholar, and had begun to develop the study of eastern European minorities, problems of geo-politics, and neglected areas of the sociology of education. By the time the depression and war were over, Roucek established the symposium as a major instrument of publication and had built a stable of contributors from outside the sociological mainstream. The job market had begun to open up, but by this time Roucek was in his mid-forties, a time when academic mobility is largely over. However, also by this time younger scholars had begun to move in and take over areas he had opened up.

The essay on Panos Bardis, which is printed herein for the first time, was undertaken in the interest of determining the extent to which the phenomena illustrated by Roucek—the achievement of a unique form of personal success outside the mainstream of sociological culture—has been possible since World War Two.

Roucek was born in Czechoslovakia, Bardis in rural Greece. Both were to complete their graduate work and make their way in the United States outside the mainstream. At the time of the study Bardis at the age of 57 had 363 items in his bibliography, not counting hundreds of book reviews. His writings comprised nine books and one novel. In addition he had written twenty songs for the mandolin and a large volume of poetry, only a fraction of which was published. Like Roucek, Bardis has been building a world of his own but in a somewhat different manner from his older contemporary.

Bardis has the habit of writing to persons who interest him for one reason or other, sending on reprints of his writings. If they reply, perhaps sending back reprints of their own or making comments on his writings, Bardis enlists them as regular correspondents. And if they seem sympathetic, sooner or later Bardis sends on reprints of his poems. As a result of such activity, together with editing, book reviewing, and writing essays, books and poems, Bardis has built up a national and international circle of scholars (corresponding with them in their own languages, for Bardis works easily in half a dozen or so). One product of these contacts is Bardis's receipt of invitations to international conferences and symposia on a variety of subjects. He has, in consequence, traveled and lectured in many parts of the civilized world.

In November of 1981, for example, Bardis was invited to participate in an International Conference on the Unity of the Sciences in Seoul, South Korea. During the same period he attended the Global Congress on the World's Religions in Seoul, presenting a paper on "Kant, Christianity, and Marxism." He also addressed the Professors' World Peace Academy Congress of Seoul with "Comments on the History of Peace," and was invited to give a lecture on "Philosophy in East and West, the Problem of World Peace and the Korean Experiment," at the University of Seoul. He also gave a seminar on irenology and polemology at the Graduate School of Social Development of Chungang University of Seoul. During this visit to Korea, the American Embassy at Seoul gave a reception in Bardis's honor.

The various addresses presented at such conferences by Bardis are eventually processed in notes and essays and published in a variety of journals. In time, reprints of them will be added to the mass of materials he sends out to his many correspondents. Moreover, in preparation for such junkets and during whatever free time he has during them, Bardis prepares himself for the experience by working up the history and folklore of the area, reviewing the traditional culture, and savoring features of the natural and social landscape. The ideas and observations that emerge from such workup and observation eventually take the form of sketches and poems, sometimes dedicated to important individuals met on his travels, which may be published in newspapers, professional newsletters, journals or the poetry magazines. And, eventually, such poems are added to the extensive material sent around to his international circle of correspondents.

In a letter from Bardis just after his return from Korea he reported: "I have to write *250 letters* after Korea (to scholars all over the world)! I've found a *mountain* of mail, which, as usual, I'll have to answer *myself*!" Since Bardis was gone about two and one-half weeks, his correspondence seems to accumulate at the rate of about 100 items per week.

Panos Bardis has developed a unique occupation for himself outside the mainstream of sociological culture: responding to an international circle of corresponding scholars, a circle he has developed himself. In the material which he endlessly processes and reprocesses through his circle of correspondents he exploits humanistic materials, particularly folklore and mythology, for ideas and develops ultra-positivist measurements and scales for the gathering of fresh empirical material. However, since the large proportion of his energy goes into the maintenance of his circle of correspondents, folklore-based hypotheses and positivistic scaling and data-gathering instruments remain largely undeveloped and unexploited. This may be the reason why potential tensions between the humanistic and positivistic aspects of his activities seem not to be a source of concern. There are many rich suggestions scattered throughout his work that may one day be exploited by others or Bardis himself.

Panos Bardis presents the astonishing spectacle of a scholar whose primary achievement has been creation of an international circle of scholars. In this he harms no one and, if one is willing to accept him simply as he is, Bardis is a source of pure delight. He is like a fountain that continuously circulates the same material—to be sure, constantly adding fresh material to replace whatever is lost through evaporation—a fountain that sends its spray into the sunlit air to descend in rainbow mists. Circles of corresponding scholars are rare these days and are no longer fashionable in the elite circles that dominate the mainstream of professional social science culture. It is a source of reassurance to see a scholar at the periphery managing to create around himself an active humanistic milieu that recalls an older time.

Notes

1. Thomas, Lewis (1979). *The Medusa and the Snail.* New York: Viking, p.3.

2. *Ibid.*, p. 4.

3. Fox, Michael W. (1974). *Understanding Your Cat.* New York: Bantam Books, p. 152.

4. *Ibid.*, p. 153.

5. Hobbes, Thomas (1949). *The Citizen.* New York: Appleton, and (1958) *Leviathan: Or, the Matter Form and Power of a Commonwealth, Ecclesiastical and Civil.* Oxford: Clarendon.

6. Locke, John (1959). *An Essay Concerning Human Understanding.* New York: Dover; and *Locke Selections,* edited by Sterling P. Lamprecht (1928). New York: Charles Scribner's Sons.

7. Turnbull, Colin M. (1972). *The Mountain People.* New York: Simon & Schuster, pp. 287-295.

8. *Ibid.*, p. 289.

9. *Ibid.*, footnote, p. 33.

10. Hume, David (1958). *A Treatise on Human Nature.* Oxford: Clarendon.

11. Smith, Adam (1966). *The Theory of Moral Sentiments.* New York: Kelly.

12. Thomas, Lewis (1974). *The Lives of a Cell.* New York: Bantam Books, pp. 128, 129.

13. *Ibid.*, pp. 126-127.

14. Thomas, *The Medusa and the Snail, op. cit.,* p. 116.

15. Cooley, Charles Horton (1956). *Social Organization: A Study of the Larger Mind.* New York: The Free Press.

16. Mead, George Herbert (1934). *Mind, Self and Society.* Chicago: University of Chicago Press, p. 216.

17. Hume, David (1927). *Selections,* edited by Charles W.Hendel, Jr. New York: Charles Scribner's Sons, pp. 83, 84, 85.

18. Kant, Immanuel (1929). *Selections.* Edited by Theodore Meyer Greene. New York: Charles Scribner's Sons, p. 77.

19. *Ibid.*, p. 78.

20. James, William (1980). *Principles of Psychology.* 2 vols. New York: Smith.

21. In James's view "*a man has as many social selves as there are individuals who recognize him* and carry an image of him in their mind." *Ibid.*, I:294.

22. Mead, *Mind, Self and Society, op. cit.,* pp. 136, 137, 138, 140.

23. Sorokin, Pitirim A. (1963). *A Long Journey.* New Haven, CT: College and University Press, pp. 243, 244.

24. Parsons, Talcott (1937). *The Structure of Social Action.* New York:

McGraw-Hill, see particularly pp. 473-697.

25. *Ibid.*, p. 251.

26. Sorokin, Pitirim A. (1966). *Sociological Theories of Today.* New York: Harper & Row, pp. 420-432.

27. Sorokin, Pitirim A. (1956). *Fads and Foibles in Modern Sociology and Related Sciences.* Chicago: Henry Regnery.

28. Sorokin, *A Long Journey, op. cit.*, p. 297.

29. Martindale, Don (1975). *Prominent Sociologists Since World War II.* Columbus, OH: Charles E. Merrill.

30. Robertson, Duncan (1982), ''The Overprotected Professors,'' *Newsweek*, February 15, p. 17.

31. Most honor societies actually begin more or less in this fashion. An individual or clique sets them up. To the extent to which they are effective in instituting genuine judgments of worth they legitimize themselves.

32. The journals involved are: *Revista International De Sociologia, Revista Espanola De La Opinion Publica, Il Politico, International Journal of Contemporary Sociology, International Journal of Sociology of the Family, Ukranian Quarterly, College Journal of Education, International Review of Modern Sociology, East European Quarterly, Journal of Political & Military Sociology, Nationalities Papers, Balkan Studies, Journal of Thought, Annali Di Sociologia,* and *Sociologia Internationalis.* Other journals sponsored by Delta Tau Kappa are: *International Journal of Legal Research, Malaysian Journal of Education,* and *Sociologia Religiosa.*

II

Max Weber:
Sociology's Last Puritan

"Max Weber," says Daniel Rossides, "is the only non-metaphysical social scientist of modern times (except Montesquieu), the only one to develop a genuinely scientific social science."[1] Although some students also have described Weber as the greatest sociologist of all time, there is no great virtue in such evaluations. Few things are more bootless than invidious distinctions in the field of science, for when a scientist of the past is turned into an apotheosized superman he is transformed into the center of a cult. The effect is at once to devalue the works of other thinkers and to transform those of the cult center into sources of dogma. Max Weber was an outstanding member of the generation that transformed sociology into a professional discipline. His work remains a part of the living heritage of sociology, still serving as a source of much vital theorizing and research. His works should not be sanctified and placed beyond use.

A Chronological Review of Max Weber's Life and Death

Max Weber was born into a middle-class family in Erfurt, Thuringia, April 21, 1864. The family on his father's side had been linen merchants and textile manufacturers. Members of his mother's family had been teachers, theologians, and small officials. Weber's father trained as a jurist, became an effective politician, serving in the municipal diet of Berlin, in the Prussian diet, and finally in the Reichstag. Max Weber was reared in the cosmopolitan atmosphere created by the many important political and academic persons who frequented the parental household and broadened by the extensive travels of the family.

After finishing the Gymnasium at Berlin-Charlottenburg in 1882, Max Weber's university studies were pursued at Heidelberg. There he joined a duelling fraternity, participating in patterns of status imitation of the Junker aristocracy which typified upper-class German university students. His undergraduate university studies were continued at Strassburg, where he served his year in the army and received his officer's commission, and then completed the requirements at Berlin and Goettingen. His studies concentrated on law, economics, and history. In 1886 Max Weber began postgraduate studies of law at the University of Berlin, completing his Ph.D. dissertation on *The History of Trading Companies during the Middle Ages* in 1889. He passed his second examination in law in 1890 and began teaching at the University of Berlin. His habilitation thesis was on *The History of Roman Agrarian Institutions*(1891). During the same period (1891-1892), he conducted an investigation of the conditions of agrarian workers in the East Elbe area for the *Verein fuer Sozial-politik,* a private reform group.

The early 1890s were a period of intensive work for Max Weber. In addition to his teaching he practiced law in Berlin and served as legal consultant in an official investigation of the stock market. Several essays on the stock market were a product of this experience.[2] He continued his researches on the agricultural workers of Eastern Germany, he participated in the Evangelical-Social Conferences on social policy, and he was active in the Christian Social Party. He was married to Marianne Schnitger, and in 1893 he became Professor of Commercial and German Law at the University of Berlin. He moved the next year, becoming Professor of Political Economics at Freiburg University (1894). In 1897 he was called as Professor of Political Science at Heidelberg University as successor to Karl Knies.

In 1897, shortly after the death of his father, Weber fell ill with a nervous disorder. For the rest of his life Weber tended to alternate between periods of nervous collapse, travel, and intense work. His state of psychic exhaustion was such that in 1898 and 1899 the university granted him leave with pay. The Webers traveled to Venice, and he returned apparently improved, but when he took up his duties he soon collapsed again more severely than before. For a short period in 1899 he entered a mental institution. The following summer he traveled in Italy and Switzerland. He felt so improved that in 1902 he was prepared to take up his teaching duties at Heidelberg once again. However, there were further setbacks, leading him to resign his professorship. He was made an honorary professor at Heidelberg in

1903.

In 1904 Weber was asked to join with Werner Sombart and Edgar Jaffe in editorship of the *Archiv fuer Sozialwissenschaft und Sozialpolitik,* which had been failing. Primarily under Weber's direction, it was transformed into the foremost social science journal in Germany, comparable to *L'Anee Soziologique* in France and *The American Journal of Sociology* in the United States. In 1904 Weber visited the United States and addressed the St. Louis Congress of Arts and Science on "The Relations of the Rural Community to Other Branches of Social Science." The same year Weber undertook intense researches and writing in connection with his editorship. He completed a major essay on methods and the problem of objectivity in the social sciences and the first half of his most famous essay, *The Protestant Ethic and the Spirit of Capitalism.*

Stimulated by the Russian Revolution the following year, Weber quickly learned Russian and produced for the *Archiv* two major essays on Russia: "The Situation of the Bourgeois Democracy in Russia" and "Russia's Transition to Sham Constitutionalism." He completed major essays on religious groupings in 1906. An analysis of historical materialism and social science methodology was carried through in 1907. An essay on "Agrarian Conditions in Antiquity" was written for the *Handwoerterbuch der Staatswissenschaften*(3rd ed., vol. 1, 1909) in 1908. Also in 1908 Weber made a survey on "The Adjustment and Selection of Workers in Large-Scale Industrial Establishments" for the Society for Social Policy. He undertook a major investigation of industrial psychology in his grandfather's linen factory in Westphalia.

In 1908 Weber also took an active part in the deliberations leading to the establishment of the German Sociological Society. He assumed responsibility (1909) for organizing and editing (for Paul Siebeck) a series of studies on the Foundations of Social Economics. His own contribution to the series, *Wirtschaft und Gesellschaft,* was published posthumously. In 1910 he played a leading role in setting the tone of the discussion and directing the research orientations of the first meeting of the German Sociological Society.

In 1911 Weber began his extensive studies of the influence of the world religions on economic ethics. These were eventually collected and published posthumously in the three volumes of *Gesamelte Aufsaetze zur Religionssoziologie.* Also, between 1911 and 1913, he worked ahead on his contribution to *Foundations of Social Economics (Grundriss der Sozialoekonomik).* His *Sociology of Law, Systematic*

Sociology of Religion, Sociology of Economics, The Sociology of Music, and the methodological discussions of *Categories of Interpretative Sociology* were all composed in this connection.

In 1914 Max Weber participated in the discussion of values sponsored by The Vienna Society for Social Policy. With the outbreak of war, as an over-age reserve officer, he was commissioned and placed as officer in charge of nine hospitals in the Heidelberg area. The bureaucratic structure he created was dissolved in a reorganization in 1915, and Weber was retired from active duty. He returned to his studies of the world religions and published in the *Archiv* (1916-1917) essays on Confucianism, Hinduism, and Buddhism.

In 1917 Max Weber accepted a visiting professorship at the University of Vienna for the summer session, returning to teaching for the first time since his breakdown. He lectured on "Positive Criticism of the Materialistic Interpretation of History" and "The Sociology of the State." He was developing into a national figure and was invited to participate in deliberations of the Ministry of Interior in Berlin. In 1918 and 1919 he lectured in behalf of the German Democratic Party and worked on essays on *Ancient Judaism.* In 1919, to the students' organization of the University of Munich, he delivered addresses on "Science as a Vocation" and "Politics as a Vocation." He was a member of the German Peace Delegation to Versailles. He also was appointed to the University of Munich as successor to Lujo Brentano. His lectures on economic history were worked up at the request of students and were published as *A General Economic History.*

A number of family crises and responsibilities accumulated for the Webers in 1919. Weber's mother died in the fall of 1919. Shortly after, his sister (whose husband had recently died in battle) also died. The Webers decided to adopt the four orphaned children of his sister, only to be plagued by later doubts which led to the delay of the reception of the children into the household. In June, 1920, Weber caught cold, and by the time it was diagnosed as deep-seated pneumonia, it was too late to hope for his recovery. He died June 14, 1920. H. Stuart Hughes raises some interesting questions about the events surrounding Weber's death:

> Weber proved a cheerful patient; he did not fight the illness. In mid-June, 1920, he lay dead.... Weber's sudden death is conventionally described as a career cut short at its very height. In terms of professional accomplishment, this is undoubtedly true.... But in personal terms, the matter is more perplexing. Did Weber have a sense that his new responsibilities were

threatening to overwhelm him? Was he in his last months living in dread of a relapse into his earlier malady, to which anything, even death, would be preferable? Did he unconsciously long for release from his sudden eminence? At this very moment, Freud was publishing his speculations on the "death instinct" in human beings. We can only wonder.[*3*]

It adds very little to one's understanding of Max Weber or of his intellectual influence to decide that he spent his life under the torments of an Oedipus complex and died from a "death instinct." Moreover, it is somewhat risky, because Weber's psychological attitude during his last illness was one of "cheerful" resignation, to take this attitude as self-evidence of the presence of a death instinct. It is characteristic that pneumonia and other serious lung ailments are often accompanied by psychological attitudes of passive resignation.

The Genesis of
Max Weber's Energies and Point of View

There is some evidence from the biography of Max Weber by his wife, Marianne, from Weber's letters, and from the accounts of personal friends and associates that the intensity of his intellectual life rested in part in the degree to which personal problems coincided with the underlying social predicament of the stratum to which he belonged. When this occurs, an individual's subjective problems are objectified in his theories and his theories are fired with personal passion.

There were some anomalies in the German middle classes to which Max Weber belonged which may be elucidated by comparison with the fate of the middle classes in some other West European nations. The middle classes were the critical strata in the rise of contemporary national society. In France, in England, and in the United States, they carried out the political revolutions which delivered the state into their hands, initiating the movement toward mass democracy. Though the German middle classes were among the first to develop in Europe, they were late in receiving political and social recognition in any way equivalent to that enjoyed elsewhere.

The German city and her middle-class strata developed early, for the Italian wave of city development was soon followed by parallel movements in German hands. At the same time, in the feudalized

Holy Roman Empire, Germany had inherited from the Middle Ages a political structure which blocked the developments of nationalism of a contemporary type and the access of the middle class to positions of political opportunity and responsibility. Germany lagged behind her Western neighbors (France and England) in the formation of a nation of contemporary type, despite the rise of cultural nationalism (in the face of frustrated political aspirations) by its middle-class strata. When the German state took shape in the early nineteenth century, moreover, it was taken over into the hands of the landed aristocrats. Middle-class, urban strata were granted only a minor voice in the destiny of the nation.

In 1830 and again in 1848 the German middle classes made their bid for equal recognition in the German state. When their aspirations were frustrated and members of the class were subject to persecution, many individuals of the German middle classes migrated to North America, bringing with them valuable professions and skills. Marx, who had begun his career as a spokesman for radical elements of the German middle classes, was embittered by the consequences of the 1848 experience. He thereafter gave up the notion that it was possible to work within the framework of the state.

Thus, while the middle classes in France, England, and, above all, the United States had moved into the center of national and economic affairs, the German middle classes found themselves blocked. In part, they compensated for the frustrations in their political and economic situation by exaggerated cultural achievement. At the same time, successful members of the upper middle class often imitated the uncultivated, agrarian crudeness all too characteristic of the Junker aristocracy. This was particularly evident in circles of upper-middle-class university students, who joined duelling fraternities and spent much time beer-drinking, gambling, getting into debt, and otherwise imitating modes of deportment identified with the rural nobility.

The effect of these developments in Germany was to establish a peculiar division in the mental set of the middle classes: polarizing them in terms of attitudes of expedient crudeness and exaggerated rank consciousness in social and political affairs, and of a principled sensitivity and religious intensity in cultural concerns.

Weber belonged to the German middle class. His worldly, secular-minded lawyer father, active in civic and national politics, oriented toward the public concerns and affairs, pragmatically ready to compromise principle whenever it was expedient, expressed one phase of orientations of this middle class. His sensitive, shy, pious mother oriented toward letters, cultural concerns, and things of the spirit, forever locating problems of principle above the expediencies of everyday affairs, epitomized the other pole in the middle-class German mentality. The conflict and estrangement which developed between Max Weber's parents was a source of keen discomfort to him. It may, perhaps, be significant that Weber's illness became acute shortly after his father's death. Prior to his father's death, a sharp altercation had taken place between father and son over the father's treatment of Weber's mother. Weber was seized with severe guilt feelings over the affair. Whatever the influence may be, two major dimensions of the middle-class mind—expediency in sociopolitical concerns and principled sensitivity in spiritual matters—were dramatized in Weber's parents.

While Germany was divided into Protestant and Roman Catholic, as was the rest of Western Europe, a number of factors cooperated to give religion a somewhat greater intensity in Germany than was usual elsewhere in Western Europe. Many observers have noted the tendency for Germans to go to extremes in religious matters; toward dogmatic atheism or religious fanaticism without convenient stopping points between.

Italy, France, and Spain were predominantly Roman Catholic; England and the United States were predominantly Protestant. Religion is not usually a major issue in a community that is religiously homogeneous. Germany, however, was fairly close to a balance, being around 55 per cent Protestant to 45 per cent Roman Catholic. Under such circumstances the possibility always remains of the community being split approximately in half over religion.

Again, during the nineteenth century Protestantism was not only made into Germany's official religion, but Bismarck entered upon the dangerous experiment of attempting to stamp out Roman Catholicism. Bismarck's use of Protestantism as an instrument of political control placed underprivileged groups (such as laborers) in the position where they were not only economically and politically deprived, but where an antireligious construction was placed on attempts at self-improvement. One consequence of such policies was to drive many laborers into opposition to all religion, leading them to embrace atheistic philosophies. Karl Marx accurately summarized the German laborer's experience when he described religion as "the opiate of the masses."

On the other hand, the same official policies that drove many German workers to atheism served to turn many genuinely religious people away from official forms of religiosity—which were cynically used for political ends—toward a more purely personal religiosity. Meanwhile, the cultural struggle between the Protestant and Roman Catholic branches of the community left a lingering concern as to the importance of religion.

The patterns of personal deportment in Germany were strongly determined after the sixteenth century by Protestantism with its point of gravity in the middle classes. Traditional Christianity promised religious salvation through observance of the sacraments and the mediation of the priesthood. The sacraments provided a religious framework for adjusting to the major life crises such as birth, marriage, and death. Priesthood was not only essential for their proper performance but stood by with the confessional to release emotional pressures. However, the perfection of the Christian life was open only to those who took a further step and turned away from the world to practice withdrawn asceticism for the glory of God and salvation of the soul. Protestantism changed all this, reducing the priesthood to a mere facilitating device not absolutely essential to salvation. It promoted the nonsacramental theory of salvation, making salvation ultimately an individual responsibility in all life spheres. Finally, it eliminated the concept of withdrawn asceticism practiced by a few as the perfection of the Christian life. It substituted the inner-worldly asceticism of all. The effect of these changes was to introduce a new religious intensity and significance to everyday conduct while responsibility was individualized.

Max Weber belonged to a generation whose members were still often reared in an atmosphere which transformed the Protestant ethos into second nature even while they were religiously emancipated.

Weber exemplified in relatively pure form the Protestant ethos when he plunged into work with something approximating a religious frenzy and spoke of "the need to feel crushed under the load of work."[4] Moreover, he reacted against the doctrines of Freud which he perceived as a disguised rehabilitation of the confessional with the scientist in the role of priest and the substitution of an ideal of "normality" or "health" for ethical responsibilities.[5] Implicit in this reaction to Freudian psychotherapy as a form of moral shoddiness is the ideal of the man of conscience.

It is not altogether clear what played the most important role in the build-up of tensions that drove Max Weber into semi-invalidism for so much of his life. Possibly the conflict between his parents had laid a foundation on which others could be arranged. His own emotional history also undoubtedly was accompanied by tension build-up. For some six years before his marriage to Marianne Schnitger, Max Weber was in love with a Strassburg cousin who had spent time in a mental hospital and who was recovering when he broke up with her. His relations with Marianne, a grand niece of Max Weber, Sr., were complicated by the fact that a friend had courted her and Max Weber found it painful to cut in. The fact that the women with whom he was emotionally involved belonged to the two branches of the family may well have served to pyramid the tensions. Persons raised on the Protestant ethic who have learned to turn the problems of their lives into purely private testing grounds of their sense of worth often lash themselves unmercifully for real or presumed shortcomings. In any case, Weber plunged into work for all the world as if in expiation for guilt and nourished a sense of inadequacy from the Sisyphean tasks he undertook. As a young scholar in Berlin, he imposed a burden of work on himself that no man could sustain for long: in addition to nineteen hours a week of teaching, he was participating in state examinations for lawyers and undertaking consultant work for government agencies and special research for private reform groups.

Weber was unusually equipped by circumstances and training to carry on his lone struggle toward self-clarification in terms of the most vital problems of his generation. The parental household was a center of intellectual and political ferment—among visitors to the household were Wilhelm Dilthey, Theodor Mommsen, H. Treitschke, Julian Schmidt, H. Sybel, and Friedrich Kapp. From the mother's branch of the family, the Strassburg branch, Weber was acquainted with theological literatures, problems, and disputes. He received his training in German universities at a time when the humanistic and historical traditions had been brought to a high level of perfection. His own degree was taken in law, where the whole historical movement had begun, but he was almost as well qualified in history, philosophy, and economics. Finally, Weber moved all his life at the center of active intellectual and artistic circles of pre-war Germany. At Berlin he was acquainted with Theodor Mommsen. While teaching at Freiburg University he came to know Hugo Muensterberg, Pastor Naumann, and Wilhelm Rickert. At Heidelberg his circle of friends included Georg Jellinek, Paul Hensel, Karl Neumann, Wilhelm Windelband, and Ernst Troeltsch. Among the visitors to the Webers were Robert Michels, Werner Sombart, Paul Hensel, Hugo Muensterberg, Karl Vossler, Georg Simmel, Paul Honigsheim, Karl Lowenstein, Georg Lukacs, Mina Tobler, Karl Jaspers, and others.

Artists, philosophers, historians, psychiatrists, musicians, and many types of social scientists were drawn to the Weber sphere.

While a surprisingly large number of the most distinguished scholars and intellectuals of his generation were drawn to Weber and while they were universally impressed with the power of his mind and personality, as Julien Freund has observed: "There is no Weberian school, as there is a Marxist, a Comtian and even a Durkheimian school."[6] This remained true in the post-war period despite the ironic fact that "Many German university teachers vaunt the illustrious title of being a former student of Max Weber."[7]

Unquestionably the failure of Max Weber to found a school was in part related to the erratic course of his teaching career. After a relatively short period Weber stopped teaching in 1903 and did not resume teaching until a few months before his death in 1920. The institutionally located professor, particularly if engaged in training Ph.D. candidates, tends to be pressed in the direction of school formation. His efficiency is enhanced if he codifies his concepts and procedures into a dogma. Even if the master does not undertake this codification, his assistants and disciples may find it useful. When his former students move out into positions of their own, the school spreads in a sort of colonization process. Hence had Max Weber spent his career primarily as an institutional rather than a private scholar it is quite possible that the pressures for school formation, if not by him, but others associated with him, might have been irresistible. After Weber's death, under Karl Mannheim at Heidelberg this process was in fact underway until interrupted by the Nazis.

However, it is quite possible that the same factors in Max Weber's personality that made teaching so difficult produced an intellectual life that resisted codification. Weber, though denying personal religiosity, never lost the Protestant, and to some extent, monkish inclination to shift the arena of decisions on all issues to his inner conscience. This was a practice that had led many of the early Protestants to stand alone, naked before their consciences and their God, against the forces of this world in defiance of princes and kings. Weber seems never to have been able to yield the power of decision and responsibility to any institution's official ideological requirements. Hence, he repeatedly found himself standing alone. Freund observes:

Indeed, on a number of occasions Weber found himself completely isolated, abandoned by those who had called themselves his best friends. This isolation was no doubt due to his political attitude and, more particularly, to his hostility to the rash undertakings of Kaiser Wilhelm II. But he was similarly isolated even on the purely scientific terrain of the discussion of the concept of ethical neutrality, for instance at certain memorable meetings of the Association for Social Policy. Some of his positions on public affairs aroused the fury of nationalist students, who went so far as to invade his classroom to prevent him from lecturing. A perusal of the pious biography written by his wife, Marianne Weber, affords but the merest inkling of the outbursts, revolts and scandals he provoked.[8]

Since Max Weber never lost the Puritan's tempermental conservatism, he was reluctant to abandon any position so long as it retained any value or any idea that retained a claim to truth. It was this conservatism rather than independence per se or exasperating ambivalence that led Weber to entertain simultaneously so many ideas and propositions that other thinkers found to be self-contradictory.

In all things and all circumstances, he was essentially independent, and this explains in part some of his apparently contradictory statements and attitudes. The same impulse prompted him to advocate both the shooting of the first Polish official to set foot in Danzig and the execution of Count von Arco, the assassin of Kurt Eisner, who had headed the revolutionary government of Bavaria. Again, although he detested Ludendorff, Weber was prepared to defend him against unjust attack. He actively opposed the exclusion of anarchists, socialists and Jews from university faculties, and had only contempt for the revolutionary movement that sprang up following the defeat of 1918. And while he came out in support of pacifist students, he advocated "chauvinism" should the peace be merely unilaterally imposed by the Allies.[9]

The temperamental inability to gloss over real or apparent contradictions seems to have been a component in turning teaching into a nightmare. When he accepted a full professorship at Freiburg University, Gerth and Mills observed: "He had an enormous load, working until very late. When Marianne urged him to get some rest, he would call out: 'If I don't work until one o'clock I can't be a professor.'"[10] Later, in 1896, when Weber accepted a chair at Heidelberg he pressed himself to even greater labors and over the summer fell ill with a psychic malady. Gerth and Mills observed: "He seemed to get better when the academic year began, but toward the end of the fall semester he collapsed from tension and remorse, exhaustion and anxiety. For his essentially psychiatric condition, doctors prescribed cold water, travel, and exercise. Yet Weber continued to experience the sleeplessness of an inner tension. For the rest of his life he suffered intermittently from severe depressions, punctuated by manic spurts of extraordinarily intense intellectual work and travel."[11] No man could hope to handle for long the task Weber imposed upon himself, to bring every real or apparent contradiction in the material he was supposed to teach into confrontation in his own mind in the attempt to resolve them.

If one were to characterize the style of the man, Weber's would seem most similar to the musical styles of the series of German composers from Bach to Beethoven. What began with the voice against voice counterpoint of Bach came to a climactic fulfillment in the polyphonic confrontations brought into the passionate synthesis of Beethoven. It was Weber's tendency to bring every apparent contradiction of theme or position or concept into confrontation and to unfold its tension as he searched for a point of unity satisfying to himself. It is little wonder that those who knew him were impressed by his external ferment but inner calm. In Freund's words: "Those who knew him say that he was like a volcano in constant eruption, at the same time retaining an inward calm which added to the confusion of those who argued with him."[12] One is inclined to observe that perhaps the image of a hurricane or typhoon with unusual violence in its outer winds and dead calm at the eye of the storm would be more appropriate.

At few times has Weber come closer to the characterization of his own style than in his perceptive essay on "Politics as a Vocation." Many of the most brilliant formulations of the essay occur in the course of the counterpointlike unfolding against one another of two contrasting styles of politics: a politics resting on an ethic of ultimate ends and a politics resting on an ethic of responsibility. A politics resting on an ethic of ultimate ends seeks only to do what is right; a politics resting on an ethic of responsibility withholds final judgment and seeks a maximum solution to the plural values in human situations. An ethic of ultimate ends often leads to tyranny; an ethic of responsibility often degenerates into pure expediency. A politics resting on an ethic of ultimate ends is a politics of the heart; one resting on an ethic of responsibility aiming at rational compromise is a politics of the head. While Weber in most ordinary cases observes, in a manner that would have won the approval of Immanuel Kant, that it is safer to follow the head rather than the heart, yet politics is not— and to this extent the proponents of a politics of ultimate ends are right—made by the head alone. Hence, so long as men continue their political activities, some will be found who maintain that they only undertake to do what is right, and if this has negative consequences it is unfortunate, but responsibility for these consequences does not fall upon them but upon those whom they serve and whose stupidity or baseness they are undertaking to eradicate. It is characteristic of the Weber style that having brought a confrontation of ideas to this point he makes the following observation. Referring to persons who advocate an ethic of ultimate ends, Weber observes:

> I am under the impression that in nine out of ten cases I deal with windbags who do not fully realize what they take upon themselves but who intoxicate themselves with romantic sensations. From a human point of view this is not very interesting to me, nor does it move me profoundly. However, it is immensely moving when a *mature* man—no matter whether old or young in years—is aware of a responsibility for the consequences of his conduct and really feels such responsibility with heart and soul. He then acts by following an ethic of responsibility...and somewhere he reaches the point where he says: "Here I stand; I can do not other." That is something genuinely human and moving. And every one of us who is not spiritually dead must realize the possibility of finding himself at some time in that position. In so far as this is true, an ethic of ultimate ends and an ethic of responsibility are not absolute contrasts by rather supplements, which only in unison constitute a genuine man—a man who *can* have the "calling for politics."[13]

The pathos of this extraordinary passage derives from the fact that Weber was not simply formulating the ultimate requirements of a calling for politics, but, as he saw them, the ultimate requirements of the calling for science as well. It was the destiny of the man of science to stand alone with only his reason and his conscience, seeking to resolve the contradictions that swept in out of the world about him. As once the old Protestants had stood with their conscience and their God against the powers of this world, the man of science stood armed only with his puny wits against the irrationalities of the world. However, he was no longer sure that God stood at his side, for he was a Puritan in a nonreligious age.

The Main Drift of Recent Western Thought

The estimate of a thinker requires more than an examination of his biography. Ultimately he must be judged with respect to intellectual and social trends. It is necessary to chart briefly the main drift of Western thought to locate Max Weber's work.

The revolutions of the late eighteenth and nineteenth centuries were the turning point in contemporary developments. The prerevolutionary world was dominated by the politics of enlightened despotism. The state was, in principle, the private property of the kings. For their part, the kings were engaged in the creation of administrative and military structures which implemented their power and economic conditions (mercantilism, cameralism) which enhanced their financial independence. The middle classes which produced much of the liquid wealth that made the monarchies workable were largely without political power or social recognition. Under the enlightened despots a type of thinking became popular which is best described as rationalistic, individualistic, and reformist. Among the major objectives of enlightenment thought was the effort to remove the traditional obstacles to the reforms required by the new political and economic institutions.

The revolutions, which swept away some of the despots and threatened the position of others, brought the middle classes to political and social prominence. The new movements toward mass democracy and socialism were spawned by the revolutionary movements. Since the ideologies of revolution were framed out of the materials of rationalistic thought, rationalism went out of fashion once the revolution was over and the task of consolidating the new social order it had created was faced. A type of thinking best described as collectivistic appeared. It had two major forms: collectivistic and conservative (illustrated by Hegel and August Comte) and collectivistic and revolutionary (illustrated by Marx and Engels).

In the prerevolutionary period society was conceived to be a conscious association (contract) of similarly constituted rational individuals. In the postrevolutionary period (for both right- and left-wing groups) society was conceived to be a superindividual entity with properties not reducible to individuals. Individuals were increasingly viewed in the postrevolutionary world as irrational and emotional. Rationality was reconceptualized as an objective property of society. In the prerevolutionary period the basic method of thought was usually conceived as a process of analysis in terms of fundamental units. Hegel and Marx set much of the tone to methodological thought in the nineteenth century by arguing that the true method both of thought (and of reality) consisted of dialectical conflicts within the whole of the mind (or of social reality) which were overcome by more comprehensive syntheses.

In the late eighteenth and early nineteenth centuries in Germany, where the middle and intellectual classes were bearers of an insurgent cultural nationalism, such theoretical collectivism and a predisposition toward dialectical-synthetic methodology were characteristic. Hegel became the great spokesman for these strata. When an embittered individualist such as Schopenhauer attempted to criticize such collectivism, he was for some time simply thrust aside.

However, when their revolutionary bids for political and social recognition were largely frustrated after 1830 and 1848, the German middle classes became somewhat disillusioned with theoretical collectivism and dialectical methodologies. For the first time Schopenhauer became popular. After the frustrations of 1870, the disillusionment deepened. In the late nineteenth century these dissatisfactions increasingly took the form of a ferment in German thought represented by neo-idealistic and neo-Kantian trends.

In somewhat different ways both the neo-idealists and the neo-Kantians called into question the collectivistic assumptions of the early nineteenth century and offered alternatives to dialectical methodologies. The neo-idealists dropped the notion that the social and intellectual world forms a single great process in which thought moves by a synthesis of opposites. Rather, they argued there is no critical difference in the thought processes which deal with the mind and with nature. Nature is known from the outside; the mind (and culture) is understood from within. The methods of explaining nature are by analysis and experiment; mental and cultural phenomena are understood by means of "ideas" specially constructed to isolate significance for each other and for man. The neo-Kantians, on the other hand, also redivided the world of thought but in terms of whether reality is comprehended as history or as science. Be it physical or psychological, science seeks to establish laws by means of experimental and mathematical-statistical analysis. History, however, is the endeavor to comprehend and causally account for the unique and particular. It requires the employment of value concepts in terms of which alone the unique can be understood. Both the neo-idealistic and neo-Kantian thinkers tended to return to individualistic theories and analytical (rather than dialectical-synthetic) methods.

Such, in schematic outline, was the primary drift in Western thought from the period prior to the middle-class revolution to the early twentieth century. The rationalistic thought of the seventeenth and eighteenth centuries in prerevolutionary Europe was individualistic in theory and analytical in method. In the postrevolutionary nineteenth-century world the pendulum swung the other way. The new national communities had to be consolidated. Thought (much of romanticism and both Hegelian and Marxian thought) was theoretic-

ally collectivistic and synthetic in method. In the late nineteenth and
early twentieth centuries during Max Weber's period, the pendulum
swung back. New versions of theoretical individualism and analytical
methods appeared. Weber was acquainted firsthand with Wilhelm
Dilthey, a major neo-idealist, from his father's household. He was
acquainted as a colleague and associate with such major neo-Kantians
as Heinrich Rickert, Wilhelm Windelband, and Georg Simmel. He
moved within the central drift of the times.

The Central Themes in Max Weber's Writings

Weber's writings may be divided into two great periods: the period of
probing and experiment beginning with his Ph.D. dissertation and
habilitation thesis (1897) and comprising various other essays and
research reports to 1903; and the period beginning with the production of his essay on "Objectivity in Social Science and Social Policy"
and the first part of his "Protestant Ethic and the Spirit of Capitalism," both of which were first published in the *Archiv fuer Sozialwissenschaft und Sozialpolitik* in 1904. The first period covered in
Weber's investigations of and writing on German agrarian problems
and the stock market. The second period coincided with his sufficient
recovery from his nervous breakdown to assume the editorship of the
Archiv and covers the unflagging productivity extending to his death.
It was in the second period that he formulated the great themes for
which he is famous.

Max Weber's Methodology

Max Weber's biography and his *milieu* cooperated to thrust him away
from the kinds of methods associated with both right- and left-wing
collectivism—that is, dialectical and synthetic methods. The starting
point for Weber's analysis in this as in other cases seems to display a
conservative bias. There is a strong tendency to start with the
assumption that whatever exists is probably right and any problems
are defects of one's personal perceptions. Weber's inclination, in
short, is always to transpose problems presented by the external
world into conflicts of conscience. Some of the characteristics of
Luther's conception of the world as God's handiwork and of the
individual's role as his "calling" persist in an otherwise secularized
outlook.

Weber's essay on "Objectivity in the Social Sciences" is a kind of methodological testament at the point in his life when he was about to undertake a mature confrontation of his problems. It also belongs in the most intimate sense to the wave of thinking of the renascent individualism which swept Western culture in the late nineteenth and early twentieth centuries. The essay is characterized by acceptance of both the neo-Kantian and neo-idealistic methodological principles and the effort to compromise their difference while preserving their insights. The parallelism between various of Weber's formulations and those of Dilthey and Rickert may illustrate this.

The cultural sciences, Dilthey had argued, analyze their material from the inside on the basis of special interpretive constructs. They differ from the natural sciences which seek mathematical and experimental knowledge of nature. Science is science, Rickert had answered, whether its content be man or nature. If there are distinctions, they are methodological. Science, which is a search for nomological knowledge, should not be confused with history, which is concerned with the unique. Special methods are appropriate to the idiographic knowledge of history in contrast to those appropriate to the nomological knowledge of science.

Weber took over from Dilthey the methodological device of utilizing special interpretive constructs or ideal types. However, with Rickert he was inclined to treat all science as a single conceptual enterprise differentiated from history.

The aim of social science, according to Weber, is to understand "the characteristic uniqueness of the reality in which we move."[14] This type of historical understanding does not constitute establishing a system of laws." As far back as we may go into the grey mist of the far-off past, the reality to which the laws apply always remains equally *individual,* equally *undeducible* from laws."[15] Socio-cultural analysis is concerned with configurations of factors arranged to form historically significant cultural phenomena. "Significance" is a value concept and the analysis of cultural science oriented to it involves a subjective element so far as it concerns events to which cultural significance is attached. Social psychological research consists of the study of many "*individual* types of cultural elements with reference to their interpretability by our empathic understanding."[16]

The type of concept construction indispensable to the cultural sciences, thus, consists, according to Weber, in framing the synthetic constructs or ideal types. Such ideal types are not hypotheses, though they may aid in framing hypotheses. "An ideal type is formed by the one-sided accentuation of one or more points of view and by the synthesis of a great many diffuse, discrete, more or less present and occasionally absent *concrete individual* phenomena, which are arranged according to those one-sidedly emphasized viewpoints into a unified *analytical* construct."[17]

Types do not supply ideals of what ought to exist but are ideal only in a logical sense serving to clarify analysis. The critical properties which remove the type from an evaluative ideal is the presence in it of relationships "which our imagination accepts as plausibly motivated and hence as 'objectively possible' and which appear as *adequate* from the nomological standpoint."[18]

Ideal types, Weber maintained, are intended for use in the analysis of "historically unique configurations or their individual components by means of genetic concepts."[19] They are indispensable for the obtaining of objectively valid empirical knowledge of social reality. "Nothing should be more sharply emphasized than the proposition that the knowledge of the *cultural significance of concrete historical events and patterns* is exclusively and solely the final end which... concept-construction and the criticism of constructs also seek to serve."[20]

In Max Weber's methodological testament at the beginning of his great period of mature work, the methodological reflections of the neo-idealists and neo-Kantians were brought into synthesis with greatest emphasis on the latter. While Weber never completely retreated from this methodological stand in his later work, he was to modify it increasingly, viewing ideal typical procedures as instruments for achieving general (lawlike) knowledge of social events and not simply as devices for estimating the unique significance of special cultural configurations.

Max Weber's Theoretical Elementarism

The substantive work which opened the mature phase of Weber's productivity was *The Protestant Ethic and the Spirit of Capitalism*. The initial conservatism which so often led Weber to begin an analysis as if on the assumption that everything that exists is essential is manifest in the *Protestant Ethic*. In scientific circles in the late nineteenth and early twentieth centuries powerful antireligious currents were present. Furthermore, thinkers of a Marxian persuasion were inclined to dismiss religion as secondary to economic circumstances. Religion was an "opiate of the masses," serving to pacify them in the teeth of economic exploitation. Critical to Weber's

analysis, however, was the recovery of a sense of the positive importance of religion for economics. This occurred despite his personal
agnosticism.

To some extent the old polarity between Weber's parents,
between a worldly father and a pious mother, may have been operating. Both attitudes were taken, so to speak, as indispensable parts of
the whole.

Theoretically, Weber's analysis of capitalism was elementaristic.
He avoided analysis of capitalistic society as a whole or historical
epoch or process, within which various forces are identified. Rather,
Weber assumes that "capitalism" is no more than a name for a way in
which some contemporary individual men behave.   The critical
questions then become: Who are the men who act in this peculiar
way? What, precisely, is peculiar about the way they act? How could
this way of acting have arisen?

A capitalistic economic action was defined by Max Weber as one
which rests on the expectation of profit by the utilization of opportunities for exchange. Where rationally pursued, economic action rests
on calculations in terms of capital represented by systematic use of
goods and personal services as means of acquisition to yield a net
profit at the close of the business period.[21] Many forms of capitalism have developed but only in the West, according to Weber, have
types appeared resting on the rational capitalistic organization of
formally free labor. This, in turn, required the separation of business
from the household and invention of rational bookkeeping.[22]

Weber maintained that the occupational statistics of any Western
country of mixed religious composition show business leaders and
owners of capital as well as higher grades of skilled labor to be
predominantly Protestant. While a larger majority of the wealthy
towns of Europe in the sixteenth century went over to Protestantism,
giving the Protestants an economic advantage, the linkage between
Protestantism and capitalism is not to be explained simply by any such
historical accident. For capitalistic economic behavior to arise, traditional forms of economic behavior had to be eliminated, and the
Reformation helped in this. However, the Reformation did more than
banish traditional controls by the church of everyday, including
economic conduct; it created new and in many ways more burdensome
systems of controls covering all phases of public and private life.

The pecularity of the social ethic of capitalism, as Weber saw it,
was the systematic rationalization of individual conduct whether such
conduct involved employment of one's personal energies or only of his

material possessions as capital. Systematic rationalization is a basic property of capitalistic economic behavior. "One of the fundamental characteristics of an individualistic capitalistic economy" is "that it is rationalized on the basis of rigorous calculation, directed with foresight and caution toward the economic success."[23] Its rational character differentiates capitalistic economic behavior from the subsistence activities of the peasant, the traditional economic behavior of the guild craftsman, and the type of capitalistic behavior of adventurers exploiting political opportunities or irrational speculation for profit. The sources of the spirit of capitalism, thus, must be found in those factors which led to the systematic elimination of traditionalism and the reorganization of everyday life on the basis of sober rational analysis. The origin of this kind of rationalization of life can be traced, Max Weber argues, to the religious idea of a "calling" and to the devotion of labor in a calling.

The conception of one's place in the world, one's calling, as a task set by God was a conception peculiar to the Protestant sects. For members in these sects it replaced the traditional concept of the monastery as the perfection of the Christian life. "The only way of living acceptable to God was not to surpass worldly morality in monastic asceticism, but solely through the fulfilment of the obligations imposed upon the individual by his position in the world. That was his calling."[24] This provided a moral justification for worldly activity. However, while he gave prominence to the idea of "calling," Luther's orientation toward everyday activity remained quite traditionalistic. His position on usury, for example, was much less favorable to capitalistic enterprise than that of the scholastics.[25] The Calvinistic interpretation gave the concept of calling its decisive form.

> The God of Calvinism demanded of his believers not single good works, but a life of good works combined into a unified system. There was no place for the very human Catholic cycle of sin, repentance, atonement, release, followed by renewed sin. Nor was there any balance of merit for a life as a whole which could be adjusted by temporal punishments or the Churches' means of grace. The moral conduct of the average man was thus deprived of its planless and unsystematic character and subjected to a consistent method for conduct as a whole.[26]

It was not Weber's argument that "the spirit of capitalism...could only have arisen as the result of certain effects of the Reformation, or even that capitalism as an economic system is a creation of the Reformation."[27] This Weber described as a "foolish and doctrinaire thesis." Rather, he argued only that religious forms played a part in the "qualitative formation and quantitative expansion" of the spirit or psychology of capitalism. In Weber's own summary: "One of the fundamental elements of the spirit of modern capitalism, and not only of that but of all modern culture: rational conduct on the basis of the idea of the calling, was born...from the spirit of Christian asceticism."[28]

Coming as it did at a critical time of his life, Weber's essay on the influence of the Protestant ethic on everyday conduct had many of the properties of a major act of self-clarification. For Max Weber was —and saw himself—as a particularly clear illustration of the Protestant ethic operating under circumstances from which—as in the cases of contemporary economic behavior—the specific religious content has melted away. In the essay he established the elementaristic orientation which remained basic to all his later work. The suggestion in the concluding paragraphs that the spirit of Christian asceticism fundamental to the ideal of calling was a basic component not only of the spirit of capitalism, but of all modern culture, is indicative of the extent to which Weber's imagination had already contemplated a program of possible scholarly investigation which could become coextensive with the range of human culture. Weber did in fact undertake the study of the rise and influence of rationalism in many other areas of life, such as in law, the state, and even in Western music.

Seen in this light, it is only a short step from the Protestant ethic to the general analysis of economic, political, legal, and cultural institutions of *Wirtschaft und Gesellschaft*. Moreover, Weber's extensive labors on the economic consequences of the religious ethics of other world religions (Confucianism, Hinduism, Buddhism, on which he was working in 1916 and 1917, and ancient Judaism on which he was working in 1918 and 1919) were a logical extension to complementary areas of the kinds of investigations undertaken in the *Protestant Ethic*.

The extent to which the kinds of problems and orientations established in the *Protestant Ethic* remained for the rest of his life is dramatically illustrated by the two famous addresses on "Science as a Vocation" and "Politics as a Vocation" delivered before the students' organization of the University of Munich in 1919. Both science and politics were approached from the standpoint of the concept of "calling" which had played the central role in the *Protestant Ethic*. It is noteworthy that Weber speaks of vocation of the scientist as if it were the last great heir of the Protestant calling. "Science today is a 'vocation' organized in special disciplines in the service of self-clarification and knowledge of inter-related facts. It is not the gift of grace of seers and prophets dispensing sacred values and revelations, nor does it partake of the contemplation of sages and philosophers about the meaning of the universe. This, to be sure, is the inescapable condition of our historical situation."[29]

Central to Weber's examination of the role of the politician in contemporary society are his contrasts between the political amateur (who lives *for* politics) and professional (who lives *off* politics) and the contrast between an ethic of absolute ends and an ethic of responsibility as alternative bases for political conduct. The formulations of this penetrating address may not unfairly be viewed as Weber's final estimation of the twin principles basic to the conflicts of his parental household: an ethic of absolute ends was implied by the attitudes of his pious, religiously oriented mother; an ethic of responsibility was implied by the attitudes of his pragmatic, politically oriented father. Weber saw the point of gravity of contemporary political life to be located in the political professional operating most effectively when, rising about principle, he seeks to discover a course that maximizes the values of all parties to the political act.

Who could doubt that for Max Weber at least his activity as a scientist had significance as a continuous effort at self-clarification?

Weber's Epitomization of His Method
and of His Theoretical Concepts

By 1910 Max Weber's productivity was in full stride. In 1909 he accepted the editorship of the encyclopedic review of the social sciences, *Grundriss der Sozialoekonomik,* agreeing to do the volume on *Economics and Society (Wirtschaft und Gesellschaft).* His contribution to the project occupied much of his time between 1911 and 1913. The manuscript included his *Sociology of Law, Systematic Sociology of Religion, Sociology of Music,* and *Sociology of Economics.* He also undertook a general restatement of his methodology and formulation of central categories of his thought in connection with *Wirtschaft und Gesellschaft.* His examination of the "Categories of Interpretive Sociology" constitutes Weber's own fullest formulation of his theoretical position.

In Weber's mature formulation of his methodological and theoretical point of view, his elementarism was made quite explicit. Sociology was defined as "the science which attempts the interpretive understanding of social action in order thereby to arrive at a causal explanation of its course and effects."[30] In this formulation the positions of the neo-idealists and neo-Kantians were at once smoothly joined. The very essence of social life (with the neo-idealists) was conceived as meaningful social actions which it was the task of sociology to interpret. However, Weber immediately went on to urge (with the neo-Kantians) that one was seeking by such interpretation a causal explanation of the course and effects of social action. It is notable in these formulations that the subjective intentions of social actors are neither conceived to be some sort of an epiphenomenon nor to constitute the sole and exclusive factor in interhuman acts.

Weber's Mature Methodology

With this definition of the task of sociology, the most fundamental of all methodological problems consists in the procedures for isolating and interpreting the subjectively intended meanings in social interaction and estimating their significance in determining the course of this interaction. Meaning, Weber observes, may be the actual meaning in an individual case, it may be the average meaning of a plurality of actors, or it may be a theoretically conceived pure type. The line between meaningful action and mere reactive behavior cannot always be sharply drawn. Much interaction (in this case of traditional or habitual behavior) is only marginally meaningful. If one asks the average man of most societies the meaning of religious rituals in which he routinely engages, he may only be able to answer vaguely. Moreover, many mystical experiences cannot be adequately communicated and are comprehended by the observer or scientist sympathetically or empathically if at all. At the same time, it is not necessary to have been Caesar to understand Caesar. There is sufficient parallelism in the range of experience of most people to permit them sympathetically to comprehend each other. Hence the interpretation of meaning which the sociologist attempts may be rational (logical, scientific, or mathematical) or emotionally empathic. When one formulates a mathematical proposition such as $2 \times 2 = 4$, this can be understood directly by anyone acquainted with the rules of arithmetic. But many religious, artistic, and emotional activities are understood by the imaginative participation of an individual in them. However, despite the fact that we rely on empathic sensitivity to estimate the meaning of many types of activities, for scientific purposes "it is convenient to treat all irrational, affectually determined elements of behavior as factors of deviation from a conceptually pure type of rational action."[31] Rationally pure types of action, however, do not represent judgment of social reality. They are methodological devices developed for convenience. In this sense only is the method of sociology rationalistic.

Many factors which have an influence upon social interaction (such as human mortality, the organic life cycle from infancy to old age, climatic and geographic factors, and so on) are devoid of meaning in that they cannot be related to action in the role of means or ends, but only constitute stimuli or favorable or hindering circumstances. Such nonmeaningful factors are often of greatest sociological importance. In the causal explanation of social phenomena these facts (including also psychic and physical phenomena such as fatigue, habituation, memory, states of euphoria, and the like) must be included. This does not, however, alter the central task of sociology of undertaking the interpretation of action in terms of its subjective meaning.[32]

Understanding in terms of subjective meaning may be direct and rational as when one understands an argument or logical demonstration directly in terms of the arguments supplied, or understanding may be explanatory in terms of motive. Explanations in terms of motive consist in placing the given act in a more inclusive context of meaning. Interpretation in terms of motive may be concerned with the intended meanings of concrete individual action, with average meanings in the case of sociological mass phenomena, or with meanings appropriate to a pure type. The interpretation of a subjectively intended meaning may be adequate on the level of meaning (when it corresponds to our habitual modes of thought and feeling) or it may be correct (when it can be shown to be not only adequate on the level of meaning but causally adequate). "The most perfect adequacy on the level of meaning has causal significance from a sociological point of view only in so far as there is some kind of proof for the existence of a probability that action in fact normally takes the course which has been held to be meaningful."[33]

Although it is often convenient to treat collectives such as states, associations, corporations, foundations, and the like as if they were individuals, for the subjective interpretation of action in sociological work such collectivities "must be treated as solely the resultants and modes of organization of the particular acts of individual persons, since these alone can be treated as agents in a course of subjectively understandable action."[34]

In these formulations Weber had not only brought the various elements taken from the neo-idealists and neo-Kantians into close formulation, but he shifted away from his earlier methodological position (formulated in the 1904 methodological essay) which would restrict sociological analysis to the estimation of unique historical cultural configurations. He now insisted:

> It has continually been assumed as obvious that the science of sociology seeks to formulate type concepts and generalized uniformities of empirical process. This distinguishes it from history, which is oriented to the causal analysis and explanation of individual actions, structures, and personalities possessing cultural significance. The empirical material which underlies the concepts of sociology consists to a very large extent...of the same concrete processes of action which are dealt with by historians.[35]

Weber's Basic Conceptual Apparatus

The most fundamental of all concepts in Weber's sociology is that of social action. Social acts are taken as the atoms or elements of all social phenomena. Social action, including failure to act when this is intended and passive acquiescence, may be directed to past, present, and expected future behavior of others. Actions toward objects are not strictly social but have a social dimension so far as they are respected or taken into account by others. Not all contacts between persons are social. Contacts may be merely reactive as when two people jostle one another in a crowd. Needless to say, such jostling may give rise to social action. However, the fact that a number of persons act the same does not make it social; it may simply be the common reaction to some nonsocial stimulus (as in the case of much crowd behavior). Much imitative behavior may be only social in a borderline sense. However, "sociology, it goes without saying, is by no means confined to the study of 'social action'; this is only...its central subject matter, that which may be said to be decisive for its status as a science."[36]

For the analysis of social events into social acts, the most fundamental distinction lies between different types. Weber isolated four basic types of action in terms of the kind of relation holding between means and ends:

> (1) in terms of rational orientation to a system of discrete individual ends (*zweckrational*); that is, through expectation as to the behavior of objects in the external situation and of other human individuals, making use of these expectations as 'conditions' or 'means' for the successful attainment of the actor's own rationally chosen ends; (2) in terms of rational orientation to an

absolute value of some ethical, aesthetic, religious, or other forms of behavior, entirely for its own sake and independently of any prospects of external success; (3) in terms of affectual orientation, especially emotional, determined by the specific effects and states of feeling of the actor; (4) traditionally oriented, through the habituation of long practice."[37]

In the end every sociological analysis consists in the determination of some one or some complex of these action types. It is noteworthy that Weber's *Protestant Ethic* reduces to a discussion of the manner in which actions of a *wertrational* type born in ascetic Protestantism eliminated traditionalistic actions and gradually generated economic actions of a *zweckrational* type. There is a clear progression in Weber's development from his 1904 essay to this theoretical formulation between 1911 and 1913.

Granted that the elements of social life are social acts, one must be able to deal with the behavior not simply of individuals but of pluralities, and one is particularly interested in the actions of pluralities that recur. The concept of "social relationship" was critical for permitting Weber to deal with such complexities and recurrences. "Social relationship" denotes the "behavior of a plurality of actors in so far as, in its meaningful content, the action of each takes account of that of the others and is oriented in these terms."[38] A social relationship from Weber's view consists exclusively in the probability that a course of social action will occur. "A 'state'...ceases to exist in a sociologically relevant sense whenever there is no longer a probability that certain kinds of meaningfully oriented social action will take place."[39]

Weber's meaning can be clarified by taking social relationship to refer to an interpersonal arrangement. For example, the interpersonal arrangement of dominance-submission requires at least two persons. This arrangement may be present in a great number of individual acts. However, the arrangement never exists *by itself* apart from action. Hence Weber's argument that a social relationship consists exclusively in the probability of the occurrence of certain kinds of social actions. Nevertheless it is of analytical value to isolate conceptually a social relationship such as dominance-submission, since it identifies a recurrent form that may be present in a large number of specific acts.

There are a number of empirical uniformities among social actions, the types of which correspond to typically appropriate subjective meanings attributable to the actors. An actually existent probability of a uniformity of social action is a *usage*. Usage is *customary* if it rests on long familiarity. Usage, however, may be purely rationally determined by employment of the opportunities of his situation in his self interest by the actor. Usage is *fashionable* when the novelty of the behavior is the basis for empirically uniform action by a plurality. As distinguished from convention and law, custom refers to empirically uniform actions not enforced by external sanctions.

Of particular importance for the formation of social actions involving social relationships into complex patterns is the existence of ideas by social actors of the existence of a "legitimate order" of social activities. The probability that action will in fact be oriented to the notion that a legitimate order exists is described by Weber as the "validity" of the order. A legitimate order consists in the recognition by the actor of a system of maxims that are binding or that form a desirable model for imitation. The fact that the person deliberately subverts the order still involves his recognition of its legitimacy, as when a thief through surreptitious acts acknowledges the validity of the criminal law. Moreover, it is quite possible for a plurality of actors to recognize the existence of contradictory systems of order both of which are valid; an individual may act out of loyalty to his family, at the same time acknowledging that his actions are violations of the criminal law. There are four bases of the legitimacy of an order corresponding to the four major types of social action: (1) because it has been established in a manner recognized as legal; (2) because of rational belief in its absolute value; (3) by tradition and belief that it has always existed; (4) by virtue of affectual (especially emotional) attitudes legitimizing the validity of what is newly revealed or a model to imitate as occurs in cases of charismatic leadership.

Social relationships may be conflicting or solidary; they may be open or closed; they may be organized in terms of representation and responsibility, giving the actions of some persons consequences for others. Social relations are conflicting when oriented to the intention of carrying out the actor's will against the resistance of others. Conflict may be peaceable as in all forms of competition, or it may in varying degrees be warlike. Social relations are solidary or communal when based on the subjective feeling that the parties belong together. Communal relations, in turn, may be associative or affectual. Associative communal relations may correspond to the first two types of social actions (rationalistic and evaluative); solidary relationships usually rest on affectual or traditional bases corresponding to the second two types of social actions.

Social relations whether communal or associative are open when access to outsiders is not denied. They are closed when certain persons are excluded, limited, or subjected to conditions. Whether a relationship is open or closed may be determined expediently, rationally in terms of values, affectively or traditionally.

Finally, the order governing social relations may determine that actions of some persons have consequences for others. In the case of solidary members, all are held responsible for the action of any one. On the other hand, actions of certain members, the representatives, may be binding on the others. Representative authority may be completely appropriated in all forms, it may be conferred in accordance with particular criteria, permanently or for a limited term, as in the case of appointment.

All these various kinds of social relations—conflicting and solidary, open and closed, representative and responsible—enter into the composition of a legitimate order. They are essential for the formation of noncorporate and corporate groups. The concept of the "corporate group" comprises a network of social relationships which are either closed or which limit the admission of an outsider by rules. When legally established, the order of a corporate group may originate by voluntary agreement or by being imposed and acquiesced in. The systems of order which govern corporate groups are "administrative orders" in contrast to the orders of noncorporate systems of action which may be described as "regulative orders." Corporate groups may be voluntary or compulsory. Among the central properties of the relations of individuals in corporate groups are power, imperative control, and discipline. Power is the probability that one actor in a social relationship is in a position to carry out his will despite resistance of others. Imperative control is the probability that a command will be obeyed by a given group of persons. Discipline is the probability that by virtue of habituation an order will receive prompt, automatic obedience on the part of a given group of persons.

An imperatively coordinated corporate group is political so far as enforcement of its order is carried out within a given territorial area by application of threat of physical force on the part of an administrative staff. An imperatively coordinated corporate group is hierocratic so far as enforcement of its order employs psychic coercion through distribution or denial of religious benefits. A hierocratic association with continuous organization is a church if its administrative staff claims a monopoly of the legitimate use of hierocratic coercion.

Such, in rather schematic outline, was the basic system of concepts ranging from social actions to corporate groups of the religious or political type by which Max Weber proposed to conduct his sociological analysis. The explanatory power of his formulations is revealed both in the great richness of his own studies and in the many researches by other scholars whom they continue to inspire. Nothing that could be said here can substantially add or detract from Weber's stature as one of the outstanding social scientists of all time. Here, for the moment, it is of more interest to note the element of human pathos never far from any of his work. This work always has the property of an act of passionate self-clarification. Always in the end there comes into view, behind his sweeping visions and enormous labors, the contours of a personality and career shaped in every detail by the Protestant ethic he so brilliantly described but operating in secular contexts from which religious hope has vanished. There remains only the lone individual condemned by the circumstances of his biography and *milieu* to bend every effort toward a salvation his mind cannot accept.

It was Max Weber's personal fate to feel compelled to transform all issues of the objective world into problems of his personal conscience. One is reminded of Nietzsche's famous passage on the madman who strode through the streets with a lantern at midday, crying that "God is dead. We have killed him." "Will we not," the madman had asked, "have to become like gods to be worthy of the deed?" It was Max Weber's personal destiny and, he thought, the destiny of all scientists to have assumed this God-like obligation, but with only the equipment of mortality for the task.

Notes

1.Rossides, Daniel W. (1972), "The Legacy of Max Weber: A Non-Metaphysical Politics," *Sociological Inquiry*, vol. 42, 3-4, p. 183.

2. For example, "Borsengesetz" in *Handwoerterbuch fuer Sozialwissenschaften*, 1st edit., supplementary volume, 1897.

3. Hughes, H. Stuart (1958). *Consciousness and Society*. (New York: Alfred Knopf, p. 329.

4. Weber, Marianne (1926). *Max Weber: Ein Lebensbild*. Tuebingen: J.C.B. Mohr, p. 249.

5. *Ibid.*, p. 379.

6. Freund, Julien (1969). *The Sociology of Max Weber*, trans. Mary Ilford. New York: Vintage Books, p. 32.

7. *Ibid.*, p. 288.

8. *Ibid.*, pp. 32-33.

9. *Ibid.*, p. 34.

10. Gerth, Hans H. and C. Wright Mills, "Abiographical View," in Max Weber, *From Max Weber: Essays in Sociology*, trans. Gerth and Mills. New York: Oxford

University Press, 1946, p. 11.

11. *Ibid.*

12. Freund, *The Sociology of Max Weber, op. cit.,* p. 33.

13. Weber, *From Max Weber, op. cit.,* p. 127.

14. Weber, Max (1949). *The Methodology of the Social Sciences,* trans. Edward A. Shils and Henry A. Finch. Glencoe: The Free Press, p. 72.

15. *Ibid.,* p. 73.

16. *Ibid.,* p. 89.

17. *Ibid.,* p. 90.

18. *Ibid.,* p. 92.

19. *Ibid.,* p. 93.

20. *Ibid.,* p. 111.

21. Weber, Max (1930). *The Protestant Ethic and the Spirit of Capitalism,* trans. Talcott Parsons. New York: Scribner's, p. 18.

22. *Ibid.,* pp. 21-22.

23. *Ibid.,* p. 76.

 Ibid., p. 80.

23. *Ibid.,* p. 76.

24. *Ibid.,* p. 80.

25. *Ibid.,* p. 83.

26. *Ibid.,* p. 117.

27. *Ibid.,* p. 91.

28. *Ibid.,* p. 180.

29. Weber, *From Max Weber, op. cit.,* p. 152.

30. Weber, Max (1947). *The Theory of Social and Economic Organization,* trans. A.M. Henderson and Talcott Parsons. New York: Oxford University Press, p. 88.

31. *Ibid.,* p. 92.

32. *Ibid.,* p. 94.

33. *Ibid.,* pp. 99-100.

34. *Ibid.,* p. 101.

35. *Ibid.,* p. 109.

36. *Ibid.,* pp. 114-115.

37. *Ibid.,* p. 115.

38. *Ibid.,* p. 118.

39. *Ibid.,* p. 118.

Selected Bibliography

English Translations of Max Weber's Writings

Ancient Judaism (1952). Translated by Hans H. Gerth and Don Martindale. Glencoe: The Free Press.

The City (1958). Translated by Don Martindale and Gertrud Neuwirth. Glencoe: The Free Press.

Economy and Society: An Outline of Interpretive Sociology (1968). Edited, revised, and partly translated by Guenther Roth and Claus Wittich. 3 vols. New York: Bedminister Press.

From Max Weber: Essays in Sociology (1946). Translated by Hans H. Gerth and C. Wright Mills. New York: Oxford University Press.

General Economic History (1950). Translated by Frank H. Knight. Greenberg Publishers, 1927; reprinted, Glencoe: The Free Press.

Max Weber on Law in Economy and Society (1954). Translated by Edward A. Shils and Max Rheinstein. Cambridge: Harvard University Press.

The Methodology of the Social Sciences (1949). Translated by Edward A. Shils and Henry A. Finch. Glencoe: The Free Press.

The Protestant Ethic and the Spirit of Capitalism (1930). Translated by Talcott Parsons. New York: Scribner's.

The Rational and Social foundations of Music (1958). Translated by Don Martindale, Johannes Riedel, and Gertrude Neuwirth. Carbondale, IL: Southern Illinois University Press.

The Religion of China: Confucianism and Taoism (1951). Translated by Hans H. Gerth. Glencoe: The Free Press.

The Religion of India (1958). Translated by Hans H. Gerth and Don Martindale. Glencoe: The Free Press.

The Sociology of Religion (1963). Translated by Ephraim Fischoff. Boston: Beacon Press.

The Theory of Social and Economic Organization (1947). Translated by A.M. Henderson and Talcott Parsons. New York: Oxford University Press.

Secondary Sources

Bendix, Reinhard. *Max Weber: An Intellectual Portrait*. New York: Doubleday Anchor Books, 1962.

Freund, Julien. *The Sociology of Max Weber*. Translated by Mary Ilford. New York: Vintage Books, 1969.

Wrong, Dennis H. *Max Weber*. Englewood Cliffs, NJ: Prentice-Hall, 1970.

III

Titans of American Sociology:
Talcott Parsons and C. Wright Mills

Discussions of outstanding men often employ roughly defined categories of first-, second-, or third-rate minds or talents. These are not necessarily invidious distinctions. A first-rate mind is one which cuts through current stereotypes and finds its way to new solutions to social or theoretical problems. In his immediate social impact, a first-rate thinker is not necessarily as significant as a second-rate thinker, who is a person with sufficient ability to understand the creators and with the capacity to work up and systematize the new positions in formulations which make the new orientation available to the times. New messages often await for their social efficacy the discipleship of the second-rate thinkers. Third-rate scholars are characterized chiefly by the industry with which they transpose the formulas of the second-rate thinkers into stereotypes for routine exploitation.

In our time, for example, Talcott Parsons, the foremost macrofunctionalist, is such a first-rate thinker. Parsons has produced some three generations of students,[1] among whom are some[2] who have transformed macrofunctionalism into semipermanent form for routine exploitation. With considerable frequency Parsons has been adjudged the most significant professional sociologist in the United States in the post-World War II period. At the time of his death, C. Wright Mills, also among the first-rate sociologists of his generation, was evolving into Talcott Parsons' great rival. While his teaching was in the college rather than in the graduate school at Columbia, preventing him general participation in the training of neophytes, Mills also was developing a considerable following, and it has been estimated by some, particularly European, students that he was the most significant American sociologist of the postwar period.

The first-rate thinkers of a generation exist in varying grades and types. They may be major or minor (depending on the importance and scope of the assumptions they transform); they may be theory or action oriented. While neither Parsons nor Mills has the scope and theoretical intensity of a Max Weber, nor the revolutionary impetus of a Marx, Lenin, or Trotsky, there is little doubt that they are or have been among the first-rate thinkers of the current sociological generation. By the 1950s Parsons and Mills had emerged as the titans of American sociology. Both men began their careers as social behaviorists; both responded creatively to the formulas of their youth and worked their way to new positions; both became centers of new conceptual ferment.

The comparison of Parsons and Mills is of special interest, because with considerable frequency they have been taken as the major antagonists expressing the fundamental polarity in postwar sociological thought. While the dimensions of current social theory are not exhausted by the alternatives supplied by Parsons and Mills, this idea testifies to their influence. To recover the picture of the full richness of current theory, it will be necessary to take account of some things on which both Mills and Parsons, despite their many differences, are agreed, but which some other social theorists do not accept.

The personal evolution of a first-rate mind occurs only when the assumptions with which it was supplied by its teachers are not adequate to its problems. A peculiar kind of intellectual courage is required to question the assumptions of one's epoch—to face up to the deepest of all forms of spiritual uncertainties. It is as if the fixed stars have vanished from their places and the universe itself falls through an immensity. It is an experience most men cannot bear for long, for it is to be lost, not as an adult may be lost, in the unshaken conviction that there is a right way which only needs to be found, but to be lost in the manner of a child before the compass points of conceptual life have been fixed. It is to be lost absolutely or *in principle*—in a manner which erases the distinction between a right and a wrong way. When the fundamental assumptions of one's time are rejected, one comes face to face with *the ultimate relativity of all human ways of life.* For *at the base of every human way of life is not a given but a taken,* an assumption, an act of faith. At the moment doubt creeps into the act of faith on which a way of life rests, most men experience an extraordinarily intense need to deny the relativity of all specifically human ways of life. *At these memoments it is necessary for men to create the gods to sustain the ways of life they have themselves invented.*

Career Comparisons: Mills and Parsons

Talcott Parsons, the elder contemporary of C. Wright Mills, was born of middle-class parents at Colorado Springs, Colorado, on December 13, 1902. Though sociology was not popular at the eastern liberal arts college to which he was sent, Parsons reports that it was here that he was converted to the social sciences as an alternative to biology and medicine.

> However, even though I was not introduced to sociology at Amherst, it was at Amherst I was converted to the social sciences. At the beginning the most important alternative was biology, and at one time I hesitated between biology and medicine. This beginning in biology has been an important influence ever since, and as an undergraduate I had a pretty good grounding in it. I was even an assistant in the laboratory of a general course in biological evolution, and I went for a whole summer to Wood's Hole, the famous marine biological laboratory.[3]

At Amherst Parsons reports among his most influential teachers Walter Hamilton and Clarence Ayers (who also influenced C. Wright Mills) and among the works to which he was introduced by these men were those of Thorstein Veblen ("for Veblen was an important mutual hero to both Hamilton and Ayers"[4]) which so impressed Mills as a young man as to lead his teacher, Hans Gerth, to say: "Mills came from Texas University with Veblen in one hand and John Dewey in the other."[5]

After graduating from Amherst in 1924, Parsons spent a year at the London School of Economics (1924-1925), while he studied with Hobhouse, Ginsberg, and Malinowski. While there he received a scholarship for study at Heidelberg (1925-1926), where he found an atmosphere dominated by the ideas of Max Weber who had died five years before. He received his doctorate from Heidelberg in 1928. From 1927 to 1931 Parsons served as an instructor in economics at Harvard. At Harvard, to which he had been invited to form a department of sociology in 1930, Sorokin reports that he rescued Parsons for sociology:

> In December, 1930, I submitted the committee's plan for the department to President Lowell. He and the administration approved it with the exception of one point: they refused to approve the appointment of Talcott Parsons as the department's faculty instructor. Somewhat surprised by this, I asked

Professor Burbank, chairman of the department of economics (where Parsons was an instructor) what could be the reasons behind this refusal. The gist of Burbank's remarks was that Parsons seemed to be less interested in economics than in sociology, that possibly for this reason his work in the department of economics was not of the best quality, that he probably would do much better work in sociology than in economics, and that therefore the department of economics would be only too glad to transfer Parsons to the new department..... I told Burbank that we were quite willing to have Parsons in the new department and asked him, Taussig, Gay, Carver, and Perry to support the committee's recommendation of Parsons to President Lowell and the administration. I also asked the members of the committee to exert all their individual influence upon the administration in this matter. Backed by their support, I did my best to convince Mr. Lowell to change his negative decision to a positive one. After two talks with Lowell I finally obtained his approval of Parsons' appointment.[6]

Some persons have been impressed by what they view as a weakness in Parsons' sociological roots: According to Edward Devereux, Parsons not only "always regarded himself as something of a maverick in the field of sociology" but has been reproached for his disregard of the founders of sociology.[7] However, though rescued for sociology by Sorokin and originally displaying a thinness of anchorage in the historical names of the field, Parsons was destined to become the most powerful figure in professional American sociology in the postwar period. He was made instructor in sociology at Harvard in 1931, assistant professor in 1936, professor in 1939. He played a major role in the reorganization of sociology at Harvard which accompanied Sorokin's resignation as chairman. Sorokin describes these changes as follows:

Some four or five years later I asked again to be relieved from this position and was again refused. Finally in 1942, for the third time, I went to President Conant with this request, but this time I took with me a copy of the recent faculty vote on this matter. According to this mandatory vote, chairmen in all departments of Harvard should be appointed only for three years--in exceptional circumstances, for five years--and under no conditions for a longer period. Showing a copy of the resolution to President Conant I said that I had already carried on the duties of chairman for more than twelve years and that morally and legally I was entitled to be freed from these duties--the more so since, while I was anxious to be rid of the chairmanship, some other members of the department were very eager to attain this position. To my great satisfaction, this time my request had to be, and was, granted. This ended my responsibility for the department and its future development. *Nunc dimittis. Feci quod potut, faciant meliora potentes.* I said to myself lightheartedly after the release from these duties.[8]

Parsons was chairman of the department of social relations at Harvard from 1946 to 1956 and was elected president of the American Sociological Association in 1949.

While Talcott Parsons was raised as the son of a Congregational minister who later became the president of Marietta College, C. Wright Mills (1916-1962) was raised in a pious middle-class Roman Catholic family of Irish and English background. Mills' youth was spent in Sherman, Fort Worth, and Dallas, Texas, in which places his parents sent him to Catholic parochial and high schools. This was as natural for Mills' parents as for Parsons' parents to dream of an Ivy League education for their son. Mills' later career has been compactly summarized by his disciple, Irving Horowitz.

After an unpleasant year as an engineering student at Texas A. & M., he went to the University of Texas, where he received his B.A. and M.A. degrees in philosophy and sociology in 1939. With the exception of his election to Phi Beta Kappa, he did not participate in any of the usual extra-curricular college activities. From Texas he went to the University of Wisconsin, where, working under Howard Becker, he received his Ph.D. in sociology and anthropology in 1941. His teaching apprenticeship began at Wisconsin, where he held a teaching fellowship during 1940 and 1941. In 1941 he was appointed assistant professor of sociology at the University of Maryland; in 1945 he was for a brief time special business consultant to the Smaller War Plants Corporation, traveling and preparing a Senate committee report on *Small Business and Civic Welfare.* Immediately after the war end in 1945 Mills was awarded a Guggenheim Fellowship and also received an appointment as assistant professor of sociology at Columbia University. Until 1948 he was director of the Labor Research Division of the Bureau of Applied Social Research, where he worked under the overall supervision of Paul F. Lazarsfeld. After that, he remained at Columbia University in the department of sociology as an associate professor.

During his later years he held visiting lectureships at Brandeis University, the University of Copenhagen, the United States Air War College, and the William A. White Institute of Psychiatry. Mills retained the specifically anthropological capacity for researching people wherever the people were. He studied health needs for the Congress of Industrial Relations in Detroit, migration patterns of Puerto Ricans in New York, personal influence and mass communication effects on midwesterners. His later travels to Latin America and Europe assisted him in expanding his vision of the human mission of sociology. Thus he became acutely aware of the threat of thermonuclear warfare during his visit to Western Europe in the early fifties, the dynamics of socialism in his later trips to Russia and Poland, and undertook to study the revolutionary process by going to Cuba at the time of Fidel Castro's emergence. This does not mean that Mills was simply a child of his experiences. It does mean that Mills' strongly pragmatic attitudes conditioned him to observe the social phenomena he was writing about.[9]

The parallelism between Parsons and Mills is rather extensive. Both men were raised in pious middle-class homes. Both came to sociology from other fields: Parsons from biology and medicine, Mills from engineering and philosophy. They shared an influence of Clarence Ayers, who introduced each to Veblen. Both men were attracted to institutional economics: Parsons through Walton, Hamilton, and Ayers, and later, by his teachers in the London School of economics, Mills through Ayers and the atmosphere at the University of Wisconsin, where the most famous student of J. R. Commons (Selig Perlman) was at the height of his powers and where the traditions of Richard T. Ely, John R. Commons, and Wesley Mitchel were still fresh. Both Parsons and Mills were introduced to Max Weber: Parsons at the London School and later at Heidelberg, Mills at the University of Wisconsin, where Max Weber's theories were zealously promoted by Hans H. Gerth. Both men made their initial reputations with translations of Weber: Parsons with *The Protestant Ethic and Spirit of Capitalism* (1930) and Mills with his co-translation (with Hans Gerth) of selected essays from Weber:*From Max Weber*(1946). Both men were to make their way to positions of prominence in great eastern private universities.

Few people would dispute the proposition that by the 1950s Talcott Parsons and C. Wright Mills had achieved foremost positions in the respective spheres of sociology they occupied: Parsons in sociology's inner professional circles and Mills in its extra-professional relations with the wider learned world. Because of his position at Harvard, as chairman of the Department of Social Relations, and his semipermanent position in the professional society, Parsons developed a power network of ties to which he was key.

> This was certainly the case with respect to Parsons' interactions with such colleagues and contemporaries as Clyde Kluckhohn in anthropology, O. H.Taylor in economics, or Samuel Stouffer in social relations. And it was still more the case in Parsons' relations with several generations of junior colleagues and graduate students who sojourned at Harvard, a changing group which in the first decade included such people as R.K. Merton, Kingsley Davis, Robin Williams, and Wilbert Moore, somewhat later included people like Marion J. Levy, Albert Cohen, David Aberle, and Bernard Barber, and in the most recent decade R.F. Bales, Edward Shils, James Olds, Renee Fox, and Neil Smelser, to mention only a few.[10]

In the 1950s Parsons would almost instantly be named as the foremost sociologist of the United States, not only by members of the profession but by most undergraduate students. On the other hand, if one

queried visiting foreign scholars and intellectuals in the mid-1950s as
to America's foremost sociologist, C. Wright Mills was almost always
named first. Parsons and Mills were the titans of American sociology
in the mid-century.

The Genesis of the Will to Succeed and Personal Style

There is a temptation to substitute a preoccupation with the human
foibles of outstanding men for the drama occurring in their minds.
The minds and often the personal lives of first-rate thinkers in all
fields are often rent by conflicts. It is impossible to imagine either C.
Wright Mills or Talcott Parsons rising to paramount positions in their
respective spheres without an extraordinarily powerful will to succeed. Each, moreover, has developed his distinctive personal style in
the course of his rise.

Too little objective information is available as yet to estimate with
any great hope of accuracy all the factors in the origins of the will to
power and the personal styles which carried each to the pinnacle of his
chosen sphere. Many persons other than Sorokin were impressed by
Parsons' drive to succeed, a drive which eventually drove Sorokin to
request relief from the responsibilities of the chairmanship at
Harvard.

> Morally and legally I was entitled to be freed from these duties--the more so
> since, while I was anxious to be rid of the chairmanship, some other mem-
> bers of the department were very eager to attain this position.[11]

At the time this author was a graduate student at Wisconsin, partly
overlapping Mills' career, he was impressed, as were others, by the
unusual power of his will to succeed. Dan Wakefield, who as an
undergraduate student at Columbia had been drawn to Mills' sphere
by the magnetic pull of his charisma and who later became Mills'
assistant and devoted follower, reports his mentor's preoccupation
with success.

> "Now, Dan," Mills counseled me once..., "you're not married yet and
> you're living alone. You must get one of your girls to come over every
> Sunday night and cook you a big stew that will last a week. You bottle it up in
> seven Mason jars, and take one out each day, and you have a good, healthy
> meal instead of that bachelor stuff." He was full of advice that was often
> valuable and always entertaining, from books I should read (he thrust James
> Agee's *Let Us Now Praise Famous Men* on me when it was out of print and
> not yet in vogue), to hints on work habits ("Set up a file"—and he showed

me how), and running through all his advice was one grand theme, which served as his own motto, an approach to the world he called "Taking it big"—by which he meant subjects, and do them in the grand manner; a philosophy he not only preached but applied to everything from eating and drinking to writing. Almost any advice he gave ended with the exhortation, "Take it big, boy!"[12]

Wakefield was convinced that Mills shared the provincial's identification of "New York City as the citadel or Headquarters of Success." He describes his mentor as an intellectual Gatsby, raised on middle-class success ideologies.

I remember once driving with Mills from his house in Spring Valley to Columbia on a bright winter morning, and as we crossed over the George Washington Bridge, he pointed to the dazzling skyline and with a sweeping gesture said, "Take that one, boy."[13]

Harvey Swados, who perhaps knew Mills more intimately and for a longer time than anyone else, was impressed by the self-absorption associated with Mills' will to dominate. He reports that Mills seemed to have utterly no memory of the activities of others unconnected with his own.

For many people this utter self-absorption was intolerable, and I must confess that there were occasions when it was for me also. But after a time it was borne in upon me that Mills could not function without the absolute conviction that what he was doing was not only right but was more important than what anybody else was doing. More than that, the unique thrust of his best work—I am thinking of the decade of the fifties, of *White Collar* and *The Power Elite*—derived directly from his egocentricity. These books would have been paltry if they had not been informed throughout with a sense of the magnetic self-assurance of their author.[14]

Swados found a parallel "between Fitzgerald's crackup and Mills' terrifying conviction at the same age that he was written out, worked out, burned out."[15] Saul Landau, who met Mills and clung to him throughout his closing days, reports similar manifestations of a career dominated by a will to succeed which has reached its limits and experiences the backwash of depression when there is no longer any place to go.

Mills embarrassed me into shaving my beard before we met Sartre and Simone de Beauvoir for lunch. He did it subtly so that I didn't realize exactly why I did it until a few weeks later. Anyway, his beard looked good. He resembled Hemingway, and although at first it was unintentional, he began to identify more and more with him. Hemingway had committed suicide a few days before and its shook Mills up. He talked about it for hours and then every day he would analyze it. It began, "obviously the man committed suicide. A man that knows weapons like he did would never point a loaded shotgun at his face. Of course he killed himself, the only way he could do it, with a hunting rifle. You know, that's the only way to do it; put the gun deep into your mouth and blast with both barrels. That's how I'd do it."

I tried to change the subject and failed. "Look, he was used up. The man hadn't written anything for ten years. He was used out. What else was there for him to do? He had done it all, and he wrote himself out. That's me." And he laughed.[16]

But it is unnecessary to establish the presence of a powerful will to succeed in Parsons and Mills. The fact that each has achieved far more than many persons intellectually their equal if not superior to them is evidence enough. The problem is, rather, to account for the genesis of such drives and the form they assumed.

One may guess that the genesis of Parsons' personal impetus rests in part in his religious and family background. The son of a Congregational minister could hardly have been unaffected by the activational complex which, since Weber, has been described as the Protestant ethic. In its nonsacramental concept of religious salvation, Protestantism tended to cast the individual on his own resources, making him individually responsible for his religious fate. Wherever this orientation appears in pure form, it carries with it the tendency by the individual to turn his activities into a testing ground of his personal worthiness. Furthermore, the individual who practices such "innerworldly asceticism" tends to measure his success in terms of objective achievement. Middle-class Americans living in a *milieu* once dominated by the Protestant ethic tend, in any case, to measure their successes in terms of achievement of their parents, and Parsons had as a personal standard a father who had made the ascent from the Congregational ministry to a college presidency. Whatever other things were operating, Parsons has shown the extraordinary capacity for hard work so typical of persons raised on the Protestant ethic, and his life also has borne the marks of an unusually intense demand for objective success.

Mills, too, may be assumed to have been personally paced by the demands for success, particularly objective success, characteristic of the American middle classes. However, Mills' drive did not possess the internalized form of an inner force in an upbuilding tension against internalized standards. His impetus was always directed outward as a rebellion against external obstacles. Despite the fact that his personal admirers, such as Swados and Horowitz, have not been impressed by the role of religion in Mills' motivations, his impetus has many of the properties typical of anti-clericalism and anti-authoritarianism. All his life Mills required external opponents: the middle classes, the power elite, and finally, anything American. One is tempted to guess that what began as anti-clericalism was successively generalized to more comprehensive contexts. Swados reports to have found in Mills

> ... a hatred, which became more ostentatious as the years went by, of everything marked Made in America. It seems to me that the last American vehicle he owned, before the MG, was that masterpiece of ingenious simplicity, the jeep."[17]

There is a close connection between the form of their respective drives, the spheres of their competition, and the personal styles of Parsons and Mills. Parsons' impetus seems to have been internalized as an up-building tension against mounting personal standards; Mills' impetus took the form of an ever more intense hatred of more and more generalized external opponents. Parsons was an in-fighter: in his department and in his university, in the official society, in the cliques of contemporary sociology. One of his long-time associates has described him as "the most masterful politician of contemporary sociology." Parsons' internal tensions led him to the psychoanalyst. Mills was a rebel against his department, against the professional society, against American society itself. Mills' personal tensions took him, not to psychoanalysists, but to the courts. His personal tensions exploded in a series of marriages and divorces and terminated in heart trouble and flight from the conflicts his actions generated.

> He hated the U.S., its politics, its culture, its "higher immorality." But he did not fit anywhere else, and he did not want to be anywhere else but in his own house, which he had built. It would be painful to be in the U.S. and read the New York Times, and face law suits, and petty professors writing personal attacks—to be in the same country that was preparing another invasion of Cuba, that would be testing bombs, and making counter-revolutions in little countries. Just reading the newspapers and not being able to do anything—it gave him chest pain.[18]

As a young man, when Mills had begun to undergo the first of his own troubles, he was fascinated by the personal problems of Charles Pierce. During the time he was a graduate student at Wisconsin, he felt a deep kinship with Pierce, not only because of Pierce's personal difficulties but of his empiricism as well. However, always in the end the personal lives of outstanding men are important for the light they may throw on the drama of their ideas.

The psychological foundations of the intellectual life of Mills have numerous superficial parallels to those of Rousseau. Like Rousseau, Mills' interests were neither purely theoretical nor purely practical. Like Rousseau, Mills was lionized by a society he despised. Like Rousseau, who worked out his intellectual destiny in the transition from enlightened individualism to romantic collectivism, Mills was gradually to abandon the individualistic social behaviorism of his early period for a collectivitistic point of view. Like Rousseau's, Mills' style is often more clear than his thought. Like Rousseau, he was a slogan maker, capable of spinning out shibboleths calling diverse groups to common action. Finally, there is some evidence that, like Rousseau, Mills had an unusual tendency to project his personal problems into his intellectual ones, giving the drama of his emotions a universal scope.

The present volume is no place to trace all the points of intersection between Mills' personal problems and his theoretical concerns. Here they have interest primarily in accounting for the generation of his intellectual energies. The projection of his personal difficulties into his conceptual problems account, as with Rousseau, for the strident call to action which hovers in the background of all of Mills' formulations. One cannot but wonder whether, given the self-conscious choice, Mills would not gladly have supplied the program for a revolution in the twentieth century comparable to the manner in which Rousseau supplied the program for the French Revolution in the eighteenth. Perhaps this is why Mills, like Rousseau, appeals primarily to the young.

Mills' intellectual evolution, like that of Rousseau, has already been subject to uncertain and, at times, contradictory construction. Some of his critics, for example, have taken the position that he was basically a Marxist. This, indeed, was Parsons' judgment. Of current sociological theories other than his own, Parsons says:

> The types of alternative theory are...various, though probably a broad neo-Marxian type...is the most prominent... Of the former type, such names as C. Wright Mills, Rolf Dahrendorf, Barrington Moore, and David Lockwood come to mind... [19]

Since the publication of *Listen Yankee*, judgments as to the essential

Marxism of Mills have become more frequent. At the same time, persons close to Mills have reported that he was taken aback at this misconstruction of this view.

If it is correct to estimate the personal styles of Parsons and Mills, respectively, as those of the astute political in-fighter on the one hand and of the rebel adept at guerrilla warfare on the other, it is quite impossible to imagine their success in spheres other than the ones they chose. Parsons' successes led him step by step to power within the profession; Mills' successes led him to ever wider audiences at home and abroad critical of one or another feature of American life. Characteristically, Mills' last truly sociological writing, *The Sociological Imagination*, before he departed permanently from its concerns, was a frontal attack upon what he viewed as all its main traditions. Swados seems unquestionably to be correct in sensing that Mills was set upon a course which involved ultimately the abandonment even of his professional role for that of sect leader. Mills, Swados urges, was entrapped by the temptation

of being simultaneously a Teddy Roosevelt and a Scott Fitzgerald, a public figure—man of action and an artist-thinker. He was becoming a leader with a following. Not merely requests to speak, but pleas for guidance and counsel came pouring in on him, and after *The Causes of World War III* they became a flood. Under such circumstances the temptation to become oracular was almost irresistible; for a man who was absolutely sure of his own insight and analysis it was inevitable.[20]

The last days of the two types of figures bear some striking contrasts. After forty-two years on the Harvard University faculty, Parsons retired. In his note of the event in the *New York Times* Robert Reinhold observed that while Parsons eschewed sermonizing his fellow men on the human predicament ''both disciples and detractors would agree that no other living scholar has had more impact on modern social thought and theory.''[21]

During the course of his service at Harvard, Parsons guided the careers of many leading sociologists such as Robert K. Merton, Kingsley Davis, Clifford Geets, Robert Bellah, Neil J. Smelser, Bernard Barber, Jesse Pitts, and Renee Fox.

Athough retiring at the age of seventy, Parsons had no intention of departing abruptly from the halls of power.

Retirement will not mean complete rest. He is in the midst of a major theoretical analysis of the American University as an institution, in collaboration with Gerald Platt of the University of Massachusetts.[22]

The last days of the rebel are another story. Swados has sensitive-
ly formulated the pathos that surrounded Mills' last days:

> I last saw C. Wright Mills in 1962, late in January, at the Nice Airport, where
> I had driven him from my French home so that he could return to America,
> after many months of fruitless wander about Europe, to die. His youngest
> child, who had been toddling about, tripped and split open his lip on the
> terrazzo floor. Mills was concerned, but unable to cope (fortunately his wife
> was). We shook hands, for the last time, and I looked back to see him
> walking slowly up and down with his child, being the dutiful parent because
> at this terrible moment he had nothing else to do with his time or with his
> life.[23]

Comparative Writing Styles of Parsons and Mills

One of the most immediately evident contrasts between Parsons and
Mills appears in their writing styles. Parsons' writing has been found
so complex and abstract, and to consist of so many finely inter-
related distinctions that Parsons insisted were equally important, as to
apparently defy summary and to lead many professional sociologists
to renounce any claim that they could fully grasp his meaning.

The actual style difficulty may be illustrated by any passage taken
at random from Parsons' writings.

> In one sense "motivation" consists in orientation to improvement of the
> gratification-deprivation balance of the actor. But since action without
> cognitive and evaluative components in its orientation is inconceivable within
> the action frame of reference, the term motivation will here be used to
> include all three aspects, not only the cathectic. But from this motivational
> orientation aspect of the totality of action it is, in view of the role of symbolic
> systems, necessary to distinguish a "value-orientation" aspect. This aspect
> concerns, not the meaning of the expected state of affairs to the actor in
> terms of his gratification-deprivation balance but the content of the selective
> standards themselves. The concept of value-orientations in this sense is thus
> the logical device for formulating one central aspect of the articulation of
> cultural traditions into the acting system.[24]

One may have to read this passage several times before one discovers
that all it says is that "action involves values and ideas as well as
pleasure and pain and the values are important."

By contrast one may consider a typical passage from C. Wright
Mills:

> The producer is the man who creates ideas, first sets them forth, possibly
> tests them, or at any rate makes them available in writing to those portions of
> the market capable of understanding them. Among producers there are

individual entrepreneurs—still the predominant type—and corporation executives in research institutions of various kinds who are in fact administrators over production units. Then there are the *wholesalers,* who, while they do not produce ideas, do distribute them in textbooks to other academic men, who in turn sell them directly to student consumers. In so far as men teach, and only teach, they are *retailers* of ideas and materials, the better of them being serviced by original producers, the lesser, by wholesalers. All academic men, regardless of type, are also *consumers* of the products of others, of producers and wholesalers through books, and of retailers to some extent through personal conversation on local markets. But it is possible for some to specialize in consumption. These become great *comprehenders,* rather than *users,* of books, and they are great on bibliographies.

In most colleges and universities, all these types are represented, all may flourish, but the producer (perhaps along with the textbook wholesaler) has been honored the most.[25]

One does not have to read this twice to discover that Mills is discussing professorial writing and that he thinks it a rather crass commercial affair.

The passage by Parsons throws up a thorny set of apparently unnecessary complications. That by Mills hacks at a point with directness and vigor. It was, perhaps, inevitable that the styles of these two giants of the 1950s and 1960s should so often be contrasted. Exposes of the pompous emptiness of Parsons' style have been carried out so often as to amount to a sort of intellectual parlor game by persons unsympathetic to sociology. With considerable unfairness it has often been suggested tht Parsons' style is characteristic of what sociology "is," while that of Mills represents what it "ought to be." Yet, despite all its display of vigor, the passage by Mills says very little more than the one by Parsons. Mills has said only that "professors produce and consume books, and the producers have somewhat more prestige."

In the course of the many exposes of Parsons' writing, it has often been hinted that he could do no better and that the prestige of Harvard had permitted him "to get away with it." It is, of course, quite out of the question that a man of Parsons' brilliance could not have written more clearly if he chose. A man does not become one of the foremost members of a professional field without outstanding abilities. **The hypothesis offered here is that PARSONS WROTE AS HE DID BY CHOICE, THAT HE DEVELOPED A STYLE AS ADAPTED TO HIS PURPOSES AS WAS THAT OF MILLS TO OTHER OBJECTIVES.**

If one traces the source of the difficulties in Parsons' writing style, one is not long in discovering a few basic devices employed with infinite ingenuity to make the grasp of his meanings difficult. New terms are coined for familiar ideas. The writing is abstract, offering virtually no concrete illustration. Sentence after sentence, paragraph after paragraph, and page after page, indefinite references are pyramided in a manner which defies keeping track of the subject without special effort. The flow of the argument is continually being disrupted by independent and dependent clauses. That he knows what he is doing is shown by the fact that Parsons rarely ever loses track of his argument.

Parsons' writing style has been described by his disciples as architectoric. One can agree that his style has architectural parallels: it is medieval and defensive. It is not medieval gothic (with its synthesis of rational and sensuous values) which belonged to the city, but medieval domestic like the rural manorial architecture of the early Middle Ages. Just as the estates of a rural lord were protected by crude and apparently unordered but effective moats and baileys, so Parsons' meanings are endlessly guarded: by his special terminology, by indefinite references, and by parenthetical clauses. It is as if he were endlessly on the defensive from attack from every possible quarter. One can only grasp his meanings by marshaling his forces and laying siege upon endlessly varied, crude, but effective defensive traps.

If one once accepts the possibility that Parsons' style is not accidental but intended, a number of additional deductions may be made. It is unusually well adapted to an inner-professional strategy. Those who have not the capacity or endurance to make the assault upon its defensive works and extract its meanings have no right to criticize. On the other hand, those who expend the extensive time and energy necessary to understand what is going on may not have learned anything very profound, but at least they have had a profoundly hard time getting there. And not many persons can admit after such expenditures of energy that it was not worth the effort. In any case, a subtle sense of profundity tends to cling to the writing simply because of the amount of effort required to master it. So successfully has his style served him that Parsons' critics have blamed the difficulty, the abstractness, and the obscurity of it not only on him but on sociology itself.

Closely tied to Mills' will to succeed was his preoccupation with self-presentation. As a graduate student at the University of Wisconsin he affected an air of breezy nonchalance of the kind that so impressed his followers later when his charisma was confirmed. He at times intimidated colleagues and teachers with a "bigger than life" illusion which Wakefield traces not only to his physical size—some six feet and two hundred pounds—but to his sense of restless energy and preference for unconventional dress.

> He commuted to Columbia in a rather bulky getup suggestive of a guerrilla warrior going to meet the enemy (which in a way he took the situation to be). He usually wore camping boots of some sort and either a helmet or a cap used for motorcycle riding, and was strapped around with army surplus duffel bags or knapsacks filled with books and notes.[26]

Mills continued to behave at Columbia as he had as a graduate student teaching assistant at Wisconsin, at a time when other instructors wore a conventional white shirt, tie and jacket, while Mills lectured jacketless with an open collar, a wide belt, and motorcycle boots.

However, Mills' preoccupation with self-presentation from his graduate student days on was by no means confined to the cultivation of a distinctive physical presence. He was, if anything, even more concerned with his writing style. Even in seminar papers he shadowboxed with professional opponents as in a public forum. His two great style models of the period were Ernest Hemingway and Thomas Wolfe. He loved the terse impact of Hemingway and the force, like carefully aimed bullets, of his sentences. But he also liked the gusty rhetorical overflow of richness in Thomas Wolfe. In the long run, I felt he belonged more to Wolfe than to Hemingway because his genius, like Wolfe's, overflowed from a surging inner ferment.

Even in the early days it was possible to set down the principles which seemed to guide Mills' selection of devices which he began to weave into a style of his own: he was attracted by Veblen's rather pretentious academicism which in Veblen's hands was a means of heavy-handed sarcasm; he also was fascinated by the device which Dos Passos had borrowed from O. Henry and named the Camera Eye (the juxtaposition of apparently objective but carefully selected materials which give the lie to one another); and the device of Kenneth Burke of the transplanting of the language and images from an area where they originated to another (for example, using the language and images of war in the sphere of love or the language and images of love to describe warfare).

The language and imagery of the marketplace, for example, are employed by Mills in all sorts of areas and spheres one does not normally think of as commercial. Academic writers, for example, are described as producers, wholesalers, and consumers of books.

Like the pharmacist who sells packaged drugs with more authority than the ordinary storekeeper, the professor *sells packaged knowledge* with better effect than laymen. *He brings to the market* the prestige of his university position and the academic tradition of disinterestedness.[27]

In cafe society the major inhabitants of the world of the celebrity—the institutional elite, the metropolitan socialite, and the professional entertainer—mingle, publicly *cashing in* one another's claims for prestige.[28]

One easily forgets that the under side of the glamour of cafe society is simply a service trade in vice. Those engaged in it—the procurers, the prostitutes, the customers, who buy and sell assorted varieties of erotical service—are often known to their associates as quite respectable.[29]

Yet prestige is the shadow of money and power. Where these are, there it is. Like the national market for soap or automobiles and the enlarged arena of federal power, the national cash-in area for prestige has grown, slowly being consolidated into a truly national system.[30]

Among those whom Americans honor none is so ubiquitous as the young girl. It is as if Americans had undertaken to paint a continuing national portrait of the girl as Queen. Everywhere one looks there is this glossy little animal, sometimes quite young and sometimes a little older, but always imagined, always pictured as The Girl. She sells beer and she sells books, cigarettes, and clothes; every night she is on the TV screen, and every week on every other page of the magazines, and at the movies, too, there she is.[31]

One can multiply the examples almost endlessly of the translations into the images and language of commerce of most diverse materials, always conveying the impression that one is dealing with a grubby, materialistic, despicable business— perhaps even worse than business itself, since it pretends to be something else.

While the style of Talcott Parsons is an instrument of defense, that of Mills is above all an instrument of offense. Parsons' style is calculated to hide its meanings behind an endless number of obstacles. Many a person has finally managed to surmount the obstacles and seize the meaning only to be informed by Parsons that he has advanced considerably beyond that position. Mills' style does not have to conceal its meanings, for it consists of demolition and assault devices intended to put its opponents to flight.

Personal Orientations to Western Cultural Traditions

No persons such as Parsons and Mills, arising to paramount positions in a major intellectual discipline of their times, can remain indifferent to its distinctive traditions. Every cultural tradition is distinguished by (1) its methods of analyzing the problems of man and society, (2) its modes of interpreting the relation of man to society, and (3) its strategies for realizing the good life. The distinctive methods of analyzing the problems of man and society in the West are the *humanistic* and *scientific*. The major interpretations of man and society are represented by *individualism* (which places primary emphasis on individual persons) and *collectivism* (which assigns primacy to society). Western individualism, in turn, is differentiated into *rational* and *nonrational forms*. Collectivism is subdivided into *right-* and *left-wing forms*. Individualism and collectivism are interpretations of man and his social life. *Liberalism* and *conservatism* are strategies for realigning the types of values made possible by social life.

As Parsons and Mills rose to their respective positions of eminence in inner- and extra-professional American sociology, they not only increasingly found themselves classified in terms of the structural features of the Western cultural tradition but found it necessary to locate themselves. To some extent the process of self-location was easier for Parsons. Since he has experienced himself and has been experienced by numerous others as representing the main stream of sociology, Parsons' task of self-orientation has primarily taken the form of locating his version of sociology. With respect to the primary value strategies of contemporary man (liberalism-conservatism), Parsons usually prefers to describe himself as a *liberal;* others, including many persons closely associated with him, describe him as a *conservative*.

The major act of self-location is accomplished by Parsons and his associates in the monumental *Theories of Society* of which he was senior editor. In this huge two-volume selection of pre-1935 sociological writings, all developments worthy of name are treated as an anticipation of the sociology of Parsons.

According to Shils, the sociology represented by Parsons "has come into its present estate because its own development bears a rough correspondence to the development of the consciousness of mankind in its moral progress."[32] Moreover, it "is not...a purely cognitive undertaking. It is also a moral relationship between the human beings studied and the student."[33] However, while "the sociological theory that grows from the theory of action is simply a more forward part of a widespread consensual collectivity,"[34] Shils urges, "it is still the proud boast of some sociologists that sociology is an 'oppositional science.'"[35] Most of these, he suggests, are form-

er or quasi-Marxists. They are said to focus on the miserable, the
homeless, the parentless, the insulted and injured, and to generalize
from them. They present an outlook "that radically distrusts the
inherited order of society."[36]

While these formulations are Shils,' not Parsons,' the latter was
senior editor of *Theories of Society* and permitted them to stand as a
definitive summary of his position. Moreover, when an invitation was
extended to Parsons in the Max Black symposium to defend his
position, he formulated his views in a manner similar to Shils.
Parsons showed somewhat more sympathy toward Marxism—at least
the early Marxism of the 1890s. Early Marxism, Parsons observed,
was an advance over the views that preceded it. However, Marxism,
in Parsons' opinion, has in turn been superseded and, because of both
its materialistic bias and its lack of differentiation, it is insufficient for
dealing with the great problems of culture, personality, and social
system in our day. Only the theory of action, that is, his own theory, is
adequate to the task of contemporary analysis.

> It is my own profound conviction, which I both believe and hope to be
> justified, that the developments under discussion in this volume are deeply
> rooted in the main trends of the intellectual developments of our age. Their
> base-line of reference is a great synthesis which was achieved in the gener-
> ation preceding ours—as the editors of *Theories of Society* have placed it,
> roughly 1890-1935.[37]

Parsons' concurrence in the judgments of Shils is quite complete.
Parsons and his associates consider their form of sociology to be a
"new forward part of a widespread consensual collectivity," and the
chief hope of mankind against all "alienated" positions such as Marxism which distrusts traditional society.

In his last works Mills, too, increasingly felt the need to locate
himself in the historical traditions of the West. His genius was not
one for the handling of pure ideas. One cannot ask of him the careful
examination of intellectual traditions, even those he claimed most
completely as his own. Nevertheless, in his last works, which are at
once his most creative and controversial, various of the Western
intellectual traditions within which and in part against which he was
working had become so important to him as to lead him to various
formulations concerning them. From *Images of Man* to the *Marxists,*
one or the other of the traditions of the West was never far from the
center of his reflections.

As intellectual history, the various presentations by Mills of the

Western traditions are seriously inadequate. In his edited volume of classical sociology, he set down what he considered to be the essence of its classical tradition:

> No one, I believe, has stated better, or more clearly, than did the company of thinkers presented in this volume the basic conceptions or theories of such matters as social stratification and political authority, of the nature of bureaucracy and of capitalism, of the scale and drift of modern life, of the ambiguity of rationality, of the *malaise* individual men so often feel.[38]

Mills' selection rigidly followed this proposal. He divided his treatment into three parts: "the first...concerns the difficulties of thinking clearly and well about man and society" (illustrated by selections from Walter Lippmann and Spencer);[39] "the second...suggests the variety of elements that go to make up a society" (illustrated by Marx's and Engels' concept of class and historical materialism and by Mosca, Michels, and Pareto's concepts of the *elite*);[40] part three "contains several of the original...statements of the crisis of individuality"(illustrated by selections from Thomas and Znaniecki on personality, Simmel on the individual in mass society, and by Durkheim on anomie, by Marx on alienation, and by Mannheim on rationality).

These are vital modern themes, though the particular writers and selections chosen do not always represent the best statement of them. However, to take this selection of writings as the most essential examples of historical sociology and as a statement of its most vital problems is at least as one-sided as the two volumes, *Theories of Society*, edited by Parsons and others. In the Parsons' treatise a large number of fragments from pre-1935 sociology had been treated as anticipation of the writings of Talcott Parsons which, in turn, were presented as the solely significant sociology of the present. Again a striking similarity appears between Parsons and Mills, in that each conceives the sole value of historical sociology to be the anticipation of himself.

In his last work, in press at the time of his death, Mills attempted to delineate Marxism in terms of various thought movements. As he saw them, the two positive intellectual traditions of the West are Marxism and liberalism.

> In their classic versions, liberalism and Marxism embody the assurances and hopes, the ambiguities and fears of the modern age. They...constitute our major, even our only, political alternatives.[41]

Their common opponent is conservatism.

> In the United States...conservatism offers only a retrogressive utopia to
> circles best described as cranky, if not crackpot. Insofar as it is not that,
> conservatism is a defensive gesture of businessmen and politicians who
> would defend the *status quo*, but who are without ideas with which to do
> so.[42]

There is a notable failure by Mills to isolate conservatism as a value
orientation from various political and social groups branded by the
term and a failure to acknowledge the quite genuine values (social
stability, peace, security) which lie at the heart of the conservative
orientation. One may, of course, believe that social harmony is not
enough and not worth the sacrifice of individuality, but that is another
story.

Finally, Mills' failure to isolate distinct idea configurations may be
illustrated by his derivation of Marxism and liberalism.

> Both Marxism and liberalism embody the ideals of Greece and Rome and
> Jerusalem: the humanism of the Renaissance, the rationalism of the
> eighteenth century enlightenment... What is most valuable in classic liber-
> alism is most cogently and most fruitfully incorporated in classic Marxism...
> Hence to confront Marx and Marxism is to confront this moral tradition.[43]

The methodological positions which have emerged at the core of
Western thought and the primary strategies of social life (individualism and collectivism) and their sub-forms (rational and nonrational
individualism and right- and left-wing collectivism) illustrate the
confusions which arise in the assignment to Marxism of the best of
humanism, liberalism, rationalism, and the ideals of Greece, Rome,
and Jerusalem. Some of Mills' attributions are doubly confusing,
since there are both individualistic and collectivistic interpretations of
Christianity and Judaism. One cannot know without specification
what is intended by the assertion that their best traditions have been
incorporated into Marxism.

Neither Parsons nor Mills presents a very accurate account of
historical Western culture or historical sociology, though Parsons is
rather more accurate than Mills. Parsons defines his position in terms
of the inner structure of the field; Mills' problem was more difficult,
for he had to define himself in opposition to a variety of positions.
While Parsons liked to call himself a liberal, it is quite evident that
anyone who views his position as "a more forward part of a widespread consensual collectivity" and is opposed to all positions that

"distrust the inherited order of society," basically views himself as having a vested interest in the *status quo* justifying the attribution of conservatism.

Parsons' theories are no longer as popular with sociologists as they once were. Young sociologists particularly shun abstract theory in preference for immediate issues which they view as relevant. In stressing the tendency of social systems to resist change, Parsons is visualized as politically conservative. Situations of confrontation and conflict impress the young, rather than situations of accomodation and equilibration, as where the action is. However, though declining in size there remains, according to Reinhold, a circle that is loyal to Parsons.

> Friends contend it is unfair to say that Talcott Parsons has removed himself
> from worldly affairs or that he is conservative. They note his strong stand
> against Naziism and McCarthyism, and the constant unselfish devotion, both
> from himself and his wife, Helen, lavished on a long parade of students.[44]

Mills, for his part, left no doubt as to his self-classification among those whom Parsons and Shils described as "oppositional" and "alienated." Mills' opposition to Parsons was direct and emphatic.

> Is grand theory, as represented in *The Social System,* merely verbiage or is it
> also profound? My answer to this question is: It is about 50 per cent
> verbiage, 40 per cent is well known textbook sociology. The other 10 per
> cent, as Parsons might say, I am willing to leave open for your own empirical
> investigations. My own investigations suggest that the remaining 10 per
> cent is of possible—although rather vague—ideological use.[45]

Apart from Parsonian theorizing, Mills maintains, sociological research is dominated by "abstracted empiricism" in which "the thinness of results is matched only by the elaboration of the methods and the care employed."[46] Mills illustrates what he views as its triviality by the World War II American soldier researches directed by the late Samuel Stouffer.

> The studies, it seems to me, prove that it is possible for social research to be
> of administrative use without being concerned with the problems of social
> science.[47]

So far as it is concerned with practical problems, contemporary sociology is characterized by "a new illiberal practicality."

New institutions...in which this illiberal practicality is installed: industrial relations centers, research bureaus of universities, new research branches of corporation, air force, and government...are not concerned with the battered human beings living at the bottom of society—the bad boy, the loose woman, the migrant worker, the un-Americanized. On the contrary, they are connected, in fact, and in fantasy, with the top levels of society, in particular, with enlightened circles of business executives and with generals having sizable budgets.[*48*]

Thus the self-locations of Parsons and Mills place them respectively in the positions of primary heirs and defenders of the sociological and social *status quo* on the one hand and the guerrilla leader laying siege upon these strongholds of "conservatism" on the other. This appears to cast Mills in the camp of the Marxists, but to the end he resisted any complete identification with Marxism.

The First Phase in the Intellectual Development of Parsons and Mills

Though Mills was fourteen years the junior of Parsons, both came to maturity in the interwar period: Parsons in the late 1920s and early 1930s; Mills in the late 1930s and early 1940s. Despite different religious backgrounds, both came from middle-class strata of the American West. In this period the dominant politico-economic philosophy was laissez-faire. The counterpart of laissez-faire economic doctrines in American thought was pragmatism. While accepting, by and large, the individualistic values and suppositions of laissez-faire, institutional economics represented the beginnings of a critique of them. Both Parsons and Mills, as has been noted, were influenced as young men by institutional economics and by pragmatism.

American sociology in the interwar period had its strongholds in the midwestern universities: at Chicago, Minnesota, Wisconsin, and Michigan. Its strongest theoretical orientations in this period were various forms of social behaviorism: symbolic interactionism and pluralistic behaviorism. Symbolic interactionism was powerfully influenced by pragmatism. Pluralistic behaviorism was strongly influenced by individualistic traditions in Europe stemming from Gabriel Tarde. Also in the American midwest other European individualistic traditions represented by formalism found a ready reception.

Both Talcott Parsons and C. Wright Mills opened their intellectual careers as adherents of social behaviorism. It was perhaps inevitable that Parsons and Mills should begin from the same basic position in view of their class derivations, the dominant *milieu* in American thought at the time, and even the particular influence on each. However, both responded to social changes in their time and played a role in transforming the intellectual climate with which they were in interaction. These responses set them on divergent courses.

Parsons' First Phase: Student Days to 1939

Having been raised in the home of a Congregational minister turned college president, Parsons was directly influenced by an atmosphere in which the Protestant work ethic was an everyday reality. When he encountered Max Weber's tradition during his days at Heidelberg and read Weber's famous work, *The Protestant Ethic,* one can well imagine that a good deal of personal and public experience seemed to be synthesized by it. His translation of it effectively opened his intellectual career. Parsons observes:

> The first thing of his I read was the essay, *The Protestant Ethic and Spirit of Capitalism* (1904-5), and it was not altogether a matter of chance that a few years later I translated it for an English language edition. This essay, along with Weber's more comprehensive comparative empirical and theoretical works, has remained a very dominant influence on me.[49]

Parsons came to full stature as a significant contemporary sociologist with his first original book, *The Structure of Social Action.*[50] It consisted of a review and an attempt at integration of the theories of Alfred Marshall, Vilfredo Pareto, Emile Durkheim, and Max Weber. This was not an easy task, since Pareto and Durkheim are organicists with collectivistic analyses of social events; Marshall and Weber are social behaviorists with individualistic analyses.

The two major points in Parsons' first system of sociology which cannot be reduced to Max Weber's form of social behaviorism are his rejection of the positivistic analysis of social action (his assignment to social behaviorism properties which resist naturalistic analysis) and his insistence that systems of social action acquire emergent properties not reducible to the units and acts which compose social systems.

> To carry unit analysis to the point of the conceptual isolation of the unit act is to break up the system and destroy this emergent property.[51]

In his first work the foundation was already being laid by Parsons for a possible departure from Weber's type of social behaviorism.

Mills' First Phase: Discovery to 1947

The early stages of the formation of Mills' views were clearly a period of discovery for him. Contrasting positions were held simultaneously as appropriate to different sides of his interests. Mills was moved by a powerful reformist drive; he was a self-avowed socialist and follower of Marx. At the same time he was strangely insensitive to the Stalinist-Trotskyite controversy which raged in left-wing student circles. Mills was an old-line Marxist and Norman Thomas a socialist in his orientation to social problems.

Theoretically, of course, Marxism is a form of scientifically oriented left-wing collectivism. The units of social life are not individuals but social classes. Individuals only achieve significance for Marxism when they act in, and in terms of the requirements of, social classes. Moreover, this left-wing collectivism was conjoined to scientism and progressivism. Marxism was optimistic and sustained by the conviction that underlying the development of classes is an even more efficient application of scientific technology to the mastery of nature. In the end, despite all counter-revolutionary activity, scientific technology drives men through the conflicts which usher in the classless society and the utopian fulfillment of history.

While Mills at this time subscribed to a collectivistic approach to social reform, he simultaneously held a social behavioristic theory of social phenomena. His social behaviorism was, in part, derived from the pragmatic orientations he brought with him to the University of Wisconsin. It was further strengthened by the pragmatism of John Dewey which dominated the University's philosophy department. At this time Mills also was influenced by Veblen and introduced by Hans Gerth to the social behaviorism of George Herbert Mead and Max Weber.

Through all forms of social behaviorism runs a strong clear vein of individualism. Veblen, Weber, and the pragmatists were, at times, socially critical, but they were also anticollectivistic. The units of social life were actions. Social groupings of all sort (including classes) are not new kinds of entities with greater importance than individuals, but social strategies of pluralities. The Marxian theory of history tends to dissolve in their analyses into a maze of now larger, now smaller encounters of individuals and cliques and organizations.

The main impetus, more unconscious than conscious, of Mills' intellectual life in this period was the search for a formula which would

fuse the Marxian and social behavioristic positions. The point at
which they seemed to be common appeared to be that both were to
some extent socially critical. That they presented different critiques
with quite distinct consequences was passed over in silence. Characteristic of the lines along which such fusion tended to occur was Mills'
modification of the social behavioristic theory of motivation in a manner which transposed it into general social-critical form. This was first
worked out in articles and eventually transplanted to *Character and
Social Structure,* written in collaboration with Hans Gerth.

Since Mills was fundamentally concerned throughout his career
with the place of the individual in the social order, his conception of
the individual lies at the very core of his interests. His contributions
to the theory of motivation belong to his first, most purely individualistic, rationalistic, and scientific phase. His handling of the problem,
however, demonstrates how uneasily he wore the mantle of individualism.

> Motives are generally thought of as subjective "springs" of action... But
> there is another way to think of them... We may consider motives as the
> terms which persons typically use in their interpersonal relations.[52]

> Sociologically...a motive is a term in a vocabulary which appears to the actor
> himself and/or to the observer to be an adequate reason for his conduct...
> Conceived in this way, motives are acceptable justifications for present,
> future, or past conduct.[53]

> When a person confesses or imputes motives...he is...usually trying to
> influence others.[54]

> No one vocabulary of motives is accepted by everyone, so the alert individual
> must use one or the other tentatively, until he finds the way to integrate his
> conduct with others, to win them as allies of his act.[55]

> The terms which the person uses to refer to his own feelings are socially
> confirmed by their use by other persons. Self-knowledge that is not socially
> confirmed, not yet disciplined by interaction with others, is not secure
> knowledge.[56]

As shocking as Mills would have found this characterization, he leaves
little doubt that to him the problem of motivation concerns not the
inner person (who, Mills argues, achieves reality only when his personal terms are confirmed by others) but interpersonal strategies.
Vocabularies of motive are implements of social influence.

Even at this early stage in his thinking, Mills was in flight from social behaviorism. His treatment of motivation is not the argument of a man who will eventually assign, with Weber or Veblen or Mead and the other pragmatists, primary reality to the individual. The core of individuality was being hollowed out and assigned only schematic significance. Mills was in evolution away from social behaviorism, for even at this stage he was beginning to visualize individuality as a dangerously chaotic principle.

Parsons and Mills first established their intellectual orientations as social behaviorists. Each, however, shows the response and partial reception of collectivistic elements: scientific socialism in the case of Mills, the organismic sociology of Pareto and Durkheim in the case of Parsons. Ironically, in the first stage of their development Parsons showed a strong resistance to the positivistic (scientific) traditions in social science, while Mills identified himself with the ultra-positivistic philosophy of Charles Pierce. In his insistence that systems have emergent properties not reducible to unit acts, Parsons began showing signs of resistance to social behaviorism comparable to that of Mills in his early distrust of individualism.

Transitions in the Theories of Parsons and Mills

Talcott Parsons: Phase II

The possibility was already laid down in *The Structure of Social Action* for a departure from its confines. There are some indications that as early as 1939 preparation for this departure was already under way. In any case, by the time of his essay on sociological theory for the symposium of Georges Gurvitch and Wilbert E. Moore, the modification of his earlier social behaviorism was occurring.

In his second phase Parsons was inclined to break with various nominalistic elements in his earlier formulation. He became somewhat more critical of the theories of Max Weber that he had been earlier, somewhat more sympathetic with those of Durkheim. The primary task of sociology was no longer located in the analysis of social action, but in the analysis of the interrelation of institutions. Parsons was beginning to suggest that sociological analysis ought to proceed from the standpoint of the whole. This phase of Parsons' work falling between 1939 and 1949 displays a strong thrust toward a realistic position and a growing sympathy with positivism.

C. Wright Mills: Phase II

It is interesting to speculate as to how the second phase of Mills' work will eventually be viewed. At present any estimate is difficult, for his ultimate importance depends upon what happens to the traditions with which he worked. If the work in Mills' third and final phase becomes, as it could, the starting point for a new theory of sociology, his ultimate importance will undoubtedly be that of a creator and pioneer of new orientations. However, if it does not, Mills' significance will be found in his second period, in which he will be viewed not as a founder of new traditions but as an elaborator and interpreter of established views.

The central factor in Mills' second period consists in the carrying through of the program which was only envisioned in his student and immediate post-student days—the attempt to integrate the traditions of old-line Marxism and socialism with those of social behaviorism. This took the form of a review of the central problem of the left-wing collectivists (the problem of classes) in terms of the new tools of the social behaviorists (Veblen and Weber particularly).

Three major books belong to this period of Mills' development: *The New Men of Power, White Collar,* and *The Power Elite.* In these volumes three essentially socialistic themes were taken up and dressed in new terminologies. *The New Men of Power* rests on the Marxist and socialistic thesis that those persons who use the tools of production and their leaders hold the future in their hands. In *White Collar* the Marxian thesis that as the final phases of the class struggle draw near the middle classes will wither away is reviewed and modified by tracing the rise of the new white-collar workers. The volume opens with the apocalyptic vision of their powerlessness. The impotence and shallow pretensions of the new middle classes are developed in terms borrowed from Veblen's theory of conspicuous consumption. The implication for the new middle classes is that they must either join the group that holds the future in its hands or become lackeys of powers that will exploit them. Finally, in *The Power Elite* the old socialistic and Marxian vision of the *bourgeoisie* exploiters of contemporary society is restored to its old position. Instead of capitalistic exploiters, the ruling strata are described as a *power elite.* However, the old evil vision of a conspiracy at the top remains. Veblen's ideas of conspicuous consumption were employed earlier.

In Mills' second phase, as in the case of Parsons, the continuing modification of social behaviorism with collectivistic perspectives is obvious. Mills was showing an increasing tendency to reduce materials drawn from Veblen and Weber to "tools of analysis," while the substantive theories of social life to which he subscribed were increasingly drawn from left-wing collectivism.

The Period of Fulfillment: Parsons and Mills

Talcott Parsons: Phase III

It is a matter for speculation whether the rapid evolution of Parsons' thought from an individualistic to a wholistic form may not have been considerably related to the role of Pitirim Sorokin at Harvard. Sorokin has made an interesting case for this.

> Reading *Toward a General Theory of Action,* especially its most important part: "The General Theory of Action" representing the collective work of all the participants of the volume: T. Parsons, E. A. Shils, G. W. Allport, C. Kluckhohn, R.A. Murray, R.R. Sears, R.C. Sheldon, S.S. Stauffer, E.C. Tolman; and then reading T. Parsons' *The Social System,* I was pleasantly surprised at finding the readings in some parts easy and feeling myself in these parts pasturing on very familiar grounds. The more I read these works, the more familiar I felt, at least in their basic conceptual framework and in their main concepts. Soon I discovered the reason for this familiarity. It was a striking concordance between the basic conceptual scheme of the authors and my own conceptual framework. In a preliminary form my sociological framework was published first in my Russian two-volume *System of Sociology* (1921). In its fully developed form I have been hammering it in my courses at the Universities of Minnesota and Harvard since 1928; and since about the same time in several of my publications. Finally, it was published in its final form in first three volumes of my *Social and Cultural Dynamics* (1937) and then in its fourth volume (1941). Then it was reiterated in an abbreviated form in my *Sociocultural Causality, Space, Time* (1943) and in my *Society, Culture, and Personality: Their Structure and Dynamics* (1947)...
>
> While there is a multitude of dissimilarities between two conceptual systems, there is hardly any doubt that the basic framework of the authors exhibits a notable resemblance to my framework.[57]

Following this statement Sorokin presented some eight-and-a-half single-spaced pages of comparisons between key notions from Parsons' works and his own of earlier publication. Sorokin stated in summary:

> The total body of these similarities is so evident that though my theories are neither mentioned nor referred to in both volumes, I contend that none of the

numerous theories gratefully mentioned by the authors (M. Weber, V. Pareto, S. Freud, E. Durkheim, L. Henderson, and others) are so similar to the framework of the authors' as the conceptual framework developed—logically and empirically—in my courses and publications. Even more, there is no sociological, anthropological, or psychological theory in the whole field of psychosocial sciences as similar to the basic conceptual framework of two volumes discussed as my framework or, more exactly my re-formulation, development and test of the theories of many earlier eminent social thinkers. The basic framework of the new volumes is notably different even from that of T. Parsons' *Structure of Social Action*. His new framework shows a very tangible departure from the semi-nominalistic and singularistic standpoint of the *Structure of Social Action* with its main axis of the "means-end-schema." Now this standpoint and schema are practically abandoned in favor of "a more generalized level" of analysis (S.S.,9) and the Weberian semi-nominalistic and singularistic framework of "actions," "actors and roles" is embraced by a more adequate "realistic standpoint" of "social system," "cultural system" and "personality system," or by the larger framework of "the whole play" in which "roles, actions, and actors" are but components. This shift explains why Parsons' present framework is more similar to my basic system than to that of his *Structure of Social Action*.

Side by side with the basic similarities there is a multitude of dissimilarities between two sociological theories compared. These dissimilarities concern though important but mainly secondary points. Among many factors for these dissimilarities, one is due to Parsons' uncompleted transition from his previous standpoint to the new one. For this reason "the sins" of the previous framework continue to visit upon, to crop in, and to vitiate the new framework. Hence a peculiar eclecticism of his new standpoint. The incompatible elements of two different frameworks, put together, clash and do not allow a consistent logical integration into one system. They fill the new basic framework with many "logico-meaningful congeries." "It is earnestly hoped that the transition will eventually be completed and will lead to an elimination of these congeries.[58]

Quite apart from possibly establishing the influence of Sorokin's "wholism" on Parsons, Sorokin's statement has interest in independently documenting Parsons' transition from individualism to collectivism. Sorokin also independently confirms the conflict of points of view which marks the transition period in Parsons' theories and which, as he indicates, persists into the third phase of Parsons' work.

Sorokin's conclusion to a parallel discussion in *Sociological Theories of Today* is an excellent summary of Parsons' development in his third phase: an increasing abandonment of the individualism and atomism of his earlier period and the integration of its form of wholism or functionalism. Parsons, for his part, has come quite explicitly to visualize his views as a form of collectivism.

Parsons' new framework shows a very tangible departure for the seminominalistic and singularistic standpoint of his *Structure of Social Actions* with its
"unit act" and its voluntaristic "means-end schema." This standpoint and
schema are now practically abandoned in favor of a more "generalized"
level of analysis (SS9), and the Weberian seminominalistic and singularistic
framework of actions, actors and roles is replaced by a more adequate
"realistic" framework of social system, cultural systems, and personality
system or by the "whole play," of which roles, actions, and actors are but
components.[59]

Substantively, Parsons' theories of society were worked out by way
of a conception of pattern variables conceived as dimensions of the
social system which was, in turn, conceived to be the primary social
reality. Personality, society, and culture were conceived as independent boundary-maintaining systems. Finally, the social system was
conceived as a set of forces in equilibrium, divided into component
subsystems. The great subsystems of society were conceived as
receiving influences from one or more of four sources (physical
nature, the biological organism, personality, and culture) and, like a
great factory, processing these influences into some sort of output.
The integrating summary of his conception of the social system was
presented by Parsons in one of his contributions to *Theories of Society*
in 1961.

The presuppositions of his functionalistic theory are compactly
summarized by Parsons in the Max Black symposium. Parsons maintains that an action system is constituted by the internalization in
personality and the organism and the institutionalization in society
and culture of patterns of meaning. Patterns of meaning comprise
feelings, values, and ideas. The goals of the units of the action system
(that is, of the people who act) must, Parsons insists, represent contributions to the functioning of the whole. To the extent that an action
system becomes differentiated, a balance must be struck between
definiteness in the relationships between the units and flexibility with
regard both to the system and to extra-system factors. Such a balance
(between the needs of individuals and the needs of society) is achieved
by the institutionalization of generalized normative patterns compat-
ible with the varied requirements of special situations. Such an action
system, moreover, is subdivided into four functional subsystems between which direct interchanges may occur.[60]

At the time of his formulations in *Theories of Society* and his
summary statement for the Black symposium on his theories, Parsons'
functionalism was virtually complete. His activities since have consis-

ted largely in working out the details and planing down the rough spots in the conception of society as a system within which all subparts operate interdependently to realize the values of the whole. In the newspaper report on Parsons' retirement, Robert Reinhold called attention to the biological analogies in terms of which Parsons had ordered his conception of society.

> Like biological systems, he argues, social systems have regulatory mechanisms that allow them to return to equilibrium after each disturbance. Thus, while many conflicting forces are crossing through the body of the system, the mechanisms of social control tend to keep the system as a whole in dynamic equilibrium.
>
> One of the main cornerstones of Parsonian theory is what he calls the "four-function paradigm." According to this concept, a social system's structure is governed by the way it meets four basic needs. The system differentiates into subsystems that serve to satisfy these needs.
>
> The four are: "goal attainment," or the methods by which the system mobilizes to achieve its goals; "adaptation," or adjustment to the environment for survival and to acquire facilities, such as capital, to reach the goals; "integration," the internal relations of the units of the system to each other, designed to reconcile conflicts and maintain cohesion; and "pattern maintenance," the means by which the actors deal with pressures to deviate from accepted norms.[61]

C. Wright Mills: Phase III (1958-1962)

Some persons, even some close to Mills, are already visualizing phase II of Mills' intellectual development as his greatest period. One estimate of *The New Men of Power, White Collar,* and *The Power Elite* runs as follows:

> These books were sociology in the classic sense of "the study of society" rather than the new, compressed, and jargon-ridden styles of the profession which Mills so brilliantly analyzed but dismissed in *The Sociological Imagination*... But in the last few years Mills was doing something further, in short, books that he did not present as sociology but which nevertheless were attacked for not being sociology. He thought of these books, *The Causes of World War Three* and *Listen Yankee,* as a high order of "pamphleteering" which frankly included exhortations as well as analysis.[62]

Perhaps in the long run it may be true that phase II of Mills' work will be viewed as his most important period. If so, he will drop to comparatively minor significance in the total picture of the development of sociological theory. On the other hand, there is little question that the work in his third phase was most original. However, how the work of Mills' third phase will eventually be evaluated does not depend on him alone, but on what happens to the tradition which does or does not flow from it.

The effect of a man's place in the tradition on the evaluation of a theorist may be clarified by two examples. E. A. Ross wrote brilliant semiclassical studies (his *Social Psychology* and his *Social Control*) while adhering to a branch of social behaviorism. He then shifted his forces to a branch of sociological formalism, which later died out. In the evaluation of Ross' work by later thinkers, there is a tendency simply to dismiss that large part of a lifetime of work. Alfred Vierkandt displays a different fate. After brilliant contributions to positivistic organicism, Vierkandt shifted the main impetus of his work of phenomenological sociology which he pioneered. Late developments in phenomenological sociology are still under way. While Ross has some of the properties of a man who missed his deepest calling, Vierkandt does not.

In the third phase of his work Mills achieved a kind of fulfillment of the impetus already discernible to those of us who knew him as a graduate student toward bringing his reformist and theoretical inclinations together into a single formulation. Moreover, there seems to be no justification whatsoever for separating Mills' formulations in his article for the Llewellyn Gross *Symposium,* in *Images of Man,* and in *The Sociological Imagination* from the formulations of *The Causes of World War Three, Listen Yankee,* and *The Marxists.* The latter group of works are applications of the position theoretically argued in the former. These works belong together as a single unified point of view. of works are applications of the position theoretically argued in the former. These works belong together as a single unified point of view.

In the Gross *Symposium* Mills announced his radical break with empiricism.

> Now I do not like to do empirical work if I can possibly avoid it. It means a great deal of trouble if one has no staff, and, if one does employ a staff, then the staff is often more trouble than the work itself... In our situation, empirical work as such is for beginning students and for those who aren't able to handle the complexities of big problems; it is also for highly formal men who do not care what they study so long as it appears to be orderly.[63]

One could not have a more forthright break with the pragmatism and social behaviorism of Mills' early period than this. His one-time idols, Pierce and Weber, whose empiricism was deeply entrenched, must have turned over in their graves at such an utterance.

Later the same year, Mills generalized his anti-empiricism into an attack on science itself.

> The cultural meaning of physical science...is becoming doubtful... The obvious conquest of nature...is felt by men of the over-developed societies to be virtually complete. And now in these societies, science—the chief instrument of this conquest—is felt to be foot-loose, aimless, and in need of reappraisal... Many cultural workmen have come to feel that "science is a false and pretentious Messiah."[64]

The break with the pragmatists and social behaviorists was growing more trenchant. It assumed a most direct form in his passionate rejection of the individualism of one of his youthful idols, Max Weber.

> In the more political essays of Max Weber, I am inclined to believe the classic tradition in sociological thinking comes to a moral climax, a crisis of orientation, which we have by no means overcome. In fact, we have not even confronted it squarely. Weber presents the social world as a chaos of values, a hopeless plurality of gods; his is the pessimistic world of a classic liberal of supreme intelligence and enormous knowledge, thinking at the end of the liberal era and finding no basis for decision, no criterion other than his own personal will and integrity.[65]

No conservative has ever rejected individuality as a principle with greater violence! In the same context Mills welcomes all evidence of support of his own growing antirationalism—another aspect of his youthful theoretical orientation which he was in process of rejecting.

> Karl Mannheim's essay on rationality contains the seeds of the most profound criticism of the secular rationalism of Western civilization. He did not work it out in just this way, but the passage given here is among the best writings of a man who is, I believe, one of the two or three most vital and important sociologists of the inter-war period.[66]

With the rejection of empiricism, science, individualism, and finally, rationalism, Mills' departure from the ranks of the social behaviorists is complete and irreversible. His violent attack on the branches of current sociology as he defines them flows from his identification of them as empirical, scientific, individualistic, or rationalistic, as the case may be. A single sentence in *Images of Man* sums up the foundation of his opposition: "The moral crisis of this humanist tradition, reflected in sociology, coincides with the retreat of our generation of social scientists into 'mere fact.'"[67]

However, the rejection of individualism, science, empiricism, and rationalism did not exhaust Mills' message in the period of 1959-1962. He also outlined his positive views of the intellectual tradition and society. At the same time that he rejected scientific sociology ("all sociology worthy of the name is 'historical sociology.'")[68] and denied in principle its capacity to make lawlike generalizations of a scientific type,[69] he made claims of an extremity almost unparalleled since August Comte for sociology as the intellectual synthesis of modern man.

> I am going to contend that journalists and scholars, artists and publics, scientists and editors, are coming to expect...the sociological imagination... The social sciences are becoming the common denominator of our cultural period, and the sociological imagination our most needed quality of mind.[70]

Since sociology has been denied a scientific character, it can only have—for Mills—a moral and ethical character. Mills leaves no doubt as to his view of the proper task of sociology.

> As social scientists, we located ourselves... It is...the political task of the social scientist...to address his work to the other three types of men I have classified in terms of power and knowledge... To those with power and with awareness of it, he imputes...responsibility for such structural consequences as he finds...influenced by their decisions and their lack of decisions... To those whose actions have such consequences, but who do not seem aware of them, he directs whatever he has found out about those consequences. He attempts to educate and then, again, he imputes responsibility. To those... regularly without power and whose awareness is confined to their everyday *milieux*, he...states what he has found out concerning the actions of the more powerful.[71]

In short, the task of sociology is to supply the moral guidance required by the times.

It is difficult to see how *The Causes of World War Three* and *Listen Yankee* can be described as something other than sociology for Mills. To be sure, they are propaganda. But that is precisely what Mills maintains *true* sociology to be. *The Causes of World War Three* is a shrill call for action.

> The withdrawal of cultural workmen from politics, in America especially, is part of the international default, which is both cultural and political, of the Western world today. The young complacents of America, the tired old fighters, the smug liberals, the shrill ladies of jingoist culture—they are all quite free. Nobody looks them up. Nobody has to.... They do not examine

the U.S.A. as an over-developed society full of ugly waste and the deadening of human responsibility, honoring ignorance and the cheerful robot, pronouncing the barren doctrine and submitting gladly, even with eagerness, to the uneasy fun of a leisureless and emptying existence.[72]

Listen Yankee contains interesting proposals, such as:

The U.S. Government should at once and unilaterally cease all further production of "extermination" weapons—all A- and B- bombs and nuclear warheads included. It should announce the size of its present stockpile, along with a schedule for reducing it and converting it, so far as it technically possible, to devices for peacetime uses.[73]

Mills' proposals take so little account of the organization of nation-states as to amount to empty rhetoric which, at best, offers some comfort to the Soviet bloc of nations.

However, it is in *Listen Yankee* that Mills' positive views of society in his period of fulfillment are most fully expressed. *Listen Yankee* is not about "what is really happening in Cuba" at all; it is too filled with inadequate, partial, and even false information for that. Nor is *Listen Yankee* the voice of the Cuban revolutionary which C. Wright Mills only reports. Mills' hypothetical Cuban revolutionary expresses too many judgments which no Cuban revolutionary ever thought, judgments which could only have been furnished by Mills himself.

The hypothetical Cuban revolutionary in *Listen Yankee* is a vehicle permitting Mills, for once, to speak positively out of his own dreams. Mills is not the first outstanding man who spoke most directly and forcefully for himself only in those moments when he presented himself as the mouthpiece, or interpreter, or reporter, or the prophet of his god. Among nineteenth-century thinkers one is reminded of Kierkegaard, who spoke most fully for himself through various pseudonyms, each of which permitted the expression in relatively pure form of some aspect of his highly ambivalent nature. Or again, Nietzsche spoke most powerfully for himself as Zarathustra.

Listen Yankee is no very significant or authentic account of the revolution in Cuba. Its hero is the mouthpiece, not of the Cuban revolutionary, but of Mills. *Listen Yankee* is essentially a religious-morality tale manufactured out of some events and fragments of items drawn from recent Cuban experience. Its religious-morality character is shown by the blackness of its agents of darkness. (U.S. capitalists and the American State Department ready to sustain the pressure of innocent Cuban peasant girls into prostitution as a by-product of their

imperialistic plans) and the unstained goodness of its agents of light
(Castro and the revolutionaries). The limited potential of Cuba for
industrialization is thrust aside, the pressure of its population on its
resources is ignored. Cuba is visualized as a potentially self-sufficient
land of plenty. This plentitude is to be achieved by such devices as a
happy, productive chicken coop in every yard. To criticize this as
impractical, however, would be to miss the essentially utopian
character of the society which Mills visualizes the Cubans as creating.

One of the most striking of all properties of *Listen Yankee* is the
emergence of Fidel Castro as an apothesized superman, as a living
savior, a god on earth. No slightest hint of criticism ever attaches to
his figure or actions in Mills' account.

> Fidel Castro...promotes not the cult of the individual but the facts of the
> revolution... He is the most directly radical and democratic force in Cuba...
> Before any problem is solved, Fidel spends long hours on the TV... He
> explains and he educates, and after he speaks almost every doubt has gone
> away. Never before has such a force of public opinion prevailed for so long
> and so intimately with power... His speeches actually create the revolution-
> ary consciousness—and the work gets done. It is fantastic to see how, as it
> goes along, the revolutionary process transforms one layer after another of
> the population. And always there is Fidel's anti-bureaucratic personality.[74]

The touching spectacle emerges of a Columbia professor, one of
the outstanding contemporary sociologists, an author of world renown,
an ever-so-ready critic of everyone else, subordinating himself to the
authoritarian figure of a Cuban revolutionary leader. Surely the
atmosphere is religious, and the spirit medieval. The high point of
Mills' expression of those sentiments is appropriately contained in a
chapter entitled "Revolutionary Euphoria," and surely no better
description could be made of his mood than his own.

> Everyone has day dreams, but for most people these dreams are never
> related to their everyday life. By our revolution, we Cubans have made The
> Big Connection, between fantasy and reality, and now we are living in it. To
> us to live in this connection, that is the fact of our revolution.[75]

Formulations such as these which appear over and over again in
his last works show that Mills had found his own fulfillment. The final
position achieved by him thus can be seen as a form of left-wing
humanistic collectivism. Mills was quite correct in objecting to the
designation of his position as Marxist—for in contrast to the Marxists
he has rejected science and the fusion of left-wing collectivism and

science, which are peculiar to Marxism and all other forms of scientific socialism.

Even stylistically the last phase of Mills' work has the properties of a fulfillment. One of the clearest signs of the collectivist is that he is most at home when he deals with mass themes for which a generic, slogan-like style is most appropriate. On the other hand, the true collectivist is least sure of himself when he deals with individuals and the problems of personal psychology. The reverse is true of the person who by temperament and training is individualistic—masses always seem like empty categories and the language appropriate to them is made up of shibboleths which defy rational analysis.

Mills' temperamental collectivism (appearing in the inverse form of a strident, anti-authoritarianism in his early period and as the surprising subordination to Fidel Castro as an authoritarian symbol in *Listen Yankee*) is manifest in the inadequacy (notable in a mind so brilliant) with which he handles all issues of individual psychology. A striking incapacity to take the role of the other is manifest throughout *White Collar*, for example, where negative characterizations are assembled for one group after another. Particularly significant along the same lines is the almost complete lack of understanding of the psychology of women. From his earliest writings to his last, women appear in Mills' writing either as the most innocent and pure angels, defenseless and subject to cynical commercial exploitation, or they appear as the most hardened tramps. The subtle richness of feminine psychology finds no place in Mills' writings. He is most at home when individuals are reduced to categories. It is from this point that Mills' reduction of the problem of motivation to strategies of deceit must be viewed. He did not understand individuals, and in the end cast out individuality as a chaotic principle.

Similarly, Mills' style approaches its most characteristic form in his later works. Despite its vigor, his style is not stripped down and terse. There is a kind of oratorical excess about it. Mills does not draw out his analyses, nor systematically explore themes so much as to make an assault upon them. A sort of oratorical build-up is followed by the firing off of volleys of sloganlike phrases. In his latest works, these phrases assume a stereotyped form and the number of capitalized words increases. It is as if a tense, strident mood expressed itself naturally in upper case letters.

However, explorations such as these must be left to Mills' biographer. Here such style notes are only tentatively taken as possible further evidence that the last phase of Mills' work was not a deviation, as has been suggested, but a fulfillment.

Final Notes on Mills and Parsons

Talcott Parsons, Mills' foremost opponent on the current American scene, also began his career as a social behaviorist. There were, to be sure, differences. Parsons was partly influenced by Marshall in a manner not true for Mills. Mills was influenced by Veblen to a degree that seems to find no counterpart in Parsons. However, they share an influence by Weber.

It may be possible that their common social behaviorism was a product of a combination of their middle-class derivation, the intellectual *milieu*, and the Great Depression which had seriously shaken men's faith in the infallibility of the collective, while in America, at least, not replacing it with a new faith in left-wing collectivism. Whatever the cause, since World War II both Parsons and Mills have been in evolution toward collectivistic positions. Parsons has moved to right-wing collectivism and scientism, which has placed him in the stout position of defender of the *status quo*. By contrast, Mills has been in evolution toward a left-wing collectivism, but without the old optimistic faith in scientific progress of Marxism and scientific socialism. Ironically, in their orientation to science Parsons and Mills have exchanged positions. Parsons opened his career with a forthright attack on positivism (the scientific tradition in social science), but as his functionalism neared perfection he quietly re-introduced positivistic orientations in strengthened form. Mills opened his career with an almost doctrinaire adherence to the logical positivism and scientism of Charles Pierce, and closed it with violent attacks upon science as ''a false and pretentious Messiah, or at least a highly ambiguous element in modern civilization.''[76]

In the 1960s events have been moving beyond the redoubtable warriors of the fifties. C. Wright Mills was cut down by an untimely death. Even before this, developments in Cuba, including Castro's identification with Russian Communism, had betrayed the accuracy of Mills' interpretations. If Harvey Swados, Mills' most intimate friend, reported correctly, Mills' response to these developments betrays the essentially religious character of *Listen Yankee*. He maintains that Mills at the end:

> ...was torn between defending *Listen Yankee,* as a good and honest book, and acknowledging publicly for the first time in his life that he had been

terribly wrong... the tension was too much, the decline of the revolution, atop his personal pains, was too much. I can only add that he declared to me in his last weeks that he was becoming more and more impressed with the psychological and intellectual relevance of nonviolent resistance and absolute pacifism.[77]

With rather horrifying speed Castro turned out to be Mills' "god that failed." Swados seems to suspect that this was a component in Mills' last fatal heart attack.

The fate of an in-group politician rarely displays the same pathos as that of a rebel guerrilla and leader of an unorthodox transient sect. He may, as has Parsons, acquire a considerable estate in the profession which he is able to administer gracefully at long last above the conflicts of the hour. That Parsons seems inclined to assume this role appears in the closing pages of self-defense against his critics of the Black symposium.

> To me, what I call the theory of action was, in its core—which I take to be the social system in its relation to the personality of the individual—founded in the generation of Durkheim, Weber, and Freud, with of course a very complex set of other influences, a few of which have been mentioned here. With the very perceptible fading of the influence of the older economic individualism—in its scientific rather than political reference—and the older personality-individualism, it is a striking fact that *general* orientations in this field have, in recent years, tended increasingly to polarize between a non-dogmatic and non-political "Marxian" position and one which in the broadest sense may be called one or another version of the theory of action. The most important exception to this is probably the influence of the "culture and personality" school which is an attempted direct *fusion* of the atomistic and idealistic trends, as distinguished from what I have symbolized as a "marriage."[78]

One must never forget that what Parsons (and earlier, Shils) calls the "theory of action" is his name for functionalism. It is a form of wholism or collectivism which has little to do with the social action theory of Max Weber which is an individualistic (or atomistic) form of social behaviorism.

This statement by Parsons, made in 1961, amounts to an admission that Parsons' theory is not the sole legitimate heir of sociology after all, for neo-Marxian conflict theory is undergoing a revival and becoming an increasingly important rival of functionalism. Moreover, the same statement admits that all individualistic (or atomistic) positions are not as antiquated as was once assumed. Parsons has been correct. As the 1960s have unfolded, the number of attacks upon functionalism have increased. Forms of neo-Marxian conflict theory have continued to develop. Moreover, all forms of social behaviorism have shown unexpected vitality.

Even Parsons' position in the profession has been subjected to what amounts to symbolic assault and transformation. In 1963 some persons, outraged at the failure of the nominating committee of the American Sociological Association to place Parsons' old rival at Harvard, Pitirim Sorokin, on the ballot for the presidency, threatened a write-in campaign. As pressure built up, the nominating committee was forced to reissue a new slate of candidates including Sorokin. The society responded by electing Sorokin the next president of the Association.

It would be a mistake to view Sorokin's election to the presidency of the American Sociological Association as a ''rejection'' of Talcott Parsons. It would be as misleading to draw the conclusion that Parsons is being rejected as to interpret the numerous tributes and memorial volumes to C. Wright Mills as a posthumous attempt by professional sociologists to join Mills' peculiar form of antiscientific sectarianism. The insistence upon the part of the professional society of extending to Parsons' old rival the highest honor it is able to bestow amounted to acknowledging him to be an elder of equal honor. It implied that in the minds of many, Parsons was now but one of the elders. And the tributes and memorials to C. Wright Mills amount to the claim by the profession to the remains of one of its own prodigal sons.

The 1970s may develop new proponents to represent the great divisions, but Parsons and Mills will remain the titans of the 1950s and 1960s as sociology's heroes who, at the mid-twentieth century, epitomized better than most men in their theories and their careers the contrast and tension between the scientific and humanistic wings of contemporary American sociology.

Notes

1. Martindale, Don (1959). ''Talcott Parsons' Theoretical Metamorphosis from Social Behaviorism to Macrofunctionalism,'' *The Alpha Kappa Deltan,* XXIX, no.1, Winter, pp. 38-46.

2. See Edward C. Devereaux, Jr., ''Parsons' Sociological Theory,'' in *The Social Theories of Talcott Parsons,* ed. Max Black. Englewood Cliffs, NJ: Prentice-Hall, 1961, p. 6.

3. Parsons, Talcott (1959). ''A Short Account of My Intellectual Development,'' *Alpha Kappa Deltan,* Winter, p. 3.

4. *Ibid.*, p. 4.

5. Gerth, Hans (1962), mimeographed statement read at a Memorial Meeting, Columbia University, April 16, p. 3.

6. Sorokin, Pitirim A. (1963). *A Long Journey.* New Haven, CT: College and University Press, pp. 243-244.

7. Devereux, *op. cit.*, p.4.

8. Sorokin, *op. cit.*, p.251.

9. Horowitz, Irving Louis (1963), ed. *Power, Politics, and People.* New York: Oxford University Press, pp. 6-7.

10. Devereux, *op. cit.*, p. 6.

11. Sorokin, *op. cit.*, p. 251.

12. Wakefield, Dan (1961). "Taking It Big: A Memoir of C. Wright Mills," *Atlantic,* September, p. 66.

13. *Ibid.*, p. 68.

14. Swados, Harvey (1963), "C. Wright Mills: A Personal Memoir," *Dissent,* Winter, p. 37.

15. *Ibid.*, p. 40.

16. Landau, Saul(1963), "C. Wright Mills—The Last Six Months," *Root and Branch,* Berkeley, CA., Spring, pp. 7-8.

17. Swados, *op. cit.*, p. 38.

18. Landau, *op. cit.*, p. 14.

19. Parsons, Talcott (1961), "Comment on Llewelyn Gross' Preface to a Meta-theoretical Framework for Sociology," *The American Journal of Sociology,* LXVII, No. 2, September, p. 138.

20. Swados, *op. cit.*, p. 41.

21. Reinhold, Robert, "A Mentor of Sociologists Retires After 42 Years at Harvard Post," *New York Times,* 14 June, 1973. Reproduced in *ASA Footnotes,* August, 1973, p. 3.

22. *Ibid.*

23. Swados, *op. cit.*, p. 35. As a young parent, Swados observed, Mills was completely indifferent to his infant offspring, observing that at this stage they were without personality and not worth bothering with until a few years later.

24. Parsons, Talcott (1951). *The Social System.* Glencoe: The Free Press, p. 12.

25. Mills, C. Wright (1953). *White Collar.* New York: Oxford University Press, p. 132.

26. Wakefield, *op. cit.*, p. 65.

27. Mills, *op. cit.*, p. 133. Italics mine.

28. Mills, C. Wright (1956). *The Power Elite.* New York: Oxford University Press, p. 72. Italics mine.

29. *Ibid.*, p. 82.

30. *Ibid.*, p. 83.

31. *Ibid.*, p. 82.

32. Shils, Edward A. (1961). "The Calling of Sociology," in *Theories of Society,* ed. by Talcott Parsons, Edward Shils, Kaspar D. Naegele, and Jesse R. Pitts. New York: The Free Press of Glencoe, vol. 2, p. 1410.

33. *Ibid.*, p. 1413.

34. *Ibid.*, p. 1420.

35. *Ibid.*, p. 1422.

36. *Ibid.*

37. Talcott Parsons in Black, ed., *op. cit.*, pp. 362-363.

38. Mills, C. Wright (1960). *Images of Man*. New York:George Braziller, pp.4-5.

39. *Ibid.*, p. 11.

40. *Ibid.*, p. 12.

41. Mills, C. Wright (1962). *The Marxists*. New York: Dell, p. 13.

42. *Ibid.*, p. 16.

43. *Ibid.*, pp. 13-14.

44. Reinhold, *ASA Footnotes, op. cit.*, p. 3.

45. Mills, C. Wright (1959). *The Sociological Imagination*. New York: Oxford University Press, p. 49.

46. *Ibid.*, p. 32.

47. *Ibid.*, p. 53.

48. *Ibid.*, p. 95.

49. Parsons, "A Short Account," *op. cit.*, p. 4.

50. Parsons, Talcott (1937). *The Structure of Social Action*. New York: McGraw-Hill.

51. *Ibid.*, p. 740.

52. Gerth, Hans H. and C. Wright Mills (1953). *Character and Social Structure*. New York: Harcourt, Brace, p. 114.

53. *Ibid.*, p. 116.

54. *Ibid.*, p. 117.

55. *Ibid.*, p. 122.

56. *Ibid.*, p. 127.

57. Sorokin, Pitirim A., "Similarities and Dissimilarities between Two Sociological Systems," mimeographed, Notes on T. Parsons and E.A. Shils, eds., *Toward a General Theory of Action*. Cambridge: Harvard University Press, 1951, and T. Parsons, *The Social System*. Glencoe, IL: The Free Press, 1951, p. 1.

58. *Ibid.*, pp. 9-10.

59. Sorokin, Pitirim A. (1966). *Sociological Theories of Today*. New York: Harper & Row, pp. 431-432. In this volume Sorokin extended the comparison between his own and Parsons' theories in the mimeographed paper widely circulated throughout the society several years earlier. Also see Parsons' own formulation in the Black symposium, p. 360.

60. Talcott Parsons, in Black, ed., *op. cit*. This is a summary of Parsons' argument appearing between pp. 342-344.

61. Reinhold, *op. cit.*, p. 3.

62. Wakefield, Dan (1962), "C. Wright Mills," *The Nation*, 14 April, p. 331.

63. Mills, C. Wright (1949), "On Intellectual Craftsmanship," in *Symposium on Sociological Theory*, ed. Llewellyn Gross. Evanston, IL: Row, Peterson, p. 35.

64. Mills, *The Sociological Imagination, op. cit.*, pp. 15-16.

65. Mills, *Images of Man, op. cit.*, p. 7.

66. *Ibid.*, p. 12.

67. *Ibid.*, p. 7.

68. Mills, *The Sociological Imagination, op. cit.*, p. 146.

69. *Ibid.*, pp. 149-150.

70. *Ibid.*, pp. 5-13.

71. *Ibid.*, p. 185.

72. Mills, C. wright (1958). *The Causes of World War Three*. New York: Simon & Schuster, p. 127.

73. Mills, C. Wright (1960). *Listen Yankee*. New York: McGraw-Hill,pp.122-123.
74. *Ibid.*
75. *Ibid.*, p. 113.
76. Mills, *Sociological Imagination, op. cit.*, p. 14.
77. Swados, *op. cit.*, p. 42.
78. Black, ed., *Social Theories of Talcott Parsons, op. cit.*, pp. 361-362.

Selected Bibliography

C. Wright Mills

The Causes of World War Three. New York: Simon & Schuster, 1958.

Character and Social Structure (with Hans H. Gerth). New York: Harcourt, Brace, 1953.

Listen Yankee: The Revolution in Cuba. New York: McGraw-Hill, 1960.

The New Men of Power: America's Labor Leaders. New York: Harcourt, Brace, 1948.

The Power Elite. New York: Oxford University Press, 1956.

Power, Politics, and People: The Collected Essays of C. Wright Mills. New York: Oxford University Press, 1963.

The Puerto Rican Journey: New York's New Migrants, with Clarence Senior and Rose K. Goldsen. New York: Oxford University Press, 1950.

The Sociological Imagination. New York: Oxford University Press, 1959.

White Collar: The American Middle Classes. New York: Oxford University Press, 1953.

Talcott Parsons

American Sociology, editor. New York: Basic Books, 1968.

Economy and Society, with Neil J. Smelser. Glencoe, IL: The Free Press, 1956.

Essays in Sociological Theory: Pure and Applied. Glencoe, IL: The Free Press, 1949.

Essays in Sociological Theory, rev. ed. Glencoe, IL: The Free Press, 1954,1967.

Family, Socialization, and Interaction Process, with Robert F. Bales, James Olds, Morris elditch, and Philip E. Slater. Glencoe, IL: The Free Press, 1955.

Politics and Social Structure. New York: The Free Press, 1969.

Social Structure and Personality. New York: The Free Press, 1964.

The Social System. Glencoe, IL: The Free Press, 1951.

Societies: Evolutionary and Comparative Perspectives. Englewood Cliffs, NJ: Prentice-Hall, 1966.

Sociological Theory and Modern Society. New York: The Free Press, 1967.

Structure and Process in Modern Societies. Glencoe, IL: The Free Press, 1960.

The Structure of Social Action. New York: McGraw-Hill, 1937.

Theories of Society, co-editor with Edward Shils, Kaspar D. Naegele, and Jesse R Pitts, 2 vols. New York: The Free Press, 1961.

Toward a General Theory of Action, with Edward A. Shils. Cambridge: Harvard University Press, 1951, 1962.

Working Papers in the Theory of Action, with Robert F. Bales and Edward A. Shils. Glencoe, IL: The Free Press, 1953.

IV

Pitirim Sorokin:
Soldier of Fortune

Pitirim A. Sorokin's bibliography as of January, 1963, consisted of thirty-five books (some of them multivolume works) and more than four hundred articles, essays, editorials, and papers published in scientific journals of various countries. A large number of Sorokin's books have been translated into other languages: *Contemporary Sociological Theories* has been translated from English into eleven of the major languages of mankind; *The Crisis of Our Age* into eight; other volumes into a lesser number of languages. By 1963, forty-two translations of Sorokin's published volumes had been completed. Other translations were in preparation, and Sorokin was composing other books.

In terms of comparative productivity and numbers of translations, no other sociologist equals Sorokin. Talcott Parsons, who is held by numerous contemporary scholars to be the foremost sociologist in America, had, as of 1960, a bibliography of ten books (which included two translations, jointly edited volumes, and re-published volumes of essays). Parsons had at this time also a total of eighty-two published articles. Little of Parsons' work had been translated into other languages at the time. C. Wright Mills, who is sometimes claimed to be the most important sociologist of America's post-World War II period, had a total productivity of eleven volumes (which included one joint translation, two co-authored volumes, an edited anthology, and a book of essays published posthumously). A bibliography including every essay, review, book note, and comment compiled by Mills' disciple still brought Mills' published bibliography to only 205 items.[1] A total of eighteen translations had been made of Mills' works at that time. Sorokin's productivity in books, in articles, and in the number of translations greatly outdistanced that of Talcott Parsons and C. Wright Mills, for each of whom greater significance often has been claimed. Sorokin—so far as this can be checked—seems to have been the most productive and most translated sociologist who ever lived.

Sorokin was founder, first professor, and then chairman of the department of sociology at the University of St. Petersburg (Leningrad). He published five volumes in law and sociology between 1920 and 1922. After his final arrest and banishment by the Soviet government, he became professor of sociology at the University of Minnesota. During his occupancy of this position (1924-1930), he published five major works. He left Minnesota to become founder of the department of sociology and the first chairman at Harvard University. In 1948 he established the Harvard Research Center in Creative Altruism, of which he remained director until his retirement from Harvard.

During a long productive career Sorokin played a major role in founding a number of sociological areas such as the sociology of revolution, the sociology of mobility and stratification, the sociology of calamity, and the sociology of major contemporary sociologists who worked with him as graduate students or came within his sphere of influence. In his autobiography Sorokin offered the following list of contemporary sociologists influenced by him.

> When, in January, 1962, Charles and Zona Loomis' *Modern Social Theories* was published, in my letter to the authors I observed that practically all the sociologists whose theories are examined in the volume (Kingsley Davis, G. C. Homans, R. K. Merton, T. Parsons, R. Williams, and including Professor Loomis himself and W. E. Moore, the editor of the Van Nostrand series in Sociology) were either graduate students of an instructor (T. Parsons), or an associate (G. Homans), or a visiting lecturer (H. Becker) in the department during my chairmanship. To these names of the leading American sociologists I can add several others, such as Professors C. A. Anderson, R. F. Bales, B. Barber, W. Bash, R. Bauer, C. Q. Berger, R. Bierstedt, G. Blackwell, R. Chamblis, A. Davis, N Demerath, N. DeNood, J. Donovan, R. DuWors, J. B. Ford, R. Hanson, D. Hatch, H. Hitt, L. Haak, J. Fichter, W. Firey, H. Johnston, F. Kluckhohn, J.B. Knox, M. Levy, V. Parenton, A. Pierce, B. Reed, J. and M. Riley, E. Schuler, T. Lynn Smith, C. Tilly, E. A. Tiryakian, N. Whetten, Logan Wilson, and others who did their graduate work in the department during my chairmanship.[2]

And yet Sorokin never became the center of a school or founded a movement.

Fortunately, Sorokin has left an unusually full record of the events of his personal life, including *Leaves from a Russian Diary*, *A Long*

Journey, and the autobiographical introduction to *Pitirim A. Sorokin in Review.*

The Major Events of Sorokin's Life

Few sociologists living today can boast of lives of such variety as Sorokin whose destiny took him from the frontier of northern Russia through the stormy events of the Russian revolution to the position of the world's most eminent sociologist in the 1960s.

Sorokin was one of three boys born to an Urgo-Finnish peasant girl and an itinerant artisan Russian father. He was born in the northern Russian Province of Vologda among the Komi people on January 21, 1889. His mother died when he was three years old. The Komi were peasants who supplemented their subsistence agriculture by hunting, trapping, lumbering, and fishing. They lived in village communities with a clergyman teacher, medical practitioner, policeman, mayor, and clerk. Their agrarian communities were self-governing like the German *Gemeinschaften* and Russian *mir* and *obschina.* Land was held in common by the villagers and periodically redistributed among individual families as their conditions changed. The elective authorities were charged with such tasks as the building of schools, medical centers, and the housing for cultural activities. Though many beliefs, legends, and rituals persisted from their pre-Christian pagan past, the Komi were Russian Orthodox. Families were close-knit, serving as a mutual welfare institution with their obligations of mutual aid to family members.

At the time of the death of Sorokin's mother, his younger brother went to live with a maternal aunt. Sorokin and his elder brother remained with their father, assisting him in his work as an itinerant craftsman. Wherever the father received assignments, the boys were temporarily placed in school. Also, from time to time during his childhood years Sorokin periodically vacationed or found temporary refuge with his mother's people.

Sorokin's father was born in the ancient city of Veliki Ustyug, where he became a master craftsman in gold, silver, and iron ornamental work. Sorokin and his brother accompanied him as he moved from village to village in search of assignments. Sorokin reported that his father had the reputation for being a reliable, honest, and comparatively skillful workman. However, as the years went by periods of sobriety were punctuated by excessive drinking that at times resulted in delirium tremens. After one unusually violent period which led to attacks on the boys (Sorokin was eleven at the time, his brother fourteen) they set out as independent itinerant artisans. For two years Sorokin's elder brother guided their mutual affairs, securing sufficient commissions to survive. Sorokin's brother continued to seek an education, and the two separated when Sorokin won a scholarship to a "normal" school. He did so well there as to win encouragement and support for entrance into a seminary.

Both of Sorokin's brothers eventually became involved in the Russian revolution. The elder brother continued to practice the trade of an itinerant craftsman for a time, then moved to St. Petersburg, working as a craftsman, salesman, and clerk. In 1918 he was arrested by the communists for anti-revolutionary activities and executed. Sorokin's younger brother remained with a maternal aunt until he was drafted in to the Russian army and was stationed in a Russian city. Until termination of his military service, this brother remained in the city, becoming successively a bookkeeper, clerk, and salesman. He married and raised two children. He was arrested with little justification, Sorokin believed, for subversive activities and was sent to prison, where he died.

Sorokin's itinerant life with his father and elder brother made formal schooling a hit-and-miss affair. However, he was systematically enrolled in various village schools in which his father and brother secured commissions. Moreover, since the work of the itinerant artisan was usually secured from the priest or some other member of the village intelligentsia, Sorokin came into contact with the highest cultural and intellectual traditions of the region. Moreover, travel from place to place supplied a wide base of comparative experience. Sorokin stated that he often received encouragement in his studies and the loan of books from teachers, clergymen, and more enlightened peasants with whom he came into contact.

When an advanced grade school was opened in Gam village, where Sorokin and his elder brother were working, Sorokin volunteered for the entrance examinations, which he passed with flying colors. He was awarded a scholarship of five rubles ($2.50) which paid his room and board for an entire year! The scholarship was renewed for each of the three years of the school curriculum.

At this time in Russia one of the few avenues to higher circles open to bright peasant and artisan youths was through the church. Sorokin's peasant relatives were pious Russian Orthodox in religion. Moreover, his travels with his father and brother took him primarily to the village churches for commissions. The church emerged as the single most glamorous institution of Sorokin's childhood. The village priests, for their part, often took an interest in the avid motherless youth, loaning him books and encouraging his reading. Sorokin remembered much reading in an old quarto volume of the lives of the saints which impressed him as an ideal outlet for his own abilities. He became a lay preacher at neighborhood gatherings of peasants on long winter evenings.

> If there are elements of mysticism in my theories, as several scholars assert, such mystic and tragic strains were set therein at an early age by the tragic mysteries of the Mass and by the trying experiences of my life.[3]

The spell of a clerical career and his success in the schools of his native province led Sorokin to ascend the primary route up and out of his peasant-artisan background. When in 1903, at the age of fourteen, he graduated from the Gam school, he won a scholarship for the Khrenovo Teachers Seminary in Kostroma Province. The Seminary was a denominational school under the jurisdiction of the Holy Synod of the Russian Orthodox Church. It trained teachers for the Synod's elementary schools.

In 1904, under the impact of the Russo-Japanese War, and in 1905, under the influence of the Revolution, the theological seminaries were shaken by the winds of doctrine. Within two years after his move to the Seminary, Sorokin reported that his previous religiosity had been replaced by a "semi-atheistic rejection of the theologies and rituals of the Russian Orthodox Church."[4]

Under the influence of the new revolutionary ferment, Sorokin became a member of the Social Revolutionary Party. At schools and in nearby villages he preached the Social Revolutionary gospel, as earlier he had preached religious orthodoxy to pious peasants. He was arrested and thrown into jail by the czarist police, but was—as was usual for political prisoners at the time—well treated. In jail he came into contact with the intoxicating excitement of the political prisoners and intellectuals. "Daily discussions and an intensive reading of the works of Mikhailovsky, Lavrov, Marx, Engels, Bakunin, Kropotkin, Tolstoi, Plenkhanov, Tehernoff, Lenin, and other revolutionary classics acquainted me with various revolutionary theories, ideologies, and problems."[5] He also reported that he became acquainted with the writings of Charles Darwin and Herbert Spencer at this time. During the four months of his imprisonment, he opined, he learned much more than he could have during a semester at the Seminary.

Because of his political activities, Sorokin was expelled from school. However, he was welcomed in revolutionary circles. He now engaged full time in political agitation among the peasants. Soon perceiving that this was a dead end, he moved to St. Petersburg, where he supported himself as a tutor. He also entered night school to prepare himself for the university. In 1909 Sorokin passed the entrance examinations and enrolled in the newly opened Psycho-Neurological Institute in which courses in sociology were given by two internationally famous scholars: M.M. Kovalevsky and E. de Roberty. He succeeded in acquiring the position of secretary and research assistant to Kovalevsky. In addition to Kovalevsky and de Roberty, other scholars from whom Sorokin took work at the Institute included Leon Petrajitsky (law), Tugan-Baranovsky (economics), N. Rosin and A. Jijilenko (criminology and penology), M. I. Rostevtzeff and N. O. Lossky (history and classics). In addition to serving as private secretary and assistant to Kovalevsky, Sorokin also became teaching assistant to de Roberty and co-editor with him of a series of studies of *New Ideas in Sociology*.

Sorokin also stated that Petrajitsky and Bekhterev employed him as co-editors of *New Ideas in the Science of Law* and of a *Journal of Psychology and Criminal Anthropology*. Through Kovalevsky and Petrajitsky, Sorokin met leaders of the Liberal and Constitutional Democratic Parties as well as statesmen and members of the Duma. The last time he was arrested by the czarist police (1913), he was soon released through the efforts of Kovalevsky. Sorokin thus had the rare good fortune to arrive on the scene at a time when an emerging Russian social science was in the budding stage and to serve a number of notable scholars as a student assistant.

Sorokin received a fellowship to facilitate his studies for a master's degree in criminal law under N. Rosin, A. Jijilenko, and N. Lazarevsky. This appointment covering the years 1914 to 1916 permitted him to devote full time to his studies. He passed his master's oral examination in the fall of 1916, planning to submit his volume on *Crime and Punishment* (1913) for the degree of magister of criminal law. The time for public defense of his thesis was set for March, 1917. However, the onset of the Revolution made this impossible.

As the Revolution deepened and the communists came into power, conditions worsened. The government abolished scientific degrees in 1918. They were later restored, and after changes in plans and the survival of the Revolution, Sorokin offered his two-volume *System of Sociology* (1920) as a doctoral dissertation. It was defended successfully, and he was awarded the doctor of philosophy degree on April 22, 1922.

Meanwhile, the passing of his master's oral examination won Sorokin the degree of magistrant of criminal law, entitling him to become a *privat-docent* (private lecturer) paid out of student fees. In the period of 1914 to 1916 his status as a graduate student, and, later as an instructor exempted him from service in the World War I Russian army. However, Sorokin reported that during World War I he served on committees formed to assist the mobilization of the nation's economic resources and service to the recreational and educational needs of invalids and veterans. Moreover, he delivered morale-building, patriotic lectures to military and civilian audiences.[6]

Even while engaging in such patriotic activities, however, Sorokin stated that he was occupied with others of like mind in preparing plans for the defeat of the Russian army by the Germans and for the imminent downfall of the czarist regime.[7]

The fullest report of the events of Sorokin's life during the Russian Revolution (1917-1922) is contained in his *Leaves from a Russian Dairy*. His position as a lecturer at the University of St. Petersburg put him in direct touch with persons who were to play a major role in the Revolution. His membership in the Social Revolutionary Party tied his fortunes to those of the group who were to play the major role in the first phase of the Revolution. The fall of the Kerensky Provisional Government and the assumption of power by the Bolshevists radically reversed the fortunes of the moderate revolutionaries.

In March and April, 1917, Sorokin has reported, the leaders of the Social Revolutionary Party decided to found a newspaper to mold public opinion in a desired direction. Sorokin was one of a committee of five appointed to serve as editors of *Delo Naroda* (*The Affairs of the People*), as the paper was called.[8] Because of sharp differences of opinion with the other editors, Sorokin soon resigned his position and helped to organize another Social Revolutionary paper, the *Volia Naroda* (*The Will of the People*).[9]

Sorokin by no means confined his activities to newspaper editing. He stated that he was offered three posts under the provisional government: assistant minister of the interior, director of the Russian telegraphic service, and secretary to Prime Minister Kerensky. He accepted the position as Kerensky's secretary.[10] Also in his home province of Vologda, he helped organize the electoral campaign for the Constitutional Assembly. He was, thus, one of the founders of the

All Russian Peasant Soviet. He reports that peasant conventions in three districts of Vologda Province unanimously nominated him as deputy. This nomination was concurred in by the Social Revolutionary Party of Vologda.[11]

When Kerensky was defeated and the Bolshiviki assumed power, Sorokin's roles as Kerensky's former secretary and as representative of the Province of Vologda became negative assets. Meanwhile, continued publication of the Social Revolutionary Party paper that he had helped organize and that he continued to serve as editor became dangerous. Sorokin wrote that his first arrest by the Bolshevists occurred in the offices of *The Will of the People* on January 2, 1918.[12]

After fifty-seven days in jail, an old friend from his early Social Revolutionary days who was now cooperating with the Bolshevists secured Sorokin's release. Upon release from prison Sorokin reported that he continued to engage in anti-Bolshevist activity with various Moscow groups. He assisted in the publication of an anti-Bolshevist newspaper (*Regeneration*). However, when the first copy appeared, Bolshevist agents raided the office, destroyed the copy, broke up the forms and matrices, and smashed the presses. The tension between the two groups of revolutionaries continued to mount, and by the end of May, 1917, members of the Constitutional Assembly and of the League for the Regeneration of Russia who opposed the Bolshevists began to flee Moscow.

Sorokin reported that he participated in plans for an anti-Bolshevist revolt in Archangel and set out for that city. He never reached it. The Bolsheviks had learned of the revolt and put out a dragnet for the conspirators. After a period of hiding from the Bolshevist police, Sorokin decided to give himself up to the authorities. He was in prison for four months under sentence of death. There were daily executions from among his cell mates. An old student intervened for him, and Sorokin's release was secured by the direct intervention of Lenin, who wrote an article in *Pravda* urging that intellectuals such as Sorokin could be useful as educators to the new Communist order.[13]

Sorokin was permitted to return to the Psycho-Neurological Institute and was elected professor of sociology in both the Agricultural Academy and the Institute of Public Economy. Because of the extra rations, he accepted both positions. At the same time two large cooperative organizations not yet nationalized asked him to write textbooks in law and sociology.[14]

In the spring of 1920 Sorokin was transferred to the Agricultural

Academy of Czarskoe Selo. Shortly after this he published his two-volume *System of Sociology* which, he stated, caused a temporary flurry among the Chekhists (secret police). Official persecutions were not systematically organized at this time but were whimsical and arbitrary, varying by the day. However, if one were picked up he could stay in jail indefinitely. Hence with the excitement over possible subversion in his *System of Sociology,* he deemed it wise to drop out of sight for a couple of weeks. As he had anticipated, the flurry died down, and he was able to submit and defend his text as his doctoral dissertation.

Sorokin witnessed the Great Famine of 1921 which brought the prestige of the Bolshevist government to a low ebb. In May, 1922, he published a book on *The Influence of Hunger on Human Behavior.* It was severely censored beforehand, and its appearance coincided with renewed vigor in the Soviet's propaganda campaign against opposition on the home front. Once again Sorokin thought it expedient to drop out of sight for a while. A wave of arrests of scholars was under way, but they were routinely being banished rather than executed or sent to prison. Since the police in St. Petersburg were relatively more severe, Sorokin decided to give himself up to the authorities in Moscow in the hope of banishment rather than imprisonment or execution. It all worked out as planned, and Sorokin was banished to Czechoslovakia.

In Prague he offered a series of public lectures which were published as *The Contemporary State of Russia* (Prague, 1922). He also worked up a volume of *Essays on Social Pedagogy and Politics.* He participated as editor and contributed to a journal on *The Peasant's Russia,* published in it a series of studies of agrarian problems. He undertook work on the manuscript that was to become his *Sociology of Revolution*(1925).

Sorokin's intellectual activities in Prague attracted the attention of international scholars. This resulted in the extension of invitations from Edward C. Hayes of the University of Illinois and from Edward A. Ross of the University of Wisconsin to come to North America and deliver a series of lectures on the Russian Revolution. After Sorokin's arrival in the United States, his predicament as a penniless *emigre* was learned by Henry Noble MacCracken, president of Vassar College. MacCracken invited him to be the guest of Vassar for a few weeks with complete freedom to study English and work up his lectures.[15

Upon completion of his lecture series at the University of Wisconsin and Illinois in 1924, Sorokin was invited by F. Stuart Chapin to teach in the summer session at the University of Minnesota. His success in teaching there led to his appointment as full professor. During his six years at Minnesota, Sorokin published six works: *Leaves from a Russian Diary*(1924); *The Sociology of Revolution* (1925); *Social Mobility* (1927); *Contemporary Sociological Theories* (1928); *Principles of Rural-Urban Sociology* (with C.C. Zimmerman, 1929); and the three volumes of *A Systematic Source-Book in Rural Sociology* (with C.C. Zimmerman and C. J. Galpin, 1930-1932).

In 1929 Sorokin was invited to deliver a series of lectures at Harvard University. These turned out to be exploratory prior to inviting him to join the faculty and establish a department of sociology. In addition to serving as chairman, Sorokin continued his program of research and writing. Harvard assisted him by financial grants (amounting to some $10,000) in securing the assistance of specialists in the history of painting, sculpture, architecture, music, literature, science, philosophy, economics, religion, ethics, law, war, and revolution. Sorokin was compiling evidence from all such areas of rates and forms of cultural change. This project, which he had conceived while still at Minnesota, eventually was published as his four-volume *Social and Cultural Dynamics*. A large part of the work in assembling material from special cultural areas was done by displaced Russian scholars. Sorokin was able both to secure excellent skills and talents at bargain prices and to assist many refugee scholars in the difficult transition period in the New World. Meanwhile, he established and strengthened the Harvard department and enhanced its attractiveness with invitations to many eminent specialists. He eventually gave up the chairmanship in 1942.

Four years after retirement from the chairmanship at Harvard, Sorokin received a letter from Eli Lilly offering him $20,000 to finance research on the topic of the moral and mental regeneration of contemporary humanity. At the suggestion of President Conant, the grant was made (for tax exemption purposes) to Harvard University, though the money was entirely at Sorokin's disposal. Using only a fraction of the fund, Sorokin produced a volume on *The Reconstruction of Humanity* (1948). Lilly was so impressed that he made an additional grant of $100,000 at the rate of $20,000 a year for the next five years. The grant led to the establishment in 1949 of the Harvard Research Center in Creative Altruism with Sorokin as director. Thereafter his time was equally divided between his teaching duties in the sociology department and directorship of the center. Ten years later, when the fund was exhausted, the Lilly Foundation granted an additional $25,000 for continuation of the work of the center and to finance publication of the Proceedings of the First International Congress for Comparative Study of Civilization, of which Sorokin was president, at Salzburg in 1961.

In April, 1950, Sorokin gave the Cole Lectures on ''Recent Philosophies of History'' at Vanderbilt University. These were published as *Social Philosophies of an Age of Crisis*(1950). In January, 1955, he retired from teaching but continued to act as director of the Harvard Research Center in Creative Altruism until he was seventy. His publications accelerated in volume after his retirement, illustrated by *Fads and Foibles in Modern Sociology* (1956), *The American Sex Revolution* (1956), and *Power and Morality* (1959).

After his retirement from teaching Sorokin attended many national and international congresses, and was elected the first president of the International Society for the Comparative Study of Civilizations (1961). He was elected president of the American Sociological Association in 1965.

In 1966 Sorokin returned to the special field of sociological theory for the first time since his 1928 review. It is a testimony to his flexibility and his movement toward personal synthesis that he completely scrapped his earlier typology redividing the theories into nominalistic-singularistic-atomistic, on the one hand, and systemic on the other. He located his positions, which he described as integral theory, primarily among the systemic theories, but as a more comprehensive form of theory which integrates the other two.

> In their sound parts, the singularistic-atomistic theories of social, cultural and personal congeries are reconcilable and complement the sound body of systematic theories: Each class of these theories gives a real knowledge of the singularistic and systematic forms of the total superorganic reality.[16]

Sorokin continued giving additional lecture series and working on additional publications until his death in 1968.

Sorokin's Intellectual Development

In his autobiography Sorokin undertook to trace the development of his own ideas. There is not the slightest reason to doubt the accuracy of his self-estimate. He divided his intellectual development into three phases.

Traditional Religiosity

Like many another simple peasant or artisan youth with special intellectual aptitude at the same time and place in Russia, young Sorokin had begun to climb the one major ladder up and out of his peasant-artisan background. He had won a fellowship at one of the seminaries which trained individuals for teaching or the priesthood. To win such opportunities young Sorokin had to demonstrate not only intellectual acumen but special interest in things religious. He reported that he was spellbound by the lives of the saints and took them as an ideal. He plunged intensely into activities as a youthful teacher-preacher among the peasants. At this stage of his life Sorokin stated his mentality was dominated by Russian Orthodox Christianity.

> This religious climate...served as a stimulus and outlet for the development of my creative propensities... I learned *verbatim,* prayers, psalms, and scriptural texts as well as the details of my religious services... This knowledge was also partly responsible for my becoming a teacher-preacher at the neighborhood gatherings of peasants during the long winter evenings... The moral precepts of Christianity, especially of the Sermon on the Mount and the Beatitudes, decisively conditioned my moral values not only in youth but for the rest of my life... All in all mine was an idealistic world-view in which God and nature, truth, goodness, and beauty, religion, science, art, and ethics were all united into one harmonious system.[17]

It was the combination of intellectual acumen and traditionalistic piety which gave peasant and artisan youth in Czarist Russia access to the theological and teaching seminaries. Stalin, too, had started up this particular ladder. Traditionally such young men would have normally ended up in the village *intelligentsia* or priesthood. However, at that particular time and place the theological and teaching seminaries were becoming hotbeds of revolutionary excitement.

Positivistic Organicism

The alertness and impressionability that had led young Sorokin to isolate the religious element of his peasant artisan surroundings as its most dramatic and exciting component could hardly have remained untouched by the intoxicating atmosphere of revolution. All the evidence suggests that Sorokin gravitated immediately and spontaneously to the centers of excitement.

Inasmuch as czarist monarchism was locked together with Russian Orthodox religiosity into a traditional complex, revolutionary opposition to the regime usually had an anti-religious bent. How far young Sorokin went along with this trend is indicated by what he describes as his "semi-atheistic rejection of the theologies and rituals of the Russian Orthodox Church," his abandonment of religion for science, and adherence to the czarist monarchy and capitalism for "republican, democratic, and socialist views."[18] He embraced the tenets of revolution with religious intensity and became an active missionary among worker peasant groups for his new gospel.

While the prevailing atmosphere in the Russian universities at the time Sorokin was an undergraduate was not characterized by active revolutionary ferment, it, too, differed rather markedly from the traditional religiosity of Sorokin's childhood. His most admired teachers, Kovalevsky and de Roberty, were more liberal than revolutionary. They led Sorokin to the sociological classics. In Sorokin's own estimation the result was a modification of his revolutionary inclinations toward a position close to that of such classical sociologists as Comte, Spencer, and Durkheim.

> Philosophically the emerging system was a variety of empirical neo-positivism or critical realism based upon logical and empirical scientific methods. Sociologically it represented a sort of synthesis of Comteian-Spencerian sociology of evolution-progress corrected and supplemented by the theories of N. Mikhailovsky, P. Lavrov, E. de Roberty, L. Petrajitsky, M Kovalevsky, M. Rostovtzeff, P. Kropotkin, among the Russian social thinkers, and by the theories of G. Tarde, E. Durkheim, G. Simmel, M. Weber, R. Stammler, K. Marx, V. Pareto, and other western social scientists. Politically, it was a form of socialistic ideology, founded upon the ethics of solidarity, mutual aid, and freedom.[19]

Inasmuch as the classical sociologists conjoined a confidence in scientific methods as adequate to the study of society with an organismic theory of society and faith in its progress or evolution, the position has been described as positivistic organicism. Sorokin's position in his own estimation was, at this time, a form of classical theory, differing only in its socialistic coloration. "I did not," Sorokin observed, "foresee then that this 'scientific, positivistic, and progressively optimistic' *Weltanschauung* soon would be found wanting by the crucial test of historical events and would engender the second crisis of my world outlook."[20]

Integralism

In the twentieth century the naive confidence in the classical sociological theories of progress was seriously shaken. It was difficult to reconcile wars and revolutions with the concept of progress. However, even before the close of the nineteenth century the balked aspirations of many groups were accompanied by increasing dissatisfaction with the classical synthesis of positivism, organicism, and progress. World War I and the backlash of disillusionment that accompanied the Russian Revolution delivered the final blows to the prestige of sociology's first synthesis. Indication of the state of the popular mind was the enormous popularity of Spengler's *Decline of the West.*

Sorokin characteristically attributed his own reactions to his independent assessment of world events rather than to any change in world opinion.

> Already World War I had made some fissures in the positivistic, "scientific," and humanistic *Weltanschauung* I had held before the War. The Revolution of 1917 enormously enlarged these fissures and eventually shattered this world-outlook with its positivistic philosophy and sociology, its utilitarian system of values, and its conception of historical process as a progressive evolution toward an even better man, society, and culture.[21]

Sorokin reported that the revision of his point of view was virtually complete by the end of the 1920s. "It resulted in what I now call the *integral system* of philosophy, sociology, psychology, ethics, and values."[22] Integralism, Sorokin maintained, was systematically extended and expressed in the volumes he published in the last three decades.

Sorokin's *magnum opus* in which his integralism was brought for the first time into mature synthesis was his four-volume monograph, *Social and Cultural Dynamics,* on the cultural changes in Western civilization. This project was conceived in 1929 and eventually brought to completion with the publication of the fourth volume in 1941. Sorokin believed his publications after *Dynamics* were renewed formulations and extensions of the same point of view to new calamities of the 1950s and attempts to round out his integral system of philosophy, sociology, psychology, and ethics. Such volumes as *Man and Society in Calamity* (1942), *Socio-Cultural Causality, Space and Time*(1943), *Society, Culture, and Personality*(1947), and *The Meaning of Our Crisis* (1951) are somewhat simplified formulations and popularizations of the views of *Social and Cultural Dynamics.* The numerous volumes done or supervised for the Harvard Research Center in Creative Altruism were primarily conceived as the exploration of alternatives to the decadence of contemporary culture; they were practical applications of integralist theory intended as a basis for social reconstruction.

Comte's Positivism and Sorokin's Integralism

Since by his own admission Sorokin's position in his inexperienced youth was close to that of the classical sociologists, it is not unfair to compare his views with those of the founder of sociology to see how far in fact his integralism departs from the classical formula.

Comte drew premises for his own system from both the idealistic and empiricist traditions of philosophy. The essence of human society, he believed, is constituted by ideas. Moreover, such ideas are not the isolated notions of individuals but collective formations. Comte's successor, Durkheim, built directly on Comte in this respect and made the concept of collective representations as the basic facts of society quite explicit. Comte, furthermore, did not draw a sharp distinction between society and culture. Humanity or mankind consisted of the collective mind of all men living and dead. It has an organic unity. The central clue to its unity is provided by the prevailing mode of thought of a given time and place. This mode of thought of mankind progresses through three grand stages: theological and priest-dominated, metaphysical and philosopher-dominated, and positivistic and scientist-dominated. The unity in the various aspects of mankind is displayed in the presence of the basic presuppositions of the dominant mode of thought in all the various spheres of socio-cultural life: religion, economics, politics, and so on.

The similarities between Comte's position and Sorokin's integralism are numerous. Like Comte, Sorokin believed that systems and supersystems of sociocultural life form dynamic, interrelated wholes. Moreover, like Comte at the highest level (the supersystem), the lines between society and culture are blurred. The primary difference at this level between Comte and Sorokin is the latter's shift toward a vaguely theistic position. For Comte, humanity itself became the substitute for God. Integralism, according to Sorokin,

> views total reality as the infinite X of numberless qualities and quantities: spiritual and material, everchanging and unchangeable, personal and super-personal, temporal and timeless, spatial and spaceless, one and many... its highest center--the *summum bonum*--is the Infinite Creative X that passes all human understanding.[23]

Comte's early formulations thrust theology aside as a primitive stage in human thought. However, in the end Comte substituted humanity for God and transformed sociology into applied theology, hopelessly confusing the lines between science, philosophy, and religion. Sorokin,too, blurred the lines between these disciplines. The essence of his point of view, he urged, is the same as that of the philosophical thought of Taoism, the Upanishads, the Bhagavad-Gita, the writings of Hindu and Mahayana logicians, the Zen Buddhists, the great Muslim thinkers and poets, the philosophies of Heraclitus and Plato and to a lesser extent Aristotle, the philosophies of Plotinus, Porphyry, the Hermetic, Orphic, and Christian Church fathers and mystics and the philosophies of various rationalists.[24]

Though Comte's early system of sociology rejected religion, he came to the view that only religion was able to provide the essential unity to society. Prior to Comte's association with Saint-Simon, he seems to have accepted the traditional Catholicism in which he was reared. Sorokin, too, seems to have undergone a similar series of developments starting with traditional religious orthodoxy, becoming for a time an atheist, eventually subscribing to religion once more. Though there were differences, both Comte and Sorokin came to subscribe to nonstandard faiths:Comte to the religion of humanity, and Sorokin to an amalgam of elements drawn from the great religions and philosophies of the world.

Comparable to Comte's view that a peculiar set of ideas and methods of·thought provided the order to the stages of the development of mankind is Sorokin's view that the essence of every cultural system (and, incidentally, system of ethics, religion, and philosophy) is the peculiar set of values taken as of central importance and the appropriate methods for the pursuit of these values.

> any great culture, instead of being a mere dumping place of a multitude of diverse cultural phenomena, existing side by side and unrelated to one another, represents a unity or individuality whose parts are permeated by the same fundamental principle and articulate the same basic value. The dominant part of the fine arts and science of such a unified culture, of its philosophy and religion, of its ethics and law, of its main forms of social, economic, and political organization, of most of its mores and manners, of its ways of life and mentality, all articulate, each in its own way, this basic principle and value. This value serves as its major premise and foundation. For this reason the important parts of such an integrated culture are also interdependent causally: if one important part changes, the rest of its important parts are bound to be similarly transformed.[25]

For Comte there were three great historical systems of humanity: theological, metaphysical, and positivistic. These followed one another in a progressive series. For Sorokin, too, there were three great systems depending on the value which forms their integrating point. The two major contrasting types were the ideate, a civilization integrated around a supersensory value such as the love of God, and sensate, a civilization integrated around .sensual values. Just as Comte's metaphysical society was transitional between the theological and positivistic, Sorokin's idealistic civilization was transitional between ideate and sensate.

However, while Comte's systems were thought to represent a progressive series, Sorokin emphatically rejected the concept of progress. The impetus for change in Comte's view was the application of man's intelligence to the solution of his problems and the increasing control of the emotions by reason. Sorokin, however, had no equivalent confidence in human reason or similar notion of the relation between reason and the emotions. "No finite form, either ideational or sensate, is eternal. Sooner or later it is bound to exhaust its creative abilities. When this moment comes, it begins to disintegrate and decline."[26] The basic mechanism of change for Sorokin appeared to be the property of "exhaustion of creative abilities."

For Comte the millennium was being ushered in by the application of science to social affairs, but for Sorokin the disintegration of civilization, the salient property of our epoch, was in large measure a product of the application of science. While Comte reversed the medieval philosophy of history, Sorokin in many respects returned the theory of history to a formulation closer to that of St. Augustine with whom, in fact, he was fond of identifying. The contemporary crisis of society and culture is traced to the corruption of a sensate culture in a manner that would gladden the heart of a medieval theologian. For example, contemporary art, Sorokin insisted, "is primarily a museum of social and cultural pathology. It centers in the police morgue, the criminal's hide-out, and the sex organs, operating mainly on the level of the social sewer."[27] The corruption of contemporary civilization is even manifest in its methods of thought. There has been, Sorokin maintained, "an increasing relativization of sensory truth until it becomes indistinguishable from error."[28] Society has undermined its own values "through a progressively thin and narrow empiricism divorced from other social values—religion, goodness, beauty, and the like."[29] Ultimately even science is said to have "distinctly impaired our understanding of reality."[30] In the fields of ethics and law the crisis of sensate culture is said to have resulted in transforming values into "mere 'rationalizations,' 'derivations,' or 'beautiful speech reactions,' veiling the egotistic interests, pecuniary motives, and acquisitive propensities of individuals and groups."[31] Ethical norms have ceased to be guides to behavior, becoming instead a smoke screen for lust and greed. Legal norms have been converted into devices for exploiting the weak by the powerful.

The crisis of contemporary civilization, Sorokin insisted, runs through all institutions: family, government, economic institutions, cultural institutions. Even international relations have been in crisis. Accompanying the crisis has been a rise in the rates of suicide, criminality, war, and revolution. Contemporary culture as a whole is said to be characterized by chaotic syncretism, quantitative colossalism, and the loss of creativeness.

Somewhat parallel to the manner in which St. Augustine had held out *The City of God* as an alternative to the decay of the earthly city, Sorokin held out the promise of a possible reconstruction of humanity. the remedy required "replacement of the withered root of sensate culture by an ideational or idealistic root, and eventually in a substitution of a full grown and more spiritual culture for the decadent sensate form."[32] However, despite many similarities, Hans Speier calls attention to the error of identifying Sorokin's theories too closely with those of the Church fathers. He described Sorokin's position as

a modern vulgarization of early Christian thinking. The distinction between senses, reason, and faith is retained as a universal principle of division of the types of man, cultures, and "systems" within each culture. The hierarchization of these values, however, is blurred. The idea of a supreme good is given up in favor of a relativistic point of view, tempered by eclectic professions of absolute standards. Throughout his work some kind of hierarchy of the three values is implied, as is particularly evident from the expressions of contempt, disgust, and revulsion in which Sorokin indulges whenever he describes the "sensate sewers" of our time. However, it is not the truth of faith which ranks highest, as one might expect from familiarity with the tradition which Sorokin follows in distinguishing the three values. Rather, he "prefers" idealism to ideationalism. Again, ideationalism is constructed as a compromise between sensation and idealism, which blurs the distinctions further. Finally, the methods used in *Social and Cultural Dynamics* are those of "sensate science," which has induced a malicious critic to remark that the work may be a satire on modern social science.[33]

So long as Sorokin's analysis remained within the framework set by *Social and Cultural Dynamics*, Speier's criticism is well taken. In the end Sorokin's position remains a form of cultural relativism, for even granting that one replaces the root of sensate culture by an idealistic or ideational form, this would only be for a time. According to Sorokin's own principle, sooner or later it is bound to exhaust its creative abilities.

However, there is some possible indication that Sorokin was moving toward a conception of the final deliverance of mankind in the form of an integralistic system of civilization which is superior to the three inevitable forms (ideate, sensate, and idealistic).

> From the integralist standpoint, the present antagonism between science, religion, philosophy, ethics, and art is unnecessary, not to mention disastrous. In the light of an adequate theory of true reality and value, they are all one and all serve one purpose: the unfolding of the Absolute in the relative empirical world, to the greater nobility of Man and to the greater glory of God. As such they should and can cooperate in the fulfillment of this greatest task.[34]

This would seem to bring Sorokin even closer to the position of the Church fathers.

In his autobiography Sorokin insisted that at least in his personal life he succeeded in "reuniting into one *summum bonum* the supreme Trinity of Truth, Goodness, and Beauty.... Integralism has given me a firm foundation for maintenance of my integrity and has wisely guided my conduct amidst the bloody debris of the crumbling sensate civilization."[35]

Sorokin's last book, *Sociological Theories of Today,* indicates that he had no intention of leaving integralism at the level of a purely personal philosophy. The various conceptual developments of his work were clearly being codified. The following estimate sums up the differences between his earlier and later treatments of theory.

> Sorokin's earlier review of sociological theory, *Contemporary Sociological Theories* (1928), was completed prior to the synthesis of his distinctive theoretical position in his *magnum opus,* the *Social and Cultural Dynamics* (1937-1941, 4 vols.).
>
> The primary difference between the two reviews of theory, apart from the survey of new developments in sociology from 1928 to the present, is the introduction of a new classification of theories and the application of a consistent critical position to all material reviewed.
>
> In *Sociological Theories of Today* Sorokin divides sociological theories into three types:(1) Singularistic-Atomistic, (2) Systemic--divided into Systemic theories of culture and Systemic theories of society with numerous sub-divisions--and (3) the Integral System of structural and dynamic Sociology.

Much of the material earlier contained in *Fads and Foibles in Modern Sociology*(1956) is summarized under the Singularistic-Atomistic type of theory. Most of the recent developments in the theory of culture and society are subsumed under Systemic types of theory. There is, apparently, only one true example of Integral theory, namely, Sorokin's own. Integral theory is claimed to synthesize whatever is valuable in all other methodologies and substantive theories, bringing the methods and values of the senses, the reason and intuition, and the interpretations of corresponding forms of personality, society, and supersystems--cultures and civilizations--in which these various methods and values are embodied into balanced perspective.

All new major developments in sociology since the 1920's are reviewed to determine the extent to which they are false or redundant, that is the extent to which they disagree or agree with the Integral System of Sociology.[*36*]

Sociological Theories of Today leaves little doubt that Sorokin was bringing the diverse strands of his thought into unity.

Soldier of Fortune

The nearest counterparts to Sorokin's system of ideas are found in Hegel in philosophy and Comte in sociology. Sorokin's writing has a vigorous and forthright character and is inspired by a zest for the destruction of popular idols. He often conveyed the impression of rather naive heedlessness, and many a person had been lured into battle only to discover himself *vis-a-vis* with a battle-wise campaigner. One often discovered that Sorokin was able to quote chapter and verse from his writings apparently in direct refutation of charges which a moment before had seemed almost self-evident.[*37*]

Although Sorokin appeared to have a unified system of ideas, unity was provided by the Absolute which, in principle, is placed outside manifest experience as an ultimate reality not directly accessible except by intuition. The Absolute comprises all dynamisms, all changes, all contradictions, which arise in the unfolding experiences of everyday life.

Sorokin conceived of the senses, the mind, and the spirit as three basic realities, each with its special form of knowledge and truth. The three methods comprise the empirical methods of science, the logical methods of reason, and the intuitive methods of the spirit. Each of the three basic realities supplies its distinctive value to human endeavor: the sensory, the value of reason, and the super-rational, super-empirical value of faith. On the basis of these three types of value, meaning, and truth, Sorokin projected the existence of distinctive types of civilization and personality (men of science, men of reason, and men of faith).

In examining the manner in which various social and cultural phenomena are related to one another, Sorokin apparently subscribed to a holistic position. In fact, he described himself on occasion as a holist. Holism is inseparable from the view that in some sense the whole is a causal component in the development and change of its parts. In this connection, the exchange between Louis Schneider[38] and Sorokin is of special interest.[39] Quite in accord with the assumption that Sorokin's concept of sociocultural systems was holistic, Schneider saw him as accounting for change primarily on the basis of an internal dialect (that is, change is brought about by the structure of the sociocultural system itself without any requirement of extra-system factors). While Sorokin did not altogether accept Schneider's interpretation, he agreed that he accounted for change primarily in dialectical terms.

While Sorokin's holism appeared to be complete in every respect, whenever he was criticized for failing to account for various categories of events which failed to obey his principles, he was able simply to point out that he had insisted that not all sociocultural phenomena are integrated into supersystems. There also are partly organized systems, contradictory systems, and collections of elements that form mere congeries without any system at all. Hence one was left quite in the dark as to when Sorokin's holism would or would not apply, and he was free to use or not use it as he moved from case to case and from argument to argument.

Treating the objects of sense experience, of logical reasoning, of faith as three categories of reality, each with its appropriate methods of study (scientific empiricism, logical reasoning, and intuition), seems very plausible in terms of various ancient notions of human thought and experience. However, whenever one considers the actual reasoning processes of men, this treatment of these as equal and parallel forms of truth establishment leads to considerable confusion. In actual cases of scientific investigation various empirical, logical, and intuitive (in some senses of this highly ambiguous term) elements are simultaneously present. To treat the intuitions and revelations of mystics as in some sense parallel to the deductions of a logician or the experimental investigations of a scientist is to blur very significant differences between them and in no way to solve the problem that arises when, for example, the suggestions of intuition are in direct contradiction with the other so-called modes of truth establishment.

On the other hand, to ignore such contradictions and, perhaps, assign them to the Absolute in which all contradictions are ultimately resolved, is to solve the problem by irrational means.

Sorokin's procedure of placing the three so-called realities on a parallel plane (objects of sense, reason, and faith) leveled down the distinction between values and facts. This in turn became a license to load his writing with all sorts of supercharged value judgments. Moreover, he was simultaneously left free to pursue any tack he pleased and did not hesitate, for example, to quantify all sorts of matters which even some rather extreme positivists found rather hair-raising while attacking attempts at measurement and quantification by other researchers. Riley and Moore, for example, observe:

> ...notwithstanding his continuing concern with problems of measuring qualitative variables, he ridicules as "metrophrenia" the solutions to these problems worked out by serious and competent scholars. His gratuitous attack on Guttman scaling, for example, serves only to demonstrate his fundamental misunderstanding of the meaning of scalability and his own failure to recognize the procedure as an important complement to his own work. Thus the reader can find passages in his critical writings which seem to support almost any standpoint--or its opposite![40]

Sorokin described his political position as that of a "conservative, Christian anarchist."[41] Presumably his anarchism (which ordinarily is an intransigent form of individualism) coexisted without any sense of conflict with his holism (which is ordinarily an intransigent form of collectivism). Sorokin's "conservatism" also apparently coexisted without conflict with his "nonconformism" and "revolutionism." He was, in fact, inordinately proud of his "idiosyncrasies" and his "bullheadedness and deviationism."[42] Finally, his Christianity coexisted with the lack of any church affiliation and the inclination to pick and choose bits at will from any religion or philosophy that interested him.

As many a person has discovered, the farther one goes in Sorokin's writing in the attempt to work out its internal system, the more certain he is to encounter difficulties or to become bogged down in its quicksands. This resistance to systematization, in fact, seems to be the basic reason why Sorokin has never become the founder of a school. Despite its pungent slogans and battle cries, his integralism resists the kind of codification into a dogma which is so critical for school formation. At the same time, the very property of Sorokin's thought which made it unusable for purposes of sect formation emphasizes the striking fact that in his hands his set of notions constituted an unusually effective instrument.

All these considerations suggest that the ordinary modes of estimating bodies of theory do not apply to Sorokin's integralism. At the
same time, the judgment that, despite all the many genuine insights
that Sorokin scattered so liberally throughout his work, his ideas were
in fact an eclectic patch and paste collage, though in a sense correct,
seems also to miss the point. The one estimate that seems best to fit
the complex of notions that constituted Sorokin's integralism is that
they were the arsenal of a soldier of fortune.

Sorokin himself represented his life as "a sort of continuous 'way-
faring' through most different occupational, social, economic, cultural, political, and ethnic positions and group affiliations."[43] After
the loss of his mother when Sorokin was three, he was taken with his
father and elder brother on their itinerant route from village to village.
After the break with their father, the two boys (aged ten and fourteen)
were able to maintain themselves in the same itinerant trade. Adeptness at taking advantage of the opportunities around him made it
possible for Sorokin to obtain as good an education as was available to
a youth on the Russian frontier. He was also able to start on the route
up and out of his peasant-artisan background through the teaching
seminary. The same acceptance and eye for the main chance guided
Sorokin in his participation in the two Russian revolutions with his
imprisonment three times by the czarist government and three times
by the communist government. He managed to found departments of
sociology at Leningrad, the stronghold of communism, and Harvard,
the intellectual stronghold of capitalism. Sorokin summed up his own
individualistic adaptability as follows:

> Sternly disciplined for many years in this sort of school, I became, to a
> notable degree, a self-reliant, independent, now and then nonconformist
> individual who in his search for truth does not accept any authority, any
> theory, any belief, or any value until it is tested and verified by all the
> relevant evidence available.[44]

Since Sorokin's list of the various forms of truth included the empirical, the rational, and the intuitive, he was quite free to accept or reject
just about anything he pleased, unworried about contradictions, since
in the Absolute, which includes everything, all contradictions are
resolved. The truth of this last notion is apparently given in intuition.

Sorokin was one of the types cast up by revolution, a soldier of
fortune, an ideologist produced by successive displacements (from
peasant-artisan to seminary student; from potential candidate for

the church school or clergy to revolution; from revolutionary to servant
of Bolshevism: from servant of Bolshevism to celebrated American
professor of sociology). He managed to survive these successive
displacements with a combination of skill, intelligence, and good
fortune. He became increasingly adept in the techniques of
ideological combat. He came, also, to locate his objectives in himself
alone. In short, Sorokin became sociology's primeval rebel without a
cause, its revolutionary without a revolution.

As a warrior of a primitive type, Sorokin was an individual fighter
rather than the disciplined member of a combat team. Moreover, as a
primitive warrior he early learned to live off the land. Few sociologists
have been more adept in exploiting every personal experience for
publication purposes. Thrown into prison for anti-czarist activities,
Sorokin came into contact with a variety of ordinary and political
criminals and turned the experience into intellectual assets.

> They were largely responsible for the topic of my first book, *Crime and
> Punishment, Service and Reward* (published in 1913) and for my choice of
> criminology and penology...as the field of my first specialization at the
> University of St. Petersburg.[45]

After surviving arrest by the communists and being permitted to teach
at St. Petersburg, Sorokin accepted the commission to write a *System
of Sociology*,[46] which he used as his Ph.d. dissertation (1920).

The great Russian famine of 1921 apparently convinced Sorokin,
along with many others, that the Bolshevist regime could not survive.
At the same time and with typical economy, he made sociological
capital of his observations of the famine with a book on *The Influence
of Hunger on Human Behavior: on Social Life and Social Organization*
(1921). Had Sorokin been correct in his assumption that the famine
was about to bring down the Bolshevist regime, this book would
probably have been a major life raft to survive the currents of change.

> Not much scientific knowledge did I gain in those twenty days I spent in the
> famine regions, but the memory of what I saw and heard there made me
> absolutely fearless in denouncing the Revolution and the monsters who were
> devouring Russia.[47]

However, Sorokin and various others who had assumed the imminent downfall of the Bolshevists had underestimated the extent to
which the regime had made itself crisis-proof. The Bolshevists met
the crisis by ruthlessly stamping out all forms of revolt and stepping

ıp their propaganda campaign. Sorokin reported:

> In May, 1922, my book, "The Influence of Hunger on Human Behavior"...
> began to be printed. Before publication, many paragraphs, indeed, whole
> chapters, were cut by the censors. The book as a whole was ruined, but what
> remained was better than nothing. The Soviets' "war on the ideological
> front" and terror were now being diffused with great energy. We all lived
> from hand to mouth, expecting some new blow each day.[48]

This is a considerable switch from being "absolutely fearless in
denouncing the monstors who were devouring Russia."

The currents of revolution have a way of successively tossing now
one, now another group, to leadership.   As conflict grows more
severe, violence may increase and the executioners of yesterday become the victims of today. However, the top ranks of leadership are in
most imminent danger of being cut down. Members of lower ranks
enjoy some flexibility in changing allegiance. Sorokin's survival of
earlier crises was a product not only of luck and skill but of the fact
that he was still of relatively minor importance among the revolutionaries. He reported that his younger brother was arrested primarily
because he was brother of "Communist Enemy No. 1." This judgment, however, came not from headquarters of the Bolshevist Party,
but from "the local authorities."[49] However, in becoming a professor and author and founder of a sociology department, Sorokin's
status was rising. He was well aware of the fact that this time the
outcome of arrest and imprisonment could be quite different.   He
reported that he chose to deliver himself up to the authorities in
Moscow in hopes of banishment.[50]

Escaping from Communism, Sorokin again demonstrated his capacity to capitalize on his experience. He immediately began to establish
himself in Czech intellectual circles by delivering a series of lectures
on Russia under the Revolution, and he turned his experiences as an
editor and propagandist to account by editing and contributing to a
journal on *The Peasants' Russia* (*Krestianskaiya Rossia*). Sorokin's
Contemporary Situation of Russia (*Sovremennoie sostoianie Rossii*,
1922) and *Popular Essays in Social Pedagogics and Politics* (*Popular-
nuye echerki sozialnoi pedagogiki i politiki*, 1922) were immediate
products of this activity. His *Leaves from a Russian Diary* (1924, 1950)
and *Sociology of Revolution* (1925) were started at this time though
not finished until later. His writing and lecturing on the state of
Russian society attracted internationally minded American sociologists, leading to the invitation to lecture on the subject in the United

States.

Sorokin's transition to North America and his sojourn in the midwest were accompanied with characteristic adeptness. In the American midwest the empirical and practical aspects of American sociology were in rapid evolution. Under Minnesota influences Sorokin strengthened the positivistic aspects of his sociology, even trying his hand at sociological experimentation and developing an enthusiasm for quantifying all sorts of data. Similarly, Sorokin enthusiastically entered the emerging subdiscipline of rural sociology, making contributions in his *Principles of Rural-Urban Sociology*(1929) and his *Systematic Source Book in Rural Sociology* (1930-1932). In making the transition to America, it had been necessary for Sorokin to educate himself in western and American sociology. With characteristic efficiency he converted necessity into virtue, producing his *Contemporary Sociological Theories* (1928) which long remained the standard synthesis in the area. The work was translated into German, French, Polish, Czech, Chinese, Turkish, Portugese, Hindi, and, in part, into Japanese. Also during his years in the midwest, Sorokin responded to the universal American concern with self-improvement by a ground-breaking study of *Social Mobility* (1927).

At the time of his move to the American midwest, Sorokin seems to have arrived at the final adjustment of his life formula. All throughout his life Sorokin had displayed an unusual sensitivity to the dominant elements in his environment. One can only speculate on the extent to which elements of the milieu of the American midwest were components in this life formula. There are some points of major coincidence.

The milieu of the American midwest in the 1920s was characterized by its individualism, its faith in practicality (which in social science was manifest by its positivism and faith in empirical methods), and its undertone of fundamentalistic religiosity. (Sorokin had come to the Bible Belt.) Something comparable to all of these elements entered intimately into Sorokin's personal synthesis. While he had never foregone his holism with respect to sociocultural phenomena, in his personal life he appeared to have become an anarchist at this time. Moreover, quite in accord with the persistent midwestern liberal's suspicion of "bigness" at this time, Sorokin did not seem to abandon the view from the 1920s to his death that all top political authority is suspect, for power corrupts (manifest in *Power and Morality*, 1959).

One may speculate, moreover, that the influence of the strong empiricist traditions and concern with quantification in the 1920s lay at the source of Sorokin's enthusiasm for quantifying data of all types.

Furthermore, Sorokin seemed to have shifted away at this time from what he described as his semi-atheistic middle period toward a more religious point of view. Perhaps the omnipresence of the undertone of fundamentalistic religiosity of the Bible Belt played a role in this partial return to the point of view of his childhood. In any case, from this time forward Sorokin always had an appreciative audience among Protestant clergymen. When he counterposed the ethic of the Sermon on the Mount to the spiral of degradation leading at last to the sensate sewers of the West, he awakened a responsive echo in fundamentalistic American circles.

Sorokin's Self-Image and Self-Presentation

Sorokin's explicit pride in his accomplishments has often been taken by his opponents as evidence of megalomania. Even a former student and academic assistant writing Sorokin's obituary expressed strong ambivalence at this aspect of Sorokin's personality.

> No man who writes two autobiographies (*Leaves from a Russian Diary*— 1924, revised in 1950, and *A Long Journey*—1963) can be said to be wholly self-effacing. Sorokin was not... No man who published as many books and articles as Sorokin did—in at least three original languages and countless translations—could be successfully accused of reticence. No man could, with self-activated provocation, lash out at what he regarded as sociological idiocies and would write and publish so intemperate a book as *Fads and Foibles in Modern Sociology and Related Sciences* (1956) could be thought of as having a solely dispassionate sense of the scientific enterprise... In *Sociological Theories of Today* (1966), Sorokin's most extensive, negative criticism is heaped on his most respected peer, the late Georges Gurvitch of the Sorbonne. Robert K. Merton, Sorokin's most cherished former student and one-time collaborator, also gets paternal or avuncular whacks in full measure.[51]

But to take such actions as megalomania is to miss the fact that Sorokin was first and last a warrior, not of the disciplined, reticent variety who fight in the ranks, but a lone hero as in the Greek heroic period. Primitive men of war of this type have rarely been modest about their accomplishments, nor have they been less effective when they have boasted of their prowess. It is from this standpoint that Sorokin's statements illustrated by the following must be understood.

> Since I actively participated in and directly observed two world wars and two revolutions, with their disastrous results—great famines, devastating

epidemics, and other calamities—it is comprehensible why these phenomena attracted my attention and became the topics of my investigations.[52]

Having been imprisoned three times by the tsarist government and three times by the communist government, and having come in contact inside prisons, not only with political prisoners, but also with non-political criminals, I naturally became interested in the phenomena of crime, criminals, and punishment.[53]

Since my early boyhood, being incessantly confronted with a multitude of human problems, beginning with the problem of procuring means of subsistence...I could not help becoming interested in human beings and in social and cultural problems.[54]

Since I came out of the lowest peasant-labor-stratum and had a full share of hardships and disenfranchisement common to such strata, I naturally identified myself with these classes and eventually became disrespectful toward the incapable, privileged, rich, and ruling groups.[55]

I was able [upon receiving a fellowship at the university] to give all my time to preparation for master's examinations as well as to my sociological research. With youthful vigor I earnestly devoted myself to these tasks, and in a record period of two years, instead of the usual four or more years, I succeeded in passing my master's oral examinations in October-November, 1916. Perhaps it should be stressed again that these examinations were much more rigorous than the American oral examinations for the Ph.D. degree.[56]

So far as the quantity of my output for these six years [at Minnesota] was concerned, I was satisfied; I knew that it exceeded the life-time productivity of the average sociologist—American or foreign.[57]

This is only a sample of the typical ways in which Sorokin publicly accounted for his achievements. To treat such statements as megalomania is to miss all the fun and excitement of sitting spellbound as the old warrior holds forth.

The Chance, Love, and Logic of the Warrior

If one takes Sorokin as a primitive warrior, a complex of factors in his writing and career which have often seemed to defy explanations may be seen to form a syndrome. He had been and continued until his death to be enormously productive; yet he did not appear to be driven by some inner compulsion or haunted by some "complex." He did not discriminate between his critics but was as inclined to thunder at minor ones as at major ones. He had a peculiar orientation toward chance.

Sorokin's profession was ideological warfare. This profession emerged out of a succession of experiences, not as a psychological complex but as a way of life. In the final form this ideological combat assumed, Sorokin's opponent became the secular drift of Western civilization. The only thing to be salvaged from this universal decay was his own point of view. He liked, as noted, to describe himself as a conservative Christian anarchist.

> I did not join any of the existing parties... Although a religious man in my own way, I did not join any institutionalized religion. Neither did I share the enthusiasm of various sports-fans and devotees of passing social fads and fashions. In all these and other respects I was rather an independent noncon-formist with my own theories, beliefs, standards, and values which I regard as truer, more universal, and more perennial than the transitory, local, and largely obsolescent values and ideologies of many of my colleagues and students.[58]

In short, in a world of almost universal decay, Sorokin decided to be a world sufficient unto himself.

Here, at once, is a clue both to Sorokin's enormous productivity and the fascination of his activities. Ideological combat is more than an instrument to an end; it is a way of life. In its eventual form, his "battle" assumed an attack on the secular drift of contemporary civilization. As the apparently endless stream of Sorokin's writings indicated, there was little danger of his running out of subject matter. Furthermore, since nothing will draw a crowd more quickly than a fight, Sorokin's writings never failed to arouse interest. Since in the end Sorokin was promoting no cause other than his own, he put on an enormously good show and hurt no one permanently.

The type of primitive warrior who defined combat as the important thing rather than its results tends not to draw the line between opponents who are or are not worthy of their weapons. This seems to explain the fact that Sorokin tended to turn his thunder on minor as well as on major critics. He slashed back in this manner at the critics of *Fads and Foibles* and still grumbled about the matter in his autobiography.

> Despite this "backwash" [of unsympathetic reactions by critics], the critic-isms of the *Fads and Foibles* have not been wholly ineffective. They seem to have tangibly influenced a number of American and foreign sociologists, psychologists, and psychiatrists. A few years later, in a somewhat simplified form, most of my criticisms were reiterated by C. Wright Mills in his book,

Sociological Imagination. In his personal letter to me, written soon after publication of my volume, he expressed his high evaluation and essential agreement with most of my conclusions. (For one reason or another, he did not mention my volume at all in his book, which in fact was noted and adversely commented upon by the reviewer of Mills' book in the *London Times Literary Supplement*.)[59]

In 1960 Sorokin was invited to deliver the main address at the Centenary Celebration of Herbert Spencer by the president of the American Sociological Association. He then submitted the address for publication in the *American Sociological Review,* only to receive a rejection from Harry Alpert, then its editor. In his autobiography Sorokin reproduced both the letter of rejection from Alpert and his description of Alpert to a friend.

As an office administrator he has been doing well. Now he is a dean of the graduate school of Oregon University. As a scholar he is just a third-class sociologist, who, so far as I know, wrote only one poor book about Durkheim.[60]

Many persons have found it difficult to reconcile the image of a world-famous scholar of enormous productivity with the tendency to thunder at minor and insignificant critics, to take issue over the absence of reference to his work, or to blast at the editor who dared to reject his writings. There has been a misleading tendency to identify such behavior with imbalance, but this is to miss altogether the kind of warrior he was. The question of finding opponents worthy of his weapons was simply irrelevant.

Sorokin also had considerable belief in luck. Of Lilly's unexpected and unsolicited offer of money to finance his research on altruism, Sorokin observed:

Throughout my life I have often experienced this sort of "luck" from unanticipated sources in the moments of my urgent, sometimes even desperate need. In this sense I can repeat Gandhi's remark: "When every hope is gone I find that help arrives somehow, from I know not where."[61]

Like every primitive warrior, Sorokin was deeply concerned with the nature and quality of his "luck."

How far the mark is missed when Sorokin's enormous productivity is attributed to some inner compulsion or complex, when his boasting about his achievements is conceived as megalomania, when his blasting at insignificant critics is seen as imbalance and lack of judgment, when his belief in his luck is interpreted as "mysticism." He had, rather, the firm, well-structured ego of an individualistic warrior. The personality was extroverted rather than introverted. The one thing intolerable for this type of warrior was to retire from the battle.

Sorokin's style was that of a wily combat ideologist. It had vigor rather than grace, poetic imaginativeness, or scientific economy. It often had a directness or bluntness. Sorokin, for example, liked to describe himself as "bullheaded" in the forthright manner of a man quick to admit his faults. However, it was notable that any number of synonyms, such as "stubborn," "intransigent," or "ornery," were avoided. None of these terms had quite the same capacity to disarm the opposition while, in fact, giving nothing away. Similarly, all sorts of contemporary cultural phenomena were denounced as "social sewers," disposing of these phenomena with blunt instruments. Sorokin was a rough antagonist.

There are some similarities between the styles of Sorokin and C. Wright Mills, as is to be expected, since both were assault technologists. But where Mills was a rebel, Sorokin was an old-fashioned warrior type. Sorokin's style lacked Mills' note of stridency; it was more inventive, more complex.

The movement of Sorokin's writing had a different rhythm and pattern from that of Mills'. Mills sought a weakness, striking at it with hit-and-run tactics. Sorokin made a relatively full reconnaissance of his objective. He carefully laid down a strategy and, incidentally, planned a defense and retreat route. When he was ready he mounted an offensive on the central fortifications.

Mysterious are the ways of destiny which brought Sorokin from the frontiers of northern Russia and the late nineteenth century to the pinnacle of sociology in America in the twentieth. He made enduring contributions to the discipline in virtually founding half a dozen of its subareas. Perhaps at some future time he will be seen as the last great figure of sociology's heroic age.

Notes

1. Mills, C. Wright (1964). *Power, Politics, and People,* ed. Irving Louis Horowitz. New York: Ballantine Books, p. 632.

2. Sorokin, Pitirim A. (1963). *A Long Journey.* New Haven, CT: College and University Press, pp. 248-249.

3. *Ibid.,* p. 41.

4. *Ibid.,* p. 44.

5. *Ibid.,* p. 46.

6. *Ibid.*, pp. 97ff.

7. *Ibid.*, p. 98.

8. Sorokin, Pitirim A. (1924). *Leaves from a Russian Diary*. New York: E.P. Dutton, p. 30.

9. *Ibid.*, p. 41.

10. *Ibid.*, p. 73.

11. *Ibid.*, p. 83.

12. *Ibid.*, p. 117.

13. *Ibid.*, p. 202.

14. *Ibid.*, p. 212.

15. *A Long Journey, op. cit.*, pp. 210ff.

16. Sorokin, Pitirim A. (1966). *Sociological Theories of Today*. New York: Harper & Row, p. 646.

17. *Ibid.*, pp. 40-41.

18. *Ibid.*, p. 44.

19. *Ibid.*, p. 75.

20. *Ibid.*, p. 76.

21. *Ibid.*, p.204.

22. *Ibid.*, p. 205.

23. Sorokin, Pitirim A. (1957), "Integralism Is My Philosophy," in *This Is My Philosophy*. Ed., Whit Burnett. New York: Harper, p. 180.

24. Sorokin, Pitirim A. (1963), "Reply to My Critics," in *Pitirim A. Sorokin in Review*, ed., Philip J. Allens. Durham, NC: Duke University Press, p. 373.

25. Sorokin, Pitirim A. (1957). *The Crisis of Our Age*. New York: E.P. Dutton, p. 17.

26. *Ibid.*, p. 28.

27. *Ibid.*, p. 67.

28. *Ibid.*, p. 116.

29. *Ibid.*, p. 124.

30. *Ibid.*, p. 125.

31. *Ibid.*, p. 157.

32. *Ibid.*, pp. 321-322.

33. Speier, Hans (1952). *Social Order and the Risks of War*. New York: George W. Stewart, pp. 211-212.

34. Sorokin, *Crisis of Our Age, op. cit.*, pp. 317-318.

35. *A Long Journey, op. cit.*, p. 325.

36. Martindale, Don (1967), review of *Sociological Theories of Today*, in *The Annals*, March, p. 176.

37. Recent examples appear in the Allens volume, *Pitirim A. Sorokin in Review*.

38. Schneider, Louis (1964), "Toward Assessment of Sorokin's View of Change," in *Explorations in Social Change*, ed. George K. Zollschan and Walter Hirsch. Boston: Houghton Mifflin, pp. 371-400.

39. Sorokin, Pitirim A. (1964), "Comments on Schneider's Observations and Criticism," *ibid.*, pp. 401-431.

40. Riley, Matilda White and Mary E. Moore, "Sorokin's Use of Sociological Measurement," in *Sorokin in Review*, ed. Allen, p. 223.

41. In *Sorokin in Review*, ed. Allen, p. 34.

42. *Ibid.*, p. 35.

43. *Ibid.*, p. 31.

44. *Ibid.*, pp. 35-36.

45. *Ibid.*, p. 23.

46. *Leaves from a Russian Diary*, p. 212.

47. *A Long Journey*, p. 191.

48. *Ibid.*

49. *Ibid.*, p. 26.

50. *Ibid.*, p. 193.

51. Moore, Wilbert E. (1968), "Pitirim A. Sorokin, In Memoriam," *The American Sociologist* 3, no. 2, May, p. 158.

52. *Sorokin in Review, op. cit.*, ed. Allen, p. 32.

53. *Ibid.*

54. *Ibid.*

55. *Ibid.*, p. 34.

56. *Ibid.*, p. 89.

57. *Ibid.*, p. 224.

58. *Ibid.*, p. 258.

59. *Ibid.*, p. 297.

60. *Ibid.*, p. 304.

61. *Ibid.*

Selected Bibliography

Pitirim A. Sorokin's Writings

The American Sex Revolution. Boston: Porter Sargent, 1957.

Contemporary Sociological Theories. New York: Harper, 1927.

Fads and Foibles in Modern Sociology and Related Sciences. Chicago: Henry Regnery, 1956.

Leaves from a Russian Diary. New York: E.P. Dutton, 1924.

A Long Journey. New Haven, CT: College and University Press, 1963.

Power and Morality, with Walter A. Lunden. Boston: Porter Sargent, 1959.

Principles of Rural-Urban Sociology, with C.C. Zimmerman. New York: Henry Holt, 1929.

Social and Cultural Dynamics. New York: American Book Co., 1937-1941.

Social Mobility. New York: Harper, 1927.

Society, Culture, and Personality. New York: Harper, 1947.

Sociological Theories of Today. New York: Harper & Row, 1966.

V

King of the Hoboes: Joseph Roucek, Portrait of an International Cultural Workman

With some oversimplification, students of higher education in the Western world see it dominated by three great traditions: (1) the transmission of culture and, in particular, the socialization of individuals into the higher forms of culture—this is the humanistic tradition which visualizes the basic task of the university as bringing about a change of character and supplying members of the status elite with the rudiments of a cultivated style of life; (2) the transmission of vocational and professional skills—this is the practical and pragmatic tradition which conceives the basic task of the university to be the supplying of trained personnel to man the key institutions of society, such as doctors, lawyers, career diplomats, and administrators; and (3) the advancement of knowledge—this is the scientific and scholarly tradition which conceives the basic task of the university to be the training of scholars, researchers, and scientists, equipping them with a variety of research, mathematical-statistical, and laboratory skills.

The transmission of these three traditions to the American system of higher education is sometimes traced primarily (again with some oversimplification) to the influence of the English, Scottish, and German university systems; (1) the humanistic-character building concept of higher education comes from Oxford and Cambridge; (2) the scholarly and laboratory research traditions of higher education come from nineteenth-century Germany. (This tradition in the· United States was transmitted primarily by Johns Hopkins University); (3)the practical-

pragmatic tradition of higher education comes from the Scottish universities, particularly the University of Edinburgh. (It is common knowledge that this Scottish ideal of vocational-professional training comb-
ined in the United States with the populist tradition which underwrote
the land-grant legislation and its subsequent embodiment in the land-
grant colleges.)

Although none of the three traditions of American higher education necessarily conflicts with its sustaining ideology which views
education as the vehicle of progress, in practice it is not easy to
maintain excellence at one and the same time in all three. Even if the
single individual is equally endowed for excellence in humanistic
education, training for vocational performance and research, he will
ordinarily receive most recognitiion by concentrating his efforts and
zeal primarily in one sphere. Institutions like individuals also tend to
specialize even though the larger universities pursue all three ideals.
However, it was inevitable that some ordering of priorities should
develop between these three educational traditions.

With the emergence in the twentieth century of the Ph.D. as the
criterion of academic respectability, scholarly and scientific research
and writing were confirmed as the most honorable activities of the
university. Graduate education emerged as the most prestigeful form
of training. Those professors engaged in research and writing and
whose teaching activities were largely confined to the production of
new Ph.D.'s emerged as an elite professoriate. They took the lead in
founding journals, professional societies and obtaining foundation and
government research grants, activities which in turn enhanced their
elite status.

The notion that rank and salary in the American professoriate
should be administered on the principle of "publish or perish," trans-
forms the norms of the elite professoriate into the norms of the
professoriate as a whole. In the stereotype, American higher education is a meritocracy in which the ultimate test of worth is contribution to the advancement of knowledge. Even while finding fault with
American higher education for yielding to pressures arising from the
business community, from politics, and from bureaucratized administrations, critics have unconsciously assumed the point of view and
ideals of the elite professoriate as the standard by which the whole
should be judged. Nor does it matter that the discovery is repeatedly
made that membership in the elite professoriate often depends as
much upon chance, personality, school ties (the "old-boy" network),
and political skill as on achievement. This means only that in the end

the ideals of the elite professoriate are also employed on the elite itself.

Effects on Humanistic Education

In the long run, it was inevitable that the vigorous growth of research and graduate education, on the one hand, and of vocational and professional education on the other, would occur at the expense of humanistic education. It was also inevitable that institutions of higher education would be stratified with the primary division appearing between those which carry on research and graduate education and those which do not. Since the Ph.D. had emerged as the symbol of academic respectability, the teaching institutions looked to the research institutions for qualified professors and, from the ranks of their brightest products, supplied students for the graduate programs of the research institutions. Professors and administrators at the teaching institutions who had dreams of glory, at times sponsored research programs of their own and undertook to upgrade their enterprises by developing graduate programs and offering advanced degrees. And so far as the given institution provided opportunities for graduate education and research, it facilitated the upward mobility of those professors who managed to publish and achieve professional recognition. In any case, because of shared aspirations, on the one hand, and negative sanctions from the various academic accrediting agencies on the other, if they did not increase the percentage of Ph.D.s on their faculties, the American professoriate formed a crude system in which rank was determined by distance from the elite professoriate.

In the various studies of the American system of higher education such as Veblen's 1918 study, *The Higher Learning in America,* Logan Wilson's 1942 study, *The Academic Man,* Theodore Caplow's and Reece McGee's *The Academic Market Place,* and Lionel Lewis's 1975 study, *Scaling the Ivory Tower,* there has been an understandable tendency to concentrate on the elite institutions and the elite professoriate. The failure to pay equal attention to the non-elite members of the professoriate is also quite understandable, for lower ranking members of the professoriate already had access to education, the instrument of upward mobility in America. Moreover, a few individuals have made their way up the educational ladder and into the elite against considerable odds. Dissent has in considerable measure been co-opted in the process. Moreover, as Lewis has demonstrated, lower class individuals by and large do not go to the elite institutions in the

first place and the policies by these same elite institutions of recruit-
ment of professors out of their own products, largely closes off the
possibility of penetration from the outside. In Lewis's words:

> Since the elite institutions are also more likely to hire their own graduates
> and to exclude females, it would appear that in those institutions where we
> would expect the most marked emphasis on achievement we find--with the
> rejection of those outside the middle class, those with wrong credentials, and
> females--the least.[1]

An obvious consequence of these facts is that there are individuals
with as much or more intelligence and ability among the non-elite as
among the elite professors even though it is possible that the average
level of ability in the elite professoriate is higher. (This, of course, is
an hypothesis which should be tested—it would be ironic if American
higher education turned out not even to be a crude pump for lifting
ability to the higher levels of the educational system to say nothing of
the higher levels of society.)

It could be argued that it may even be fortunate that American
higher education appears to be relatively inefficient in pumping talent
and ability to the higher levels of its stratification system. In view of
the fact that research is honored most and teaching least, teaching
ought not to be doubly underprivileged not only by gliding into the
hands of the lower ranking professors and lower ranking teaching
institutions, but also by falling to the lot of those who are low ranking
because they are incompetent. However, while I do not have hard
evidence, I do have some soft evidence of the fact that some of the
best teaching in those institutions with graduate programs in higher
education is being done by professors who are not devoted primarily
to research. Furthermore, from time to time, I have been asked by
small colleges and universities outside the University of Minnesota to
evaluate their teaching and honors programs. I have been consistent-
ly impressed both by the awe with which the University is viewed (and
the sense of inferiority with respect to it) and the strong evidence of
the superiority of their teaching programs to many of those I have
been familiar with at the University.

Ironically, the drive that had dominated twentieth-century higher
education toward the Ph.D. as the criterion of respectability may
actually be weakening its teaching traditions. For one thing, the
Ph.D. rarely receives any training in teaching methods. For another,
he is taken up by the ideal of specialization and he dreams of research

and writing. He often experiences the heavy teaching loads of the teaching institutions as a major obstacle to his career goals. Much of the time the new Ph.D. has the "misfortune" to have to take a position in a teaching institution without a graduate program. He is not encouraged to engage in research nor rewarded for publication when he manages it. Often in the personal sessions with faculty that have followed the program-reviews at the smaller colleges, I have found myself listening to the lament by the faculty of their frustrations because of heavy teaching loads and the lack of adminstrative support of research. When I have congratulated them on the superiority of their teaching programs, I have, at times, noted a flickering quizzical look of uncertainty—as if they felt that I was trying to be decent and perhaps patronizing them by praising them for something that did not count. The Ph.D., in short, has largely been trained for objectives and a level of specialization inappropriate for a role in the teaching institutions.

Increase in Faculty Ph.D.s

Meanwhile, we are rapidly approaching the point where all faculty of institutions of higher learning may possess the Ph.D. In 1900 around 400 Ph.D.s were granted; in 1960 the number had risen to 10,000; in 1975 it had risen to 36,000. Between 1960 and 1970, the percentage of faculty in institutions of higher learning possessing the Ph.D. had risen from 37 to 50 per cent. These trends were correlated with departmentalization, bureaucratization, professionalism and the emphasis on research throughout higher education. By 1970 in the fifty United States and its outlying parts, 401 institutions were offering the doctoral degree and in virtually every field more Ph.Ds were being produced yearly than the academic market could absorb. There nounce the goal of 100 percent Ph.Ds in American higher education by 1984. And there is little doubt that if the present Ph.D. programs are still in operation at anything approaching their current efficiency at that time this goal could not only be realized, but there will be many excess Ph.Ds unable to find academic positions.

Under circumstances in which all professors may soon possess the Ph.D., studies of the non-elite professoriate assume increasing importance, for discrepancies between the ideal of the educational system (as determined by the principle of achievement) and its realities (in which chance and ascription all too often determine comparative rank) will become more visible. In one way or other, moreover, the system will tend to change either by restricting access to the degree (as occurred with the medieval guild system when increasing numbers of journeymen found themselves condemned permanently to journeyman status without the possibility of becoming masters) or by actually relaxing access to the Ph.D. (as seems, in fact, to be occurring at present), but basing employment primarily on other criteria (such as publishing in a limited number of refereed professional journals). Meanwhile, the professoriate as a whole, along with other white-collar professions, potentially faces competition from an increasing army of unemployed Ph.D.s. In the words of Blumberg and Murtha:

> The industrial reserve army of unemployed workers Marx described as a central figure of capitalist organization is now being joined by a growing intellectual reserve army of unemployed and underemployed college graduates.

> The evidence accumulating in the last few years leads to these inescapable conclusions: (1) the tremendous growth of college enrollment since the 1950s has culminated in a labor market composed of increasing numbers of graduates with radically diminished job opportunities; (2) those sectors of the economy that have traditionally employed large numbers of college graduates—such as high-technology, manufacturing, education and the other professions, federal public administration, finance and insurance—have not been expanding adequately to absorb the college-educated mass; (3) the collapse of the college job market, especially since the beginning of this decade, is reflected in declining opportunities for professional and managerial positions, a great rise in the proportion of graduates working at clerical and sales jobs, a decline in the real starting salaries of college graduates, narrowing of the traditional income differential between high-school and college-graduates, and the growth of substantial unemployment among recent graduates.[2]

The situation of the alumni of graduate education is only a special case of higher education as a whole, and the professoriate is beginning to find its situation determined in part by the presence of an emerging reserve army of unemployed Ph.Ds.

Faculty Hiring Tactics During the Great Depression

During the Great Depression when higher education was victimized by hard times, there was some tendency for educational institutions to hedge against the recession and still maintain teaching services by hiring new professors, retaining them until tenure decisions had to be made, and then, letting them go to hire others at lower starting salaries. In response to these depression tactics, at the base of the professoriate a special category or stratum was in process of forming. Individuals virtually became migrant workers, living by their wits, taking on a variety of teaching and other intellectual jobs as the local situation warranted. They were not unlike the journeymen who wandered the cities in the late Middle ages, or like hoboes (the migrant workmen who wandered from job to job following the railroads during the expansion period of American capitalism, performing essential services and moving on when the job gave out). I knew individuals of this sort when I was a student and graduate student in the 1930s and early 1940s who set up special tutoring services, who hired on temporarily as researchers on a variety of projects, who started clandestine theme and thesis writing services (and wrote M.A. and Ph.D. dissertations in a variety of fields). However, the development and consolidation of such a hobo stratum at the base of the American professoriate, was slowed by the use of higher education (by both state and federal government) as a weapon to fight the Depression, by the various writers' and artists' projects, and by the outbreak of World War II, which took much of the young manpower into military and industrial service, creating a shortage of positions in academia. World War II was a lifesaver to a section of the professoriate which faced potential permanent marginality.

Not until after the 1970s have conditions in American higher education again appeared similar to those of the Great Depression. Once more at the bottom of the professoriate individuals have found themselves struggling for a declining number of jobs, facing criteria for tenure and promotion which often change by the year, taking temporary positions on research projects and non-tenure-track teaching positions, setting up research organizations as independent intellectual entrepreneurs and undertaking to secure government grants for research or to offer research services to industry, establishing private counseling services, and the like. In a volume to be published by Greenwood Press, Arthur Wilke and Eugene Griesman have coined the happy term the hidden professoriate for the stratum of the professoriate which like the academic hoboes of the 1930s is emerging.

The role of chance in academic careers is such that an individual who finds his life chances determined by conditions which produce such academic hoboes (or in Wilke-Griesman's terms a hidden professoriate) may never, despite major talents, achieve access to the ranks of the elite professoriate. However, sometimes, despite the failure to gain access to elite circles, an individual, by dint of talent and hard work, still manages to achieve considerable success. An excellent example appears in the career of Joseph S. Roucek, a career worth reviewing since it illustrates the forces on the young professor in the 1930s—forces which have their counterpart in the 1970s.

Joseph Roucek was born in Prague,[3] Czechoslovakia, in 1902. Among the most famous of his teachers at the Prague Commercial Academy was the sociologist Dr. Eduard Benes, who later became foreign secretary and then president of Czechoslovakia. While continuing his studies at the University of Prague (Charles University), Roucek was employed by the American Consular Service. In 1920 he came to the United States on his own initiative.

Though partly sustained by scholarships and fellowships during his studies at Occidental College of Los Angeles, from which he received the B.A. in 1925,[4] and at New York University[5] at which he earned the Ph.D. in 1928, Roucek was mostly self-supporting. He earned a living during the years of his education with surprising versatility. He gave piano concerts.[6] He obtained roles as an actor in such silent films[7] as *The Hunchback of Notre Dame, The Son of the Sheik, The Campus Flirt, Breakfast at Sunrise,* and *The Gaucho.* He was featured in vaudeville on western circuits and as an entertainer in summer camps in the Yellowstone Park Camps Company during summer vacations.

Roucek completed his formal education and was ready to begin teaching[8] in the year of the stock market crash, 1929, and had to make his way during the difficult period of the Great Depression. His major teaching activities were at: Centenary Junior College at Hackettstown, New Jersey (1929-33); Pennsylvania State University (1933-35); New York University (1935-39); Hofstra College at Hempstead, Long Island (1939-48); University of Bridgeport (1949-67); and Queensborough Community College of the City University of New York (1967-72). He also served as visiting professor of sociology, political science, and education in such diverse places as Kent State University (1940); San Francisco State College (1941,1942,1944, 1946); Reed College (1941); the College of the Pacific (1942); the Inter-American Workshop, New Mexico Highland University (1943); the University of Wyoming (1944); San Diego State College (1945); Occidental College (1945, 1948, 1949); the University of British Columbia (1951); the University of Puerto Rico (1952); and Portland, Oregon, Summer School (1954).

Roucek's First Book in 1928

Rather than attempt to review all of Roucek's writings, only their range and frequency will be indicated here. The same year after he completed the Ph.D., his first book was published, *The Working of the Minorities Systems Under the League of Nations* (1928). He began teaching in 1929, and, despite the unusually heavy demands of his first teaching position and the fact that publication had become more difficult because of the Depression, he published *Contemporary Roumania and Her Problems* (1932). He changed jobs in 1933, going first to Pennsylvania State and then, in 1935, to New York University, but managed to complete and publish *The Poles in the United States of America* (1937). By this time, Roucek was acquiring an international reputation as an expert on minorities. He brought out an edited volume entitled *Our Racial and National Minorities* (with Francis J. Brown) in 1937 and an original volume, *The Politics of the Balkans,* in 1939. With two co-editors he also published *Contemporary World Politics* in 1939. By the end of the 1930s, and despite the problems teachers and authors experienced during the Great Depression, Roucek had taught at one college and two universities and had authored or edited six books. Besides establishing a solid reputation in the field of minorities, he had opened up a major new area of interest in the field of comparative politics.

In 1939, Roucek began teaching at Hofstra College, where he remained for nine years—his longest stay at a single institution of higher learning to that date. One explanation for this rather rapid turnover of positions in the 1930s is that these were rough times for young teachers. Salaries were dreadfully low, and in many schools waivers and salary cutbacks became necessary. Most universities had no guarantees of tenure, and it was the practice of many colleges and universities to drop instructors after a few years' service and to hire new ones at lower salaries rather than grant salary increases. In the 1940s, World War II drained much of the nation's manpower into the military services and brought war prosperity to the nation, which finally broke the back of the Depression. This period also brought a new stability to teachers in institutions of higher learning, for they were now in short supply. Though salaries lagged, appointments tended to become more stable.

During the war years, and in some measure in response to the pressures on academics who were too old to serve in the armed forces, the Rouceks[9] set up lecture programs on contemporary world problems which they offered to service clubs, women's clubs, teachers' institutes, high schools, normal schools, college assemblies, and other organizations. Roucek gave lectures illustrated with slides and motion pictures, while his wife rendered folk songs and talked on the native art and peasant life of Eastern Europe. These activities continued into the 1950s, and in 1955 Roucek lectured at the High School of Diplomacy in Madrid and at universities in Spain, Italy, Yugoslavia, Austria, Germany, Holland, and France. The pre-Communist governments of Romania and Yugoslavia had by this time recognized Roucek's contributions to international understanding by awarding him the Order of Knighthood of the Star of Romania and the Knighthood of the Crown of Yugoslavia.

During the 1940s, in addition to teaching and the development of semi-popular programs designed to promote international understanding, Roucek wrote a book in German on the Czechs and Slovaks in the United States and edited ten books on comparative politics, political science, the problems of Central Europe, and minorities.

Level of Productivity Continues

In the 1950s and 1960s, during the periods he taught at the University of Bridgeport (eighteen years) and Queensborough Community College (five years), he also worked as an editor, contributing author, and essayist, and managed to maintain the same general level of productivity as in the two previous decades.[10] His work tended to range even further afield: political science, comparative politics, geopolitics, sociology, comparative sociology, education, comparative education, juvenile delinquency, crime, mass communications, the problems of unusual and difficult children, social control, Balkan problems, and automation were among the topics on which he organized symposia and made original contributions. Meanwhile, he served as editor[11] on a number of journals and reviewed numerous books.

Despite this enormous productivity, Roucek maintained a high level of scholarly responsibility and insight. He virtually pioneered a number of areas in the fields of minorities and Eastern European problems. In the nature of the case, he tended to rough hew a subject rather than to retain it in his subjective sphere while he undertook to achieve stylistic perfection. Hence, eventually, other less original, but more sophisticated, authors quietly took over materials that Roucek assembled and presented them in more polished versions, at times winning more acclaim than Roucek himself. Moreover, since it is the nature of intellectual theft that it is essential to ruin the reputa-

of the victim to accomplish it with impunity, from the very circles of persons who intellectually borrowed from him, in time the word was spread that Roucek was an unoriginal drudge and hack.[12] The very quantity of his work was taken as evidence for this charge.

Hence, the question is: what is Roucek? And this quickly turns into a complicated question. No categorization quite fits: he was, indeed, part confidence man and a rather ingenious intellectual entrepreneur. He had the work discipline of a fanatic; he had more than a small measure of genius. He could be enchanting or cantankerous; the soul of humility or a virtual peacock of vanity. An individual with high native intelligence, he reached maturity at a time when the contrasting cultural tendencies of the West and East clashed most decisively and in a geographical area where the problems of minorities were revealed in extraordinary combination and confrontation. It was not uncommon for inhabitants of this area to learn half a dozen or so languages as if they were so many dialects.[13] Since they found themselves in culturally marginal areas, the presuppositions of the high culture centers were lifted to rare self-consciousness, and they were able to examine each from the point of view of the other with rare objectivity.

W.I. Thomas and Florian Znaniecki have described the personality type of people living in culturally marginal areas and their personal resolutions of cultural conflict in *The Polish Peasant in Europe and America*(5 vols.,1918-20). In some cases, those who find themselves trapped between different cultures never arrive at a personal resolution of their conflicts, but rather drift back and forth from one type of behavior to another, inclining toward alienated normlessness. Such *bohemian* types contrast with the *traditionalist* types who resolve cultural conflict by clinging to the external forms of one or other of the two cultures, becoming unreflective jingoistic nationalists either for the old culture or the new. However, Thomas and Znaniecki have observed that some individuals with high native intelligence and personal resourcefulness may respond to cultural marginality by transforming the cultural alternatives into a sphere of personal opportunity. The *creative* man illustrated by Roucek makes the most of both worlds, finding his point of stability within his own personality. To be sure, types are conceptual simplification intended to epitomize dominant trends in complex social realities. The creative type may actually move between tendencies: toward bohemianism, on the one hand, and traditionalism, on the other. In the end, however, he always returns to his personal creative solutions of internalized cultural conflict.

In terms of his remarkable work discipline, his capacity to think originally outside cultural stereotypes, and his adeptness at transforming unpromising situations into opportunities, Roucek should have become an eminent member of the American social science establishment during the third quarter of the twentieth century. To verify this, one need only compare Roucek's publishing record to that of the presidents of the American Sociological Society since World War II—few can match his accomplishments. Events conspired to lock his academic fate permanently to that segment of American university professors that Wilke and Griesman have called the hidden professoriate.

The "Hidden Professoriate"

Only detailed first-hand investigation could hope to reveal all the reasons why one of the most energetic scholars of American social science became locked into the hidden professoriate and was kept there despite phenomenal productivity. Possibly the time of his graduation (at the onset of the Depression, when one had to take any job and hold on to it for dear life), his status as an immigrant (with some notable exceptions, immigrant and refugee scholars and professionals have been forced to take second- and third-rate positions in which they have been dreadfully exploited), and his graduation from a minor graduate school (in general, graduates of the more prestigious institutions tend to have first choice of the better jobs and to enjoy the patronage of the more influential members of the elite professoriate), all played a role in tying Roucek's fate to the hidden professoriate.

Once in the teaching and vocational rather than the great scholarly and research institutions of American higher education, it can be extraordinarily difficult to break out.[14] And in times of economic depression it is almost impossible. The individual finds himself confronted with a killing teaching and advising schedule. He may find it necessary quarter after quarter to work up new courses. He may have to respond to university demands on his time to perform public relations and service functions to keep his institution financially solvent. His salary is too low to support much independent research. If he applies for government or foundation funds, he finds himself at a great disadvantage compared to his more fortunate colleagues in the graduate schools of the prestigious institutions. In short, he has little time, energy, resources, or stimulation to participate in the higher rat race of research, writing, and publishing. The only way out, when there is a way out at all, is to transform one's self into a virtual work slave, to forbid one's self almost all normal pleasures, and to write and publish despite the enormous demands on one's time by the teaching and vocational universities in which the hidden professoriate serves. When one does write and publish extensively in the teaching universities, however, a new ambivalent situation develops between an individual and his colleagues. One's achievement then becomes a source of envy and fear—lest the administration also demand this in addition to its teaching and service requirements. The individual also becomes a source of mixed pride and anxiety to the administrators— lest it lead productive writers and scholars to demand salary increases and free time to pursue their researches. Teaching institutions are suspicious of productive scholars. To the scholar who manages to write and publish despite the pressures against it in the teaching institutions, life has special rewards of bitterness.

While it is standard lore in American university circles that the only way to get out of the minor leagues is to write one's way out, this is not easy and most of the time it must be accomplished, if at all, when the individual is quite young. For the individual in the hidden professoriate who conducts research, writes, and publishes, no automatic door opens to admit him to the inner circles of the elite professoriate. Publication by a member of the university minor leagues is at least as apt to be quietly pillaged by members of the major leagues as to lead to invitation to the select clubs of the top elite. Moreover, members of the elite professoriate have more facilities, resources, and skills available to them, and are usually able to package ideas with greater skill, market them with greater ease, and promote them with greater authority. During the 1930s, Roucek's blaze of youthful productivity brought not recognition by an invitation to the higher circles, but pillage and devaluation as a drudge and hack. In some measure, this was because of his most original productivity was out of step with the dominant trends: the problems of minorities and of comparative politics were eclipsed by the preoccupations of Americans during the Great Depression. The major concern of this period was with social and economic problems at home and isolationism abroad.

By the time the Depression and war were over, Roucek was forty-three years old. He had reached an age when it is unusually difficult to move from the minor to the major leagues of the American university system. By this time, he had worked out a way of life that no longer courted favor of professional and establishment sociology. He had perfected the techniques of the symposium, largely bypassing the major establishment figures and enlisting the talents of professors in the minor leagues (the teaching and vocational universities) who had not yet abandoned the ideal of contributing to the growth of knowedge. While such symposia rarely received much acclaim, they proved to be useful both as reference and textbooks, and they often served as a sort of bridge between the hidden and the elite professoriates.

It has been Joseph Roucek's destiny to become an international cultural workman, performing a role somewhat like that of the sophists of the ancient world, the wandering scholars of the Early Middle Ages, or the largely anonymous mason-architects of the High Middle Ages who wandered from city to city providing much of the work, skill, and knowledge that went into the great cathedrals. In the end, one can only conclude that Roucek is an uncrowned prince of the hidden professoriate.

Notes

1. Lewis, Lionel (1975). *Scaling the Ivory Tower.* Baltimore: The Johns Hopkins University Press, p. 146.

2. Blumberg, Paul and James M. Murtha (1977). "College Graduates and the American Dream," *Dissent,* Winter, p. 45. For a full review of the prospects for college graduates see Richard B Freeman (1976). *The Overeducated American.* New York: Academic Press.

3. Though listed in most sources as born in Prague, Roucek was actually born and raised in the town of Slany. His father was a merchant, owning a store in Slany. Roucek received the typical upbringing of a Central European, middle-class child.

4. He was attending Hastings College, Nebraska. during 1922-23 when he was granted an international scholarship for the study of diplomacy by the Bencs government. He transferred to Occidental College from which he obtained the B.A. He went to Hawaii in a steerage, lost his money gambling, looked for work in Pearl Harbor, and was offered a job on a pineapple plantation for 15 cents an hour; he returned in a steerage to San Francisco where he entered graduate school at the University of California.

5. Roucek had completed all requirements for the Ph.D. at the University of California when he was offered a Penfield Fellowship in Diplomacy at New York University. NYU accepted all of his work, including his completed thesis, and he was granted the Ph.D. in 1928.

6. He studied piano in the usual routine manner of a Central European middle-class child for some ten years. In America, he gave concerts all over the country. He was featured as a solo performer with the Occidental College Glee Club.

7. During Roucek's years at Occidental, many motion pictures were made there, especially of college life and of football (1923-25). He often participated as an extra, worked in motion pictures as an actor, and was also a stand-in for Leo Carillo.

8. As a matter of fact, to the time of his completion of the Ph.D. his dream had been to enter the Czech diplomatic service. He returned to Czechoslovakia in 1928

only to be told that he would serve the Benes cause better in the United States. He returned in 1929 to search for a teaching job.

9. Roucek married Bozena Slabey, a talented violinist, in 1928. Long before World War II started, Roucek applied the lessons he had learned as a Hollywood and vaudeville entertainer to their collective careers. He worked up a program of demonstrations, songs, and lecturers which were delivered in the hundreds, not only in the United States but also in Mexico, Canada, Czechoslovakia, Spain, and elsewhere.

10. In lists of Roucek's work compiled in the early 1960s, it is noted that he was author, co-author, editor, co-editor, and contributor to more than ninety books. He has continued to produce at the same general rate. In some decades he produced articles at the rate of around thirty per year. He wrote thousands of book reviews. At the very minimum, in his 48 years of productivity Roucek has been responsible in whole or in part for around 100 books, between 1,000 and 1,500 articles, and at least 3,000 book reviews.

11. He founded the now defunct *International Behavioral Scientist* in India. He is on the editorial staff of *Revista Internacional de Sociologia* (Spain), *International Journal of Legal Research* (Meerut, India), *Sociologia Internationalis* (West Germany), *Ukranian Quarterly* (New York), *Il Politico* (Pavia, Italy), *Malaysian Journal of Education* (Singapore), *Sociologia Religiosa* (Padova, Italy), and others.

12. In addition to a number of scholars with major reputations who originally made their mark largely by restating Roucek's work in somewhat smoother language, Roucek has noted in a letter:

Today it is quite irritating that most recent scholars working in the area of the Balkans and Central Eastern Europe seek to convey the impression that nothing on these countries has been done by Roucek, to strengthen their claims for their own 'originality' in exploring this 'neglected field.'

13. Roucek speaks German, French, English, Czech, Slovak, Romanian, and Russian.

14. In a personal letter, Roucek gives the following account of how a non-tenured member of the hidden professoriate may have most of the rewards for his original work pillaged:

when at New York University I finished my manuscript on *Racial and Ethnic Minorities in the United States*, I took it to my dean, Payne, the editor of the Education Series for Prentice-Hall. He was enthusiastic about publishing it, but, considering that I was only a Lecturer in Social Studies, he made the publication conditional on having F.J. Brown, a former preacher and his confessor, as co-author. Since my job depended on him, I had to accept Brown, who knew about the subject as much as an illiterate knows about atomic energy. The book has been selling ever since and has gone through numerous revisions and reprints. Brown received from his association with the project the position of General Secretary of the American Council on Education. When I applied for a Fulbright Fellowship, which he handled, I asked for his support—and what did you think he did—claiming that he was only the chairman of the appointing committee.(Letter from Joseph S. Roucek, Sept. 23, 1976.)

Selected Bibliography

Joseph S. Roucek

The Working of the Minorities System under the League of Nations. Prague:Orbis, 1928.

Contemporary Roumania and Her Problems. Stanford University Press, 1932.

The Poles in the United States of America. Gdynia, Poland: The Baltic Institute, 1937.

Our Racial and National Minorities. Edited with Francis J. Brown. New York: Prentice-Hall, 1937, 1939.

Politics of the Balkans. New York: McGraw-Hill, 1939.

Contemporary World Politics. Edited with Francis J. Brown and Charles Hedges. New York: John Wiley, 1939, 1940.

Introduction to Politics. Edited with Roy V. Peel. New York: T.Y.Crowell, 1942.

Contemporary Europe. Editor. Princeton, NJ: D. Van Nostrand, 1941, 1947.

Sociological Foundations of Education. Editor. New York: T.Y.Crowell, 1942.

Die Tschechen und Slowaken in Der Vereiningten Staaten. Stuttgart: Publikatiensstelle, 1943.

A Challenge to Peace Makers. Editor. *The Annals* of The American Academy of Political and Social Science, 232, March, 1944.

One America. Editor, with Francis J. Brown. Englewood Cliffs, NJ: Prentice-Hall, 1945, 1948, 1952.

Central Eastern Europe: Crucible of World Wars. Editor. Englewood Cliffs, NJ: Prentice-Hall, 1946.

Twentieth-Century Political Thought. Editor. New York: Philosophical Library, 1946.

Governments and Politics Abroad. Editor. New York: Funk & Wagnall, 1947.

Slavonic Encyclopedia. Editor. New York: Philosophical Library, 1949.

Introduction to Political Science. Editor, with George B. deHussar. New York: T.Y. Crowell, 1950.

Comparative Education. Editor, with Arthur H. Meehlmann. New York: Dryden Press, 1952.

Contemporary Social Science. Vol. I: *Western Hemisphere.* Edited with Paul Harriman and George B. de Hussar. Harrisburg, PA: Stackpole, 1953.

Juvenile Delinquency. Editor. New York: Philosophical Library, 1958.

Contemporary Sociology. Editor. New York: Philosophical Library, 1958.

Automation and Society. Edited with Howard B. Jacobsen. New York: Philosophical Library, 1959.

The Challenge to Science Education. Editor. New York: Philosophical Library, 1959.

Contemporary Political Ideologies. Editor. New York: Philosophical Library, 1960.

Sociology of Crime. Editor. New York: Philosophical Library, 1960.

The Unusual Child. Editor. New York: Philosophical Library, 1962.

Classics in Political Science. New York: Philosophical Library, 1963.

The Czechs and Slovaks in America. Minneapolis: Lerner Publisher, 1967.

The Study of Foreign Languages. Editor. New York: Philosophical Library, 1967.

The Teaching of History. Editor. New York: Philosophical Library, 1967.

VI

A Son of Odysseus:

The Aesthetic Vision of Panos Bardis

Full many a gem of purest ray serene
The dark unfathom'd caves of ocean bear:
Full many a flower is born to blush unseen,
And waste its sweetness on the desert air
　　　　　　　　　　　—Thomas Gray[1]

The role of chance—or, as it has been variously called, "luck," "fortune," and "fate"—in human achievement has not figured as prominently in interpersonal estimates in the nineteenth and twentieth centuries as in the Renaissance and Enlightenment periods. Shakespeare, in a characteristic Renaissance mode, opened one of his most finely crafted sonnets with the lines, "When in disgrace with fortune and men's eyes, I all alone beweep my outcast state..."[2] and made many observations throughout his plays on the role of chance in human affairs. Machiavelli, in both *The Prince* and *The Discourses,*[3] had many observations which suggest that he continuously took chance, or as he usually named it fortune, into account. In the eighteenth century, Thomas Gray phrased the implications of chance for interpersonal arrogance. If potential human genius is a constant in the race—a logical corollary of the widely held notion of the time that all men are approximately equal—those who achieve eminence, unless there is some special mechanism to carefully sift the ranks of mankind for those with special ability, owe much to chance or happy accident. In the view of enlightenment thinkers, traditional institutions lacked such sifting mechanisms. Hence, in his Elegy written in a country church yard, Gray observed:

> *Some village Hampden that with dauntless breast*
> *The little tyrant of his fields withstood,*
> *Some mute inglorious Milton here might rest,*
> *Some Cromwell, guiltless of his country's blood.* [4]

Though the eighteenth century revolutionaries proposed to bring a new world into being in which human affairs would rest more on native ability, training, and achievement than on inherited privilege and though few persons doubt that progress has been made in this direction, there is also little doubt that, even in the more open societites of our world, the mechanisms that pump potential ability to the surface of human affairs are quite inefficient. Chance, fate, fortune still play a major role in human affairs. A question is posed, thus, as to why so little formal attention is paid at present to the role of chance in human affairs.

The Neglect of Chance

At least three recent cultural developments contribute to the neglect of chance in human affairs: the decline of theology; the rise of probability theory; and the rise of holistic explanations of social life.

Until recent times the majority of men believed that everything that could happen was ordered in advance: determined by the stars or predetermined by God's will. There was, as Shakespeare phrased it, a "destiny that shapes our ends, rough hue them as we will." Man's knowledge of what would happen, however, was deficient. Somewhat inconsistently it was believed that if one were only able to discern God's will or discover what fate had in store, one could—if not fundamentally alter one's destiny—at least temporize with it and postpone it for a time. The oldest games of chance were not in fact games at all, but magical practices designed to determine what would happen as long as one had not the foreknowledge to prevent or avoid it. Hence experts were consulted to cast lots, roll the dice, spin the wheel of fortune, or read the cards.

However, with each new success of science in extending naturalistic explanations not only to the physical, but to the social world, theological, magical, and astrological explanations have receded, leaving diminishing room for good and bad luck based on some unfathomable fate, destiny, predestination, or will of God. And while the naturalization of areas formerly thought to be ordered only by some mysterious destiny in a sense increases the scope open to impersonal accident, it also carries with it the inclination to view "accidents" as falling into categories of risks. A sober mentality which seeks to establish the frequency of various kinds of accidents replaces awe in the face of mysterious destiny.

Finally, the rise in the last two centuries of various forms of secular collectivism—the notion that the primary social reality is the community, society, or social system rather than the individual—has entailed the view that chance and accidents are primarily risks of the individual with only occasional relevance to the collective. Society is thought of as an entity operating on laws of its own, laws which cannot be deduced from the behavior of individuals. Societies may even, as Durkheim visualized it, be healthy (solidary) or sick (anomic); in the first case individuals are employed effectively and their morale is high, in the second individuals are at loose ends and their suicide rate increases. Society, so-to-speak, gets the individuals it needs, making its own adjustments for accidents in their individual lives. If a leader, for example, dies in office his second in command takes over. If a leader is incompetent, there is an inclination for others around him to take over functions he should have performed. It was said, by way of illustration, that Nixon during the last days of the Watergate crisis was so distracted by his impending impeachment that he was unable to function and that Alexander Haig was the *de facto* president of the United States. The state of society, in fact, is a chancy factor in individual fates.

In a world where religion has largely lost its authority, where science has become the norm of thought, and probability theory has familiarized large numbers of persons with the view that chance factors are not unique, but fall into categories of risk which are in varying degrees calculable and where, finally, collectivistic theories of social life have become more prominent, chance and accident become primarily of individual rather than of social concern. And, though it is accepted that from the standpoint of the individual chance and accident are quite significant, there are understandable reasons why it should so often be passed over in silence.

Wherever ability and achievement are valued over inherited privilege success will normally be attributed to the former. Even when in the particular case an individual's position and achievements in fact owe much more to the economic and social status of his family and class or to sheer accident, there are motives for his pretending that this is not the case, for his permitting his success to "speak for itself." In a society with a legitimizing ideology of equal opportunity, there are institutional pressures against the admission that social class position and accident are often more important than merit in success. The unsuccessful individual who complains too loudly and too often that the deck is stacked against him or that the successful owe their positions to chance rather than merit, runs the risk of being discredited, as expressing the envy and resentment of the incompetent.

When elementaristic theories, which treat society as what individuals do together rather than as something over and beyond interaction are popular, the role of chance in individual fates and social events tends to be frankly acknowledged. This was true during the seventeenth and eighteenth centuries and has generally been true for elementaristic theorists since the rise of sociology in the nineteenth century. Moreover, the frank acknowledgement of the role played by chance in their own careers and in events around them has often characterized strong, psychologically secure individuals, ironically the very individuals one would assume would take maximum advantage of whatever breaks come their way. Two examples may illustrate this.

Max Weber often commented on the role played by chance in his own career and when he undertook the examination of science as a vocation, he observed that while the highest achievements of science occur only in the service of ideas, whether or not an idea comes is a matter of chance.

> Normally...an 'idea' is prepared only on the soil of very hard work, but certainly this is not always the case. Scientifically, a dilettante's idea may have the very same or even a greater bearing for science than that of a specialist. Many of our very best hypotheses are due precisely to dilettantes... Ideas occur to us when they please, not when it pleases us. The best ideas do indeed occur to one's mind in the way in which Ihering describes it: when smoking a cigar on the sofa; or as Helmholtz states of himself with scientific exactitude: when taking a walk on a slowly ascending street... Ideas come when we do not expect them, and not when we are brooding and searching at our desks... Whether we have scientific inspiration depends upon destinies that are hidden from us, and besides upon 'gifts'.[5]

In the postwar period, Sorokin, in the most important of his autobiographical statements, called repeated attention to the role played by chance at turning points in his career. While still at the height of his power, he suddenly found himself isolated and without students at Harvard. He reports that he had decided to direct his attention to the problems of love and altruism, resolving to go his lonely way in pursuit of his private research interests, when a remarkable event occurred.

> For several reasons I was reluctant to apply for a financial grant for my research to any foundation, government, or even university. I seem to belong to the 'lone wolf' variety of scholars who, if need be, can do their work alone without a staff of research assistants or funds. On a small scale and with some reservations I can repeat what Albert Einstein said of himself: "I am a horse for a single harness, not cut out for tandem or teamwork; for well I know that in order to attain any definite goal, it is imperative that *one* person should do the thinking and commanding."... In addition, being naturally "bullheaded," I valued my independence and freedom of thought too highly to adapt my studies to the questionable interests of the managers of these institutions...
>
> One day in the winter of 1946 I received a letter which, without any solicitation on my part, eventually offered me a considerable sum for assistance in my "foolish research" and, through the fund, the cooperation of a number of eminent and younger scientists and scholars... Throughout my life I have often experienced this sort of "luck" from unanticipated sources in moments of my urgent, sometimes even desperate need. In this sense I can repeat Gandhi's remark: "When every hope is gone I find that help arrives somehow, from I know not where."[6]

To Weber and Sorokin chance is as much a part of the affairs of men as it has ever been. With appealing candor neither was inclined to assume credit for sheer luck. Both had healthy skepticism for other scholars with less generous natures. However, in his personal affairs each found opportunity in situations which others might well have viewed as disasters. To both Weber and Sorokin, the measure of a man was what he did with what he had.

An Anomalous Figure in the Forums
of Current Sociological Honor

Undoubtedly in all complex societies the observation Shakespeare tossed out in jest obtains: "Some are born great, some achieve greatness, and some have greatness thrust upon 'em."[7] Under the terminology ascribed and achieved status sociologists have been particularly concerned with the first two types of eminence which are thought, respectively, to characterize medieval and modern society. The revolutions that brought the end of the domination of the feudal and monarchical worlds and the creation of the contemporary nation-state with its twin propulsions toward mass democracy and socialism were sponsored by groups which envisioned mass education as the great ladder permitting all men to ascend to the highest level in society that his native abilities permit. Education was conceived as the primary avenue of achieved status.

One of the central dramas in the development of mass education in the nineteenth and twentieth centuries has been the need to continually revise and amend it, if it is to provide the opportunity for self-improvement and social and economic ascent to all segments of society. The equal opportunity legislation in the 1960s and 1970s is only the latest chapter in the story. Racial and ethnic minorities and women are only recently obtaining equal access to higher education and only in the 1930s had lower class and working (blue collar) youth begun to enter the institutions of higher learning in any numbers.

However, even with reduction of the number of categories of persons who are largely prevented in advance from ever being able to take maximum advantage of the educational routes to highest success in the society, higher education is still an inefficient pump for moving persons of ability to the highest levels of society. Perhaps the single most important organizational condition in American higher education, with influence over achievement and recognition, is the division between the research and the teaching institutions.[8]

A rough, convenient index to research orientation by an institution of higher education is possession of a program in graduate education. Graduate degrees are, at least in principle, awarded on the basis of demonstrated capacity for research. Professors involved in graduate training, in turn, deomonstrate their competence, in theory, by their researches and publications. Persons earning higher degrees are, thus, indoctrinated to aspire to positions in institutions with graduate and research programs. The importance of graduate education to the professional establishment of sociology is revealed by the publication of a *Guide to Graduate Departments of Sociology* by the American Sociological Association.

In the foreword to the 1980 edition it was reported that the data were collected by means of a questionnaire sent to all known departments with graduate programs in the United States and Canada ($N = 305$) and that after repeated follow-up letters and telephone calls, response was obtained from 249 graduate sociology departments: 226 American, 21 Canadian. It was further reported that in the United States, 120 of the 226 reporting departments and in Canada 12 out of 21 reporting departments offered both M.A. and Ph.D. programs (the remaining 109 American and 9 Canadian departments offered the M.A. only). The American Sociological Association's preoccupation with graduate sociology appears in the fact that it does not publish a guide to departments of sociology without graduate programs.

Further evidence of the importance of graduate training and of opportunities for research usually associated with it, appears in the repeated attempts by professional educators to rate graduate education in the United States. On the basis of criteria such as the quality of the graduate faculty, the numbers of graduate degrees granted, the number and quality of publications by the faculty, the number of research grants received or in process, the number of honors and prizes won by department members, evaluations by panels of judges, and the like, from time to time, evaluations of graduate departments have been carried through and comparative ratings published. While some reservations must be attached to the specific standing of a department in the ratings in view of the unavoidable subjectivity of some of the rating criteria, importance is routinely attached to comparative standing.

It is a source of pride to a department to be in the top five, or in the top ten though not in the top five, or in the top twenty though not in the top ten. It is generally agreed that the top-rated ten constitute the elite departments, though some persons are inclined to restrict this classification to the top five. It is noteworthy that the rating of academic departments is normally not even attempted outside the top twenty.

Much informal lore has arisen on the value of belonging to the elite departments. This is seen as "having a piece of the action." In the elite departments it is far easier to stay abreast of the trends. The more remote an individual from such centers, the greater probability that he will find himself responding only to yesterday's news. Publishers and foundations and political agencies in control of research funds routinely take membership in an elite department as evidence of a scholar's standing in his profession and among his peers. The obtaining of research funds and contracts for publication is far easier for members of the elite departments than for their colleagues in more humble locations. And even though the participants in the action of the elite departments are intensely competitive—like the participants in the stock exchange, the grain exchanges or even the diamond exchange—they have a common interest in excluding outsiders.

The lack of studies of the differential role played by the opportunities available to members of the elite, in contrast to non-elite, institutions in their achievements is itself a product of closure against outsiders. The members of any elite—academic, social, financial, industrial, or political—are disinclined to reveal the means by which they sustain their monopolies. It is usually only through the disaffection of some former member of the elite who plays traitor to his class, revealing its secrets, or the occasional memoir or confessional autobiography, that some of the cruder details become known of how an elite sustains itself and frustrates or coopts its opposition.

Elite academic institutions are in the best position to recruit superior students to their educational programs in the first place and to open their ranks to persons of ability who threaten to eclipse them from the outside, coopting them before they can become a threat. Hence, one may assume that the elite institutions possess a higher level of average ability than do the non-elite institutions. However, they are not as efficient in recruiting the available talent as the professional sports organizations are in exploiting the reservoir of available athletic ability. In fact, to some extent the organization of higher education suppresses the full expression of the ability of individuals in the non-elite institutions rather than encouraging it.

One implication of these considerations is that there are individuals in the non-elite institutions (both those with and those without graduate programs) who have as much or more ability than many individuals in the elite departments. Such individuals, despite imagination and energy rarely achieve recognition equivalent to that of their elite counterparts. They find it more difficult to find publishers or to obtain research money. They often find themselves overburdened with teaching and administrative assignments; they may be quietly discouraged by their administrations and have to run the gauntlet of the critical envy of their colleagues when they insist on writing and research. Furthermore, although there is no necessary tension between teaching and research ability, equal excellence in both at the same time is rare.

A young scientist with high potential for developing into one of the outstanding specialists of his time, but who because of contingencies, begins his career in a non-elite department has to work, at least initially, doubly hard if he hopes to match achievements with those fortunate enough to start at the top. Most of the time, he must make his break-out fairly soon or reconcile himself to the prospect of never making it. Furthermore, man's youth is his springtime or growth period. An individual who has not made his way out of the non-elite institutions by his late thirties or early forties—by which time the ordinary individual's energies, imagination, and resilience have peaked and are about to begin to recede—will probably never do so. Many persons at such times finally come to terms with their situations or recycle their expectations, orienting them to other than scientific or professional spheres.

Nevertheless it would be a mistake to envision as a tragedy the quiet service in non-elite and teaching institutions of individuals who, had circumstances been different, might have achieved the highest forums of honor in their scientific fields. To be sure, they are not, as Gray eloquently observed, deserving of contempt.

> Let not ambition mock their useful toil,
>   Their homely joys, with destiny obscure:
> Nor Grandeur hear with a disdainful smile
>   The short and simple annals of the Poor.
> The boast of heraldry, the pomp of power,
>   And all that beauty, all that wealth e're gave
> Awaits alike the 'inevitable hour; —
>   The paths of glory lead but to the grave.
> Nor you, ye Proud, impute to these the fault
>   If Memory o'er their tomb no trophies raise,
> Where through the long-drawn aisle and fretted vault
>   The pealing anthem swells the note of praise.[9]

However, one need not phrase the implications of circumstances for personal fates merely in negative terms, reminding the eminent who owe so much to chance that humility is more appropriate than arrogance. The fact that in the non-elite and teaching institutions there are persons with equivalent or greater abilities than those in the elite departments means (1) that if by some accident the entire intellectual elite were wiped away, it could be completely replaced in a generation, and (2) that the inadequate manner in which the educational system pumps the finest abilities to the top means that intelligences quite equal to those displayed by the elite will be devoted to a variety of other things: teaching, administration, and social service. Furthermore, there will always be some lone star intellectuals devoted to offbeat and out-of-phase scientific concerns which have been ignored and shunted aside by the powers at the centers of action. Not infrequently such lone scientists and scholars quietly create changes that Kuhn described as scientific revolutions or paradigm shifts.[10]

Many times persons of superior ability and intelligence in the non-elite institutions are virtual unknowns outside their localities. Unfortunately, moreover, the locality is often reluctant to acknowledge major abilities on the part of one of its members on the principle that a prophet is not without honor except in his own country. Often, only after having established himself in the outside world is he a candidate for local recognition. However, it is hard to keep a good man or woman down and individuals with major abilities often manage to make their way and win recognition despite opposition by their localities, on the one hand, and lack of reception into the circles of the elite, on the other. When this occurs, they shine like individual stars outside the galaxy of the elite, dramatizing the role of chance in scientific fates and illustrating an important principle: the elites may enjoy a monopoly of recognition and a quasi-monopoly of opportunities, but it by no means enjoys a monopoly of intelligence and ability.

In view of such considerations, it is a challenge to examine in detail the career and achievements of the kind of person of whom it is spontaneously said: What is he doing outside the elite institutions?

An interesting current example of such an anomalous figure in the forums of academic honor of American sociology is Panos D. Bardis, professor of sociology at the University of Toledo. The sociology department of the University of Toledo is a non-elite department. In the 1980 *Guide to Graduate Departments* it is listed as having only eleven full-time and one part-time faculty members and as offering only the M.A. degree. It had nine full-time and nine part-time graduate students and granted only four M.A.s in 1980.[*11*]

Panos D. Bardis, however, has a record of achievement that few persons in the elite departments can match: he belongs to 47 organizations; has held 26 editorships; is listed in 48 *Who's Who*s; and had a publication list as of October, 1981, comprising more than 363 items. His publications include nine books and one novel. He writes music, having composed 20 songs for the mandolin, and poetry, only a fraction of which has been published. Yet Bardis is not thought of in connection with the sociological elite, though many persons have heard of him, as it were, in passing. Panos Bardis is a star shining in his own light outside the milky way of social science celebrity.

Who Is Panos Bardis? Why Toledo?

Panos Demetrios Bardis was born September 24, 1924, the oldest son of Demetrios George and Kali (Christopoulos) Bardis in Lefcohorion, Arcadia, Greece, a poor mountain village in the heart of the Peloponnesus with a population of five hundred. His father owned a small coffee house and a few gardens, fields, and vineyards. The holdings were small and on barren land so that despite very hard work, much of the time there was barely enough bread to eat. Meat was in short supply, usually served only twice a year, Christmas and Easter.

A major memory from Bardis's early childhood was of ragged but clean clothing, the lack of shoes, frequent hunger, and hard work.

Demetrios, his father, was plagued all his life by acute asthma and from the age of three Panos worked in the fields with his mother. A younger brother was premature and died soon after birth. His only two sisters died at the ages of two or three. Three other younger brothers survived: George and Christos grew up to become, respectively, a merchant and a civil servant in Athens; Polynices became a professor of education in a provincial college in central Greece.

Demetrios Bardis had only two years of high school, but he had been brilliant and studious and instilled an intense love of knowledge in his oldest son. Kali Christopoulos had only finished grade school, but she, too, had developed a love of learning and possessed rare aesthetic sensitivity and native artistic talent: she never sent her children to bed without songs, poems, and stories that she composed extemporaneously. Both parents were neat, methodical, creative, and with the quiet religiosity and deep appreciation of family life which finds some of its most profound expressions in peasant, rural, and small town people the world over

As so often occurs with oldest sons who arrive when the parents are still young, idealistic, and with no other children of their own to compare them with, Panos Bardis was measured by ideal norms. Later children are inevitably judged by rather more practical or average standards of child behavior in contrast to the first born. Bardis was impressed by the perfectionism of both of his parents and internalized it as the standard against which he measured himself.

As a child Bardis worked almost all the time: at home, in the fields, at school. He so seldom had the opportunity to play that in time—like many oldest children in poor families who are given much love, put to work unusually early, and made the vehicle of high expectations—that he became something of an isolate. He had so little time for the collective play of his age mates that he became awkward and uncomfortable when he had the opportunity for it. He came to view the play of his peers defensively as frivolous and preferred to take pencil and paper and wander in the wheat fields, gathering flowers, listening to the nightingales, and catching cicadas and gold bugs.

Like his mother he developed a rich fantasy life. In the loneliness of his isolated play, the wind in the grasses sometimes seemed like the dancing footsteps of mythological figures. He envisioned himself as a kin of Pan—after all, had he not been named *Pan*-os? In these solitary adventures he wrote constantly, imagining that Pan and Artemis were nearby. At times he thought he heard the echo of their songs and the dying syllables of their laughter. Sometimes he even caught a glimpse of "ethereal nymphs and ridiculous satyrs."

Also in a manner which sometimes occurs with oldest children who are not only measured against ideal norms—which in contrast to average performances can never be fully attained—but who are, at the same time, expected to work hard and required to meet high standards of achievement, Bardis early found his interests turning inward, to learning and to intellectual mastery. To a letter of inquiry Bardis replied:

> I enjoyed studying immensely. I read everything I could and always took notes, summarizing and classifying basic ideas, facts, dates, theories, and the like in practically every field. I wrote miniature encyclopedias which I called "Panianas"! I also composed artistic works—mainly poems and plays in verse in both modern and archaic Greek. I won many prizes in grade and high school... In high school (the Lyceum), the curriculum was at the college level. I did well for two years. But because it was too expensive to continue I had (to drop out) to work for my family.

Recognition for the excellence of his intellectual achievements throughout his school years, clearly was an important additional factor in confirming the shift of his interests inward. The tasks of learning and the joy of knowing were much more attractive than external accomplishments. Also adding glamour to the world of the mind was the example of an uncle and three cousins.

> One uncle and three cousins were teachers. I loved them infinitely. And because of them, I wanted to become an educator. They lent me their books and mandolins. And that was my only "happiness" throughout childhood and adolescence! I loved to read and read and read everything, especially philosophy, which fascinated me so strangely. It made me forget my hellish sufferings.

Bardis was forced to drop out after two years in the Lyceum. Not only was it expensive, but at this time a worsening of his father's asthma jeopardized the family's meager income. Moreover, at this time the economic and political conditions that accompanied World War II were becoming more chaotic and there were hungry little brothers to be provided for. Bardis had to do what he could to help the family survive. For the remaining four high school years he wandered throughout the Peloponnesus as a peddler with a donkey. He reports that he was

> ...usually starving. Cold. Slepping in the wilderness at night. Dogs would bite me. Ignorant, suspicious peasants would beat me up...it was hellish. But I kept studying on my own and taking the final examinations every June. Since I knew nothing about the exact assignments, I would assimilate all textbooks in their entirety, which amazed my teachers. (Greeks value education!)

My publications made me famous. So the communists, when in control, tried to force me to edit their communist youth newspaper, I refused. (I've always rejected all ideological extremes.) So they locked me up. When the fascists took over (perpetual political changes), they tried the same trick. They failed. They locked me up. This occurred several times.

In 1945, three years after completing high school, Bardis visited Athens for the first time. When he saw the Acropolis he was so overcome with emotion that he wept. He took the entrance examinations for law and for medical school, coming in first in each. One medical professor was so impressed that he announced publicly that "he would like to kiss a certain Mr. Bardis who wrote 'an amazing composition'"[12] (part of the entrance examination).

However, though accepted by both medical and law school, Bardis found it too expensive to attend either. He took new entrance examinations to the Panteios Supreme School of Political and Social Sciences, passed, entered, and did extremely well.

But it was hellish again. Starving. Not attending classes. Selling envelopes, a penny a piece, all day long throughout Socrates and Athena Streets. All I earned was a small piece of bread and a few olives. My diet! And I lived in an underground room-cave near Athens. Primitive conditions. No electricity. Dirt floor. No bed. Nothing! I wanted to die. Instead, I composed a long poem,"Death and Faustian Twilight Over Athens"—a tragic, melancholic, and pessimistic poem. But I kept learning as much as possible on the steps of the Parthenon.

Bardis attended the Panteios Supreme School from 1945-1947.

In a newspaper one day, Bardis read that the Anglo-American-Hellenic Bureau of Education was offering scholarships for study in the United States. He made an appointment with its representative, a Greek-American biology professor. They conversed for a time in Greek. When the representative saw how high Bardis's grades were and realized how poor he was, he promised to do everything he could to send him to the United States. Thereupon the professor for the first time addressed Bardis in English, discovering that he was unable to speak or understand a single word. For his part, Bardis had never dreamed that in going to America he would be studying in other than his native tongue. The Bureau representative was quite disappointed, but advised Bardis to study English and come to see him again in three years.

To Bardis the suggestion that he be forced to delay taking advantage of the opportunity to study in the United States for three years was catastrophic. He purchased a cheap English grammar and poured over it day and night. In a mere three months after his initial interview with the representative of the Anglo-American-Hellenic

Bureau he made an appointment to visit him again. He gives the following account of the result:

> I went to the biologist *three months* later. He was glad to see me, but he politely reminded me, in Greek, that he had said "three years." Hesitantly, I remarked in quaint English: "Forgive me, Sir, but I am tired to speak Greek for so many years. Now I wish to converse with thee in the English tongue." He collapsed! And he called everyone into the office to come and hear my "excellent English."

> He and others helped me a great deal. I passed my English proficiency examination at the U.S. Embassy. Problems, agony, impediments, but, finally, I had my ticket and everything.

But Bardis's trials were not yet over. The story of his remarkable feat of learning and of his scholarship to study abroad were widely reported in headlines in the press throughout Greece. They shouted: "Poor Little Peddler Will Soon Be a University Professor in America." However, at three in the morning on the very day that Bardis was supposed to leave for America, he reports:

> Three in the morning. Strange noises. Pandemonium! Two huge vehicles loaded with policemen. In a few moments, they took me to the police station, beat me up, then to a dry little island southeast of Athens with hundreds of communists. A blazing June day! I almost died of thirst. I drank sea water. I became deathly ill. I was in infinite agony. I wanted to die. See my lawyer? Nonsense! No individual rights!

> Why all this? A little fascist in my village, who almost had a heart attack when he heard of my scholarship, went to the fascist police and accused me of being a communist and of having murdered 20 rightists!!!

After being held for twenty-four hours of detention and subjected to continuous interrogation, Bardis and a number of others—communists or persons suspected of communism—were jammed into the hold of a dilapidated boat, forced to stand, for they were packed too tightly to sit, given nothing to eat or drink, and though desperately fatigued, were unable to sleep. Some persons were driven to suicide by the experience. They were transported to an island in the East Aegean Sea near Turkey. The place, Icaria Island, was called the "Red Rock" since communists were exiled there.

A few policemen remained on guard by the sea; the rest of the island was given over to the communists. Bardis reports that those communists who knew him burst out laughing when they saw him. They pressured him to join them, pointing out that he had nothing to lose. However, Bardis reports, he resisted their solicitations as he

had earlier resisted the inducements of the fascists. He was beginning to fear for his very sanity and invented games in an effort to
retain a sense of reality.

> I composed countless poems—mentally (no paper, no pen). I brought
> together pairs of ancient philosophers, thought of their systems and "wrote"
> in imagination a dialogue between each pair. Like the ancient mathematic-
> ians, I drew figures on the sand and gave myself mathematical problems.
> Once I made a minor geometrical discovery, the "ditoxon," which was
> published when I later came to the United States.

> At the time, I was quite religious. As I looked through the entrance of my
> cave, I could see Patmos Island, where John wrote the Apocalypse! I recited
> many of its comforting verses. You see, I knew that St. John the Divine was
> *not* talking about Babylon. As his ancient readers very well understood he
> was attacking the power of Imperial Rome. But I was thinking of fascism and
> communism.

After 29 days on Icaria Island, Bardis reports, he escaped. Returning
to Athens he finally managed to overcome all obstacles to the granting
of his scholarship and departed for study in the United States.

In the United States Bardis earned the B.A. *magnum cum laude* at
Bethany College (1950). He began graduate study at Notre Dame
University, earning the M.A. (1953), and continued his studies at
Purdue University, earning the Ph.D. in 1955. He served as a mem-
ber of the faculty of Albion College from 1955 to 1959 and joined the
faculty of the University of Toledo in 1959, rising to full professor by
1963. He married Donna Jean Decker, a mathematician, in 1964. The
Bardises have two children: Byron Galen and Jason Dante.

Panos Bardis and Pitirim Sorokin:
Some Career Parallels

Of the available autobiographical statements by sociologists, that
of Pitirim Sorokin (1889-1968) presents the closest parallels to the
early career of Panos Bardis. Bardis was born in a rural village of the
Peloponnesus; Sorokin was born in Kokvitzy village of the Vologda
Province of Russia. Both had roots among rural or peasant peoples
who were traditionally religious (Russian Orthodox in the case of
Sorokin, Greek Orthodox in the case of Bardis). Both men shared an
intense appreciation for and loyalty to the family. Illness in the people
around them played an important role for both: Bardis's father suffered from asthma; Sorokin's mother died when he was three and his
father, whom he accompanied with his older brother on assignments
as a migrant artisan who worked on the decorations and icons of
Russian Orthodox churches, suffered from increasing alcoholism and

periods of melancholy. Hard work played an important role in the youthful lives of both men.

There were some differences as well as similarities. There seemed not to be quite the same extremes of poverty in Sorokin's background. Nor does there seem to have been anything equivalent to the break between the Sorokin boys and their father in Bardis's case. And while Bardis was an oldest child, Sorokin was the middle child between two brothers. Sibling position as between an oldest and a middle child seems to make an important ·difference in the source of the norms eventually internalized to supply the structure of an individual's conscience: older children characteristically internalize ideal norms and absolute standards by which they measure their performances the rest of their lives, middle children characteristically internalize average performances and do not usually spend a lifetime worrying as to whether they measure up. Sorokin and Bardis appear to have differed in this way.

Also from the beginning Sorokin seems to have been more comfortable in the middle of events, less of an isolate than Bardis. However, one should not carry their contrasts too far: both were very bright students, in love with learning, forced to acquire much of their education on the run. Both men looked largely to learning and education as the ladder up and out of their backgrounds. Both could dazzle their contemporaries with feats of scholarship.

Sorokin's early career was far better calculated to thrust him to the center of current events, enriching his mind and experience with insight into the major social and intellectual trends of the day. At the age of 14 he enrolled in the Khrenovo Teacher's Seminary in Kostroma Province in 1903—apparently on the first rung of the ladder that might eventually have taken him to the Russian Orthodox priesthood—just in time to experience the revolutionary ferment that was agitating these institutions. Such revolutionary ferment resulted in the Revolution of 1905. Its effects on Sorokin was electric and he converted to the cause of social change.

Sorokin's active participation in this movement led to his imprisonment for radical agitation along with many of the most exciting intellectuals and political radicals in Russia at the time. Such political prisoners transformed the prisons in which they found themselves into virtual universities of radicalism. In this environment Sorokin formed ties which facilitated his movement into university circles where he became secretary to M.M. Kovalevsky and research assistant to E. de Roberty, who were among the solidest scholars in Russia at the time. During the first phase of the Russian Revolution of 1917 he was secretary to Kerensky, but did not run afoul of the Bolsheviks until later. At the time he eventually did find himself in trouble with the Bolsheviks, Sorokin was in the process of establishing a sociology department at the University of St. Petersburg. Eventually he was forced into exile.

In the course of all such experiences Sorokin ended up by the age of thirty with a Ph.D. and one of the richest educations conceivable: he had studied the classics of Russian and western thought; gained practical experience with the work habits and research skills of some of the foremost scholars of Russian social science; he had acquired practical experience as secretary to one of the major political figures of the revolutionary period in Russia; had founded, edited, and published newspapers; had written a number of books. He was well on his way to becoming the foremost sociologist of Russia at the time of his exile.

Bardis's experience before and during the war years in Greece and his struggles to complete his education after the war stand in stark contrast to Sorokin's during comparable periods. Bardis did not find himself during his impressionable years at the center of major revolutionary events in the social changes of the twentieth century. He was not surrounded by idealistic intellectuals and scholars who recruited him to their cause and who could turn periods of imprisonment into valuable learning experiences. He did not rub shoulders with some of the most able scholars of the day serving as secretary and assistant to them, learning first hand their knowledge and skills, receiving their assistance in his own research and publication. Rather, Bardis found himself in a marginal area peripheral to the main struggle between communism and fascism. Moreover, this was at a time when whatever idealism had once been present in such centers of communism and fascism had long since been suppressed. What remained was only a cynical, brutal struggle for power over men's bodies and minds. And in marginal areas such struggles often assume a particularly shabby and petty form in which only power and ideology count and these in rather impoverished form. Bardis could only hope to achieve intellectual integrity and cultural enrichment by resisting dominant pressures in his environment rather than by embracing them and experiencing them to the full.

The contrasts in the comparative fates of the two thinkers continues into their American experience. Sorokin arrived in America with his education completed, the Ph.D. in hand, major writing and research experience to his credit, and ready to employ all he had learned in a fresh start under new conditions. He was welcomed as a celebrity all over the United States, provided with support until he could learn English, extended a series of temporary appointments, and, finally, offered his first permanent position at the University of Minnesota at a time when it was the fourth highest ranked department in the United States.

That Sorokin's apprenticeship was over and he was reaching the fullness of his powers at the time of his arrival at Minnesota is revealed in his achievement in the next seven years: he completed six major books, founding at least two new fields—rural sociology and social mobility—and writing the best book on sociological theory that had been completed to that time. At the age of 41 his reputation was such that he was invited to Harvard University to found its department of sociology. By this time he had virtually solidified his own theoretical perspective which he was eventually to describe as his integral theory of sociology—a synthesis of the first theory of sociology, positivistic organicism, with Christian theology which was to inform his *magnum opus* completed at Harvard during the 1930s, the four-volume *Social and Cultural Dynamics*.

Bardis arrived in the United States in 1948, not as a mature scholar or as a celebrity, but as an undergraduate college student. When he finally completed his graduate work and was granted the Ph.D. at the age of 31, he was initially only able to obtain a position in one of the teaching institutions. When he made his way at least to one of the institutions with a graduate program, it was in a non-elite department.

The experiences of his Greek childhood and his young adulthood in the United States had quite different effects upon Bardis's ultimate mentality than did Sorokin's experiences in Russia and the United States. Sorokin's initial movement toward Russian orthodoxy had not been deep going enough to leave more than a generalized religious aura that clung to his thinking through his life, dominating it except for the brief period of the revolutions of 1905 and 1917 when he seriously toyed with materialistic and atheistic socialism and Marxism. By and large Sorokin subscribed to a modified version of positivistic organicism; his integralism can be best described as a version of the theory which had its origin in the work of August Comte, pulled somewhat in the direction of Russian Orthodox theology. Sorokin's American experience appears only to have led to minor modifications in this emerging point of view: it seems to have been pulled in the direction of positivism during the 1920s, allowed to readjust somewhat in the direction of a religiously oriented holism in the 1930s—the time of *Social and Cultural Dynamics*—finally undergoing a more forthright readaptation to religious themes and problems in the period of his researches on love and altruism.

Bardis's experiences as a child, adolescent, and young adult did not encourage his immersion in contemporary events and intellectual trends, but sent him in search of the essence of archaic Greek culture. Even more than the great period of classical Greek culture, Bardis was attracted by the archetypes and images of Greek mythology, archetypes and images which live on in rural Greece into the present. As a child he found mysterious import in the fact that his father had named him after the mythological figure of Pan. He was moved by the fact that his father had named his brother Polynices (of Oedipus and Jocasta). He undertook the study of archaic Greek more ardently as a child than most of his age mates. He wept with emotion th first time he saw the Acropolis. Despite his poverty, he found strength in the fact that he was carrying on his studies, as it were, on the very steps of the Parthenon. Overjoyed by the impression he created in achieving an impressive mastery of English on his own in a mere three months, Bardis has rather assiduously cultivated eight languages: English, French, Spanish, German, Latin, Italian, Modern Greek, and Ancient Greek. He has been toying with Sanskrit. Bardis has been treating the entire system of Indo-European languages as if they were only so many dialects of a single language.

However, while the total effect of his experience in his homeland was to thrust Bardis's mentality ever more powerfully toward the cultural matrix out of which the whole movement of western culture proceeded, he was to escape from the poverty, ideological pressure, and political harassment of his immediate environment by his flight to America midway in his college experience. The thrust of Bardis's intellectual interests in the direction of the heroic Greek past, on the one hand, and his excitement about the prospects of a scholarship to study in America, on the other, can be seen as alternative strategies for dealing with an unacceptable present: an inward psychological movement and an external flight.

Bardis's flight to America (for this, psychologically, was how his scholarship appeared—a gratuitous ticket of the fates to utopia) was, in a sense, directly comparable to Sorokin's exile from the U.S.S.R. However, it was occurring not to a scholar who had won his spurs, but to a student still in process of completing his education, having not yet arrived at the point where he must come to terms with the adult world.

The decisions an individual makes at the time he completes his education (that is his formal education) and takes up the position where he intends to remain the rest of his life, are often the most important he will ever make. For this event marks the true end of childhood and beginning of adulthood, establishment of a mature identity and, in rough outline, the parameters of his expectation. The suppositions on which these decisions rest are more or less shared by the cohort of peer group members that constitute a generation. Such shared presuppositions mark a generation off from that of their parents and, in time, will separate them from the generation of their children. Particularly in times of rapid social change when the shared assumptions of one generation differ markedly from those of the parental and children's generations, generational tensions themselves may become an important aspect of social change. A generation, for example, that comes to its majority during a major depression will never quite see eye-to-eye with one that makes its peace with the adult world in time of unusual prosperity.   A war generation never fully understands a peace generation.

When Sorokin came to the United States the type of consolidation of his point of view which characterized his generation had already occurred. He had only to modify it to apply to the conditions he found in America.   When Bardis came to the United States, this final consolidation of his adult perspective had yet to be carried through. He was about to come to terms with the adult world, not with his Greek contemporaries in the milieu of his homeland, but in the United States with people of a different language and culture and with a very different milieu from that of Greece.   America had just emerged victorious from World War II and as the most powerful nation of the world.   However, it was also about to be swept by strange paranoia and the Cold War was beginning to dominate its international relations while it was lacerated internally by domestic McCarthyism.   In the social sciences, including sociology, scientific sociology and positivism were at a peak of popularity.   Domestic witch hunting by Nixon and the House of Un-American Activities Committee and by Senator Joseph McCarthy made it prudent to maintain sociology in a neutral zone remote from the ideological struggles of the day.

From his childhood in Greece Bardis derived the impulse to clasp the culture of archaic Greece in passionate embrace; from his period in America he was inclined to pursue a relatively pure form of positivistic methodology. The result was a mentality quite distinct from that of Sorokin.

There were, nevertheless, also many parallels between the mentalities of Sorokin and Bardis. Both men had profound appreciation of the family.   Both were physically active: Sorokin was a powerful swimmer and had a rowing machine to stay in shape; one of Bardis's hobbies is bicycling.   Both men loved music: Sorokin had deep appreciation of classical music; Bardis not cnly plays the mandolin, but writes songs for it. Both Sorokin and Bardis enjoyed gardening: flower gardening is one of Bardis's hobbies; Sorokin's flower gardens were featured many times in Massachusetts newspapers and he won numerous commendations from the Massachusetts Horticultural Society.

When reviewing Sorokin's achievements in other contexts I searched for a metaphor to characterize his orientation. I found myself struck by a splendid primitive quality that is rare these days. He was like nothing so much as an old-fashioned soldier of fortune,[13] a medieval knight, perhaps, who got lost on one of his adventures and strayed into the twentieth century. If one asks what kind of moral property held Sorokin's personality and outlook together, Sorokin himself

would undoubtedly have described it as "altrusim" or even "love."
If I had pursued the metaphor I had found appropriate to Sorokin, I
believe that I would have preferred "honor" or "chivalry."

When one searches for a metaphor to epitomize Bardis one once
again soon encounters a primitive or archaic quality, but it is most
certainly not that of a soldier of fortune. Nor will "chivalry" serve as
a designation for the moral virtue that informs his personality and
perspective, though, once again, like Sorokin, he is a decided individualist and has a parallel respect for his equals. If Bardis has a
property that stands out more than any other, it is unusual flexibility
or versatility, a property that would have been instantly recognized by
his ancient Greek compatriots as akin to their own. And the virtue to
which he unconsciously aspires is a kind of generalized excellence—
aretê—of the kind archaic Greeks sought to achieve over the range of
life. In Kitto's words *aretê* connotes

> excellence in the ways a man can be excellent—morally, intellectually,
> physically, practically. Thus the hero of the *Odyssey* is a great fighter, a wily
> schemer, a ready speaker, a man of stout heart and broad wisdom who knows
> that he must endure without too much complaining what the gods send; and
> he can both build and sail a boat, drive a furrow as straight as anyone, beat a
> young braggart at throwing the discus, challenge the Phaeacian youth at
> boxing, wrestling, or running; flay, skin, cut up and cook an ox, and be
> moved to tears by a song. He is in fact an excellent all-rounder; he has
> surpassing *aretê*.[14]

If Bardis has a role model comparable to Sorokin's unconscious
emulation of the soldier of fortune or medieval knight, it is the hero of
the *Odyssey*. He is best viewed as a son of Odysseus.

The Matrix of Bardis's Science and Art

It is quite in character for a son of Odysseus to practice both
science and art although in our world of specialists this is unusual.
The question whether science and art are contradictory manifestations
of the human spirit has been both affirmed and denied. It is of some
value to review the general question before examining the manner in
which Bardis manages to accomodate himself to both.

Whenever new developments in science and art are brought under
simultaneous inspection, an overpowering impression of the identity
of the creative process wherever it occurs tends to arise. New discov-
eries in science, logic, and mathematics, for example, often arrive in a
flash of inspiration and seem to flow as they unfold as if powered by an
inner energy of their own. Such new ideas are often experiences as
"things of beauty" by their creators or discoverers (for at this level

the lines between creation and discovery mysteriously blur). In all of the arts—music, the dance, painting, poetry—the artist seems to others to be subject to trance-like states and, indeed, may later, half-embarrassed, admit that he felt "possessed" by a mysterious force. In both science and art the creative idea often initially takes the form of a leap in thought, a metaphor that restructures the mental landscape, casting all things in the sphere of its radiance into a new relationship.

However, despite the evidence of the identity of the creative process whether in science or art and the fact that many scientists have more than average aesthetic receptivity and artistic ability and many artists have obvious talent for science, any given individual tends to be either a scientist or artist, not both. Rarely does an individual—as seems to have been the case for Leonardo da Vinci—appear to be both scientist and artist. To be sure, it has been argued that even in Leonardo's case, as an artist he was a magnificent failure.

The answer as to why a given scientist-artist or artist-scientist may be brilliant in his field but only slightly above average in the other, may lie, in part, in the functional specialization of the brain; it may also lie, in part, in the nature of the scientific and artistic processes.

The functional specialization of the left half of the human brain (in right-handed people) for language, writing, and logical thinking has long been familiar. Recent brain theory and research has developed a case for the notion that the right side of the brain (also in right-handed people) is no mere spare part or back-up system in case the primary one fails, but is also specialized for a variety of activities other than speech and logical thinking. Prominent among activities centered in the right side of the brain, seems to be qualitative judgment and intuitive thinking—mental activities which seem to have particular importance in artistic activity. This suggests that highest artistic and scientific capabilities may ultimately be proven to rest on hereditary endowment or some combination of hereditary capacity and experience which differentially draws upon right- and left-side capacities. To be sure, it is already clear that the highest levels of achievement seem to require both types of capacities.

Even apart from the possible importance of hereditary endowment and experience which differentially affects brain specialization, the relative infrequency with which the highest scientific and artistic ability seems to occur in the same person, could be related to the different character of the scientific and the artistic achievement. Science is directed outward toward the external world. It stands or falls on its capacity to explain, predict, and control. However "beautiful" a scientific theory may be in its own right, it is scientifically useless and will be cast on the scrap heap if it fails in its empirical mission. The artists's creation, by contrast, though it may work with

materials that belong to the external world, is directed inward, centered on experience itself—it is an "expression," a "realization" or a
"fulfillment." Whether the world outside corresponds to the internal
world of a given work of art may be of interest for non-aesthetic
reasons, but is of no importance aesthetically. The value of an artistic
creation is *intrinsic*.

In view of this, the rarity of highest scientific and artistic achievement by the same person may not primarily be due to accidents of
heredity and experience, but to the fact that each involves something
approaching the total commitment of an individual's thought and
energy. Once total self-commitment either outwardly toward the
understanding and control of nature or inwardly toward self-realization has occurred, an individual simply may not have sufficient
resources to make an equivalent contribution to the other sphere. The
great artist and great scientist may be like many outstanding brilliantly endowed athletes, capable of superior performance in many areas,
but forced to specialize if they are to reach their highest potentials.

A modification may be required of Robert Nisbet's thesis in *Sociology As an Art Form* where he argues the identity of science and art.

> For a long time now...we have perpetuated the delusion that art and science
> are by their nature different from one another... Behind the creative act in
> any science, physical or social, lies a form and intensity of imagination, a
> utilization of intuition and what Sir Herbert Read called "iconic
> imagination," that is not different in nature from what we have learned of
> the creative process in the arts... The artist's interest in form or style is the
> scientist's interest in structure or type... Of all the Idol's of the Mind or Prof-
> ession regnant today the worst is that which Bacon might have placed among
> his Idols of the Theatre: the belief first that there really is something
> properly called theory in sociology, and second, that the aim of all sociologic-
> al research should be that of adding to or advancing theory.[15]

In the remainder of his essay, Nisbet dismisses all considerations
of social science method and theory and details various "images"
which he argues were shared by literature and social science on the
assumption that they were aiming at the same thing. This well-mean-
ing, but misguided, formulation displays no very profound understanding of either science or art. In fact, it proposes the dismantling
of social science, transforming it into an art. But Nisbet is an essayist
—rather than a researcher (scientist)—working in a genre that is
closer to art than to science. He evidently views this as qualification
for holding theory and research in contempt. Nisbet belongs among
those contemporary humanists who experience themselves as in
tension with science. His *Sociology As an Art Form* may be a bid to
assume the leadership of the anti-science faction among the
humanists.

Were one able to invent a sociologist designed to test the validity
of Nisbet's thesis, it would be difficult to improve on Panos Bardis, for
in few sociologists alive today do scientific and artistic interests coin-
cide so smoothly in one and the same individual.   Thoughout his
career, Bardis has been productive in both spheres. Needless to say,
Bardis lacks the contempt for sociological theory and research that
inform *Sociology As an Art Form*. However, at the same time, Bardis
experiences his scientific research and writing, on the one hand, and
his songs and poetry, on the other, as distinct and different, rather
than identical, expressions of his interests.

The same general substantive concerns are, to be sure, at the
center of Bardis's scientific and aesthetic activities: sex, eroticism,
courtship, marriage, faithfulness and betrayal, education, the life
crises, responses to tragedy and death. Among issues on the periphery of Bardis's scientific and aesthetic interests are: problems and
theories of economy, politics, religion (except for personal religiosity
and archaic religion which Bardis views as preoccupied with the
universal life crises), criminology, jurisprudence, militarism, stratification, power and community. If one groups the various interests of
sociologists into three general categories—socialization, the mastery
of nature, and social control—Bardis's scientific and aesthetic activities may be said to center on socialization.

Had Bardis's substantive interests been concerned with the problems of mastery of nature and social control while he remained both
artist and scientist, one could speculate that he would primarily have
devoted his aesthetic talents to the writing of novels and plays, even
possibly to the composing of operas, rather than the composing of
songs and poems. Evidence for this is supplied by his novel, *Ivan and
Artemis*, the one work of art primarily concerned with political and
economic events, the furies that haunted his young manhood.

However this may be, the general style of Bardis's scientific research and his poetic creativity presents some interesting contrasts
despite the fact that they meet in the same substantive concerns.

The first time I encountered a major example of Bardis's scientific
procedure was when I read his paper on "The Measurement of Love:
The Orpheus-Eurydice, Zeus, and Penelope Types."[16] In the 1970s
when a radical form of anti-positivism and anti-scientism was taking
shape and the scientific and humanistic branches of social science
were threatening to go their separate ways, Bardis was exploiting
archaic Greek mythology for hypotheses to test with the latest device
of positivistic measurement. Was this tongue-in-cheek humor or
satire? I composed a sonnet commentary and sent it on to Bardis.

PN + SPN = C

As Measured by the Erotometer

"This theory has been partly based on the author's *kinetic-potential theory of human needs*, namely that PN + SPN = C, where PN represents physical needs, SPN social-psychological or nonphysical needs, and C a constant quantity of human needs... This study...presented the kinetic-potential theory of love. Three love types were distinguished: Orpheus-Eurydice, Zeus, and Penelope... The instrument employed [included] the author's erotometer..." Panos D. Bardis, "The Measurement of Love: The Orpheus-Eurydice, Zeus, and Penelope Types," presented at the International Conference on Love and Attraction, University College of Swansea, Wales, September 8, 1977 (*Social Science,* Winter 1978, pp. 33-47):

> *It's love when faithful, fair Penelope*
> *Resists the cuckold of Odysseus,*
> *Or when cold, exquisite Eurydice*
> *Again lives through the lute of Orpheus,*
> *Or even when sly, lecherous old Zeus,*
> *In swan-like guise to hide his passion's fire*
> *From those chaste maidens whom he would seduce,*
> *Indulges to the full, divine desire.*
> *Now from this mythic land of love's elation*
> *Our social science strips the non-essential,*
> *And finds beneath its passion and frustration*
> *Equations both kinetic and potential.*
> > *No longer ask if he's in love with her,*
> > *But send out for an Erotometer.*

Bardis not only accepted this good-naturedly, but published it in *Social Science,* which he edits!

Upon further acquaintance with Bardis's scientific work it became clear that the operation he performed in his essay on the "Measurement of Love" was neither an accident nor a joke. His originality as a scientist rests in considerable measure on the extent to which he reviews basic folklore, mythology, and language, beginning always with those of archaic Greece, but including also the folklore, mythology, and language of other peoples and cultures, exploiting them as sources of scientific hypotheses. Then, moving to the other end of the time spectrum, the positivistic traditions of twentieth-century social science, Bardis gathers data in survey research for statistical analysis by means of positivitistic attitude scales. Furthermore, he has approached the whole range of basic human predicaments up to and including responses to death in the same manner. In Bardis's *History of Thanatology,* for example, Bardis reviews attitudes and images of death in nearly a dozen folklores and mythologies (China, India,

Persia, Mesopotamia, ancient Egypt, ancient Greece, ancient Rome, The Old Testament and Judaism, The New Testament and Christianity, Islam, The Middle Ages, etc.) and ends his survey by proposing to solve residual problems in the sociology of death by means of two novelties, one of theory, the other of method:

> For the present, the wisest attitude toward life and death [is]...the *Alcestis complex*...[which] includes two elements, a virtuous life and the willingness to sacrifice it on the altar of the welfare of other human beings.

> Construction of a *Thanatometer* (Death Measure)...a scientific instrument to measure human feelings and ideas regarding death, would supply us with a wealth of valuable data.[17]

Bardis's scientific style seeks to lock together suggestions from the oldest of cultural matrixes (folklore, mythology, and language) and the latest refinements of positivism into a single procedure. He employs the same matrixes in his art but in a reverse movement, from present experiences to expressive realization under the forms of mythology.

The Roots of Bardis's Aesthetic Vision

Among the tenderest memories of Bardis's childhood was the habit of his mother of never putting him to bed without telling him stories, reciting poems, or singing songs which she freely extemporized at the moment. This childhood experience imprinted permanently on his mind and personality the value of fantasy and the conviction that, if need be, an individual must be prepared to supply his own. An influence in the same direction was the example of his most admired relatives who played the mandolin and sang and who loaned him their instruments, permitting him to learn to play for himself.

While many children experience similar pressures to assume personal charge of their fantasy lives, not all become artists. Such influences must fall on fertile soil and be watered and nourished by appropriate environmental stimulation if they are to result in artistic creativitiy. The stimulation of his mother, the example of admired relatives, the effect of being an oldest child and raised on ideal norms with its tendency to turn the thrust of mentality inward all obviously played a part. Nor should the importance of the illness of his father which forced Bardis prematurely to assume adult roles be ignored. In a curious dialectic, an individual forced too abruptly into the external world may have a more than usual inclination to escape into his interior world.

As is not unusual for children prematurely forced to assume adult roles, Bardis found himself between two worlds: that of adults and that of children. He had little time to play and when he did have the occasion, he was inexperienced in the collective games of his age mates. While it is rarely explored in depth there is a culture of children with its own games, myths, ideologies, its oral culture, passed largely from child to child with little or no intervention of adults. The normal individual passes through it on his way to adulthood in the given society. And the individual cut off from this child's world much of the time because of adult responsibilities, finds himself in an ambivalent situation. When working, even in a minor capacity in the adult world he experiences a sense of superiority to his age mates; when free to join their collective play he may be mortified by his lack of sophistication. He may respond to his awkwardness and embarrassment by declining to join the collective play of his age mates, becoming something of an isolate, and under redoubled pressure to find a personal substitute for the normal child's world of play.

The individual "cheated out of his childhood" by being forced too soon to assume responsibilities in the adult world may, indeed, enjoy some special rewards. He may perform whatever responsibilities he has in the adult world in such an exemplary manner as to win praise for them, resulting in his being held up as a moral paradigm to them—which of course may only win the envy and jealousy of his age mates, further estranging him from them. Also, characteristically, such a child-adult learns his school lessons so much more thoroughly than his age mates that he again wins praise from adults and is viewed as disagreeable by other children. But at the same time the child-adult is still being recognized primarily as a child, for all the most important concerns and rewards of adults are outside his sphere. He is between two worlds, outside that of children, but at best only at the door of the adult world.

On occasion this condition has opened the child-adult to approach by some adult who befriends him or her often in the interests of exploitation. At times such a child-adult is recruited into the drug culture. However, Bardis's ties to his family were also too close for the first eventuality; his internalized norms too firm for the second. Rather, as a child-adult Bardis early developed the habit of immersing himself so completely in his studies that there was no room for the ache of loneliness. And already in childhood he began making up songs and composing poetry, transforming the intensities of loneliness that crept over him whenever not lost in his studies into the ecstacy of creation. And, of course, he early began to win recognition for astonishing feats of learning and for the increasing sensitivity and imagination of his poetic creations.

The poetry of Panos Bardis falls into a number of genres, though, as is true of many original artists, they at times blur into one another: (1) satiric verse; (2) lyrics and songs; (3) philosophic poems and hymns.

The satiric verse of Bardis is generally conventional in form and carefully crafted, with considerable care devoted to its rhyming and rhythmic structure. It varies from mild and rather gentle humor (illustrated by "In the Library"[18] and "English Composition"[19]) to humorous satire (see "Faculty Party," in which the latent tension between the faculty's academic interests and the administration's financial interests inadvertently surfaces), to saddened cynicism (as in "Eternal Tests"[20] in which attention is called to the kind of doddering old professor, unfortunately all too frequent a figure on the campuses of American colleges and universities, who gives the same lectures and administers the same examinations long after time has rendered them anachronistic).

As could be expected of anyone who loves all phases of education as deeply as Bardis, the criticism, direct or implied, in his satiric verse on matters of education is usually quite gentle. He is even quite moderate when confronting the image of what higher education could be if academic achievement and scholarship were accorded the same priority sports and athletics routinely enjoy ("Sophopolis University"[21]). However, whenever academic values appear to be in serious jeopardy, as seemed to be true during the "counter-culture" revolts, demonstrations, and campus sit-ins of the late 1960s and early 1970s, Bardis tends to respond with anger (see "Protesting Protest"[22]). By and large, however, when academic life is the target of Bardis's satiric verse the tone remains good-tempered and indulgent. The tone is quite different, however, on those occasions when Bardis turns his talents for satire on national and international affairs and events. As illustrated by "The Cyprus Affair"[23] and "Nixon Diction"[24] the tone can become bitter or contemptuous.

Despite obvious talents for humor and satire, this type of verse is peripheral to Bardis's major poetic concerns. He has more serious interest in a second poetic genre: the song or lyric. It differs from his comic and satiric verse in tone. That of his satiric verse varies from reproving laughter to bitter irony—there is always some sharpness, some aggression in it. The tone of Bardis's lyrics, by contrast, is one of spontaneous happy laughter or even pure ecstasy. And while the rhythmic and rhyming structure of his satiric verse tends always to be rather rigidly conventional, that of his lyrics tends to be open and more complex. Sometimes it seems almost a response to dancing feet as a repeated dominant sound emerges (illustrated by "Polonaise"[25] and "First Kiss"[26]) which blurs the melodic line of the lyric to a point where it seems like a dance upon a trampoline of sound. There are dancing bears in Bardis's lyrics and performing elephants, acrobats, and calliopes.

Moreover, like his ancestors, Bardis loved the rocky hills and stony fields of the Peloponnesus. He found pure joy in roads of golden dust that loop over the hills and meadows as they twist toward the pale blue skies. He found peace in sunwashed meadows where goats graze. It was hardly an accident that flower gardening became a hobby, for, like his ancestors, he found endless delight in the flowers of the field and roadside. To Bardis, as to his ancestors, the flowers by pond and brook, by the road, and in the fields are symbolic moments of rare beauty beckoning out of the eternal cycle of birth, growth, fullness, decay, and death. Emotional experiences decked with garlands of flowers ever and again dominate his lyric poetry and song. Characteristic of Bardis's work in this genre are "Trilliums"[27] and "Two Scarlet Poppies."[28]

The third and most important category of Bardis's poetic creations comprises hymns and philosophic poems. They are the primary vehicle of his unique aesthetic vision. The world of mythology is central to them, but here it functions in a manner quite distinct from its role in his scientific concerns. For science, Bardis ransacks the world of mythology in search of types, theories, and hypotheses. In his hymns and philosophic poems the movement of Bardis's mentality is from contemporary ideas, situations, and experiences back to the mythological matrixes of culture in acts of expressive self-realization.

Bardis reads widely, among other things, following developments in science and mathematics. There is some evidence that he is never completely satisfied that he has assimilated new developments until he has located them aong the forms, themes, and images of mythology. An excellent example of understanding by assimilation to the mythological matrix is "The Pyrrhic of the Neutrino."[29]

Bardis's hymns and philosophical poems are generally highly symbolic. They display an intensity which suggests that they originate in some overpowering emotion triggered by some person, experience, or turn of events. His aesthetic vision belongs to that of the prophets and priest-singers and poets of old who transformed the universal experiences of man into myths and religions, into the superhuman encounters and achievements of gods and goddesses which in the end are not superhuman at all, but the encounters, achievements, moments of joy and sorrow of ordinary people objectified and seen in their universality. Moments of exhilaration in the flush of victory, despair in defeat, the intensity of simultaneous love and sorrow in the moment of separation, the afterglow of a happiness realized in its full magic only after it is past—such are at the base of Bardis's philosophic poems and hymns. He responds to such experiences by immersing himself in the mythological world of his ancestors, freely creating anew—in acts of self-expression and self-realization—in terms of the archetypes of mythology. In a sentence: Bardis's aesthetic vision arises at its profoundest level out of the conviction that the most intense self-realization is only possible under the form of mythology.

In Bardis's hymns and philosophical poems, much of the time, only in incidental hints or in outline is the precipitant experience visible so complete is the artistic transformations of the poet. "Separation on the Acropolis,"[30] to be sure, celebrates the bitter-sweet separation of lovers, but there is no way to determine when or who. "The Lost Seraph"[31] expresses nostalgic longing for a lost love, but there is no way of knowing whether it celebrates the same or a different event from "Separation." And sometimes the poet's inspiration is even less discernible. In Greek myth Adonis, a favorite of Aphrodite, goddess of love, is slain by a wild boar, but permitted by Zeus to spend four months of every year with Persephone, four with Aphrodite, and four wherever he wishes. While it is clear that the poet in "The New Adonis" identifies with the hero, it is not clear whether he intends to celebrate anything other than the periodic intense loneliness of separation from those he most loves. "Ilma's Fall" is a hymn of grief at betrayal. Peleus was a king of the Myrmidon, son of Aeacus and father of Achilles. Thetis, the chief of the Nereids (fifty daughters of the sea god Nereus) and mother by Peleus of Achilles. "Peleus and Thetis"[32] seems to be the celebration of Bardis's own courtship and marriage, but in any case, it is the celebration of all, apparently impossible, but unexpectedly triumphant, courtships and marriages. "Aegean Dream"[33] is a philosophical poem envisioning love, and, indeed, life itself as a tragic-romantic, ship-like adventure on a sea of tears. "The Second Golden Age"[34] is a hymn to transience, quietly reaffirming the notion that even the gods are mortal.

While such selected examples illustrate the manner in which Bardis's most serious poetry give expressive form to contemporary experience under the form of mythology, a final illustration, "Boze Narodzenie"[35] is also worth mentioning. For one thing, "Boze Narodzenie" is one of Bardis's most recent poems. For another, it won a prize in the International Lachian Poetry Competition of 1981 and was published in a special edition of *Poet* in March. The Lachian tongues are Polish, Czech, and Slovak. Bardis's poem, for which he received the Lachian Prize, concerns a tragic love story with Polish Christmas customs as its background. The poem also won the Kulikowski Special Award from New York's Gusto Press. "Boze Narodzenie" not only illustrates once more the manner in which Bardis's most significant poetry gives expressive form of mythology, but the manner in which he had tended to move beyond the sphere of archaic Greek mythology to embrace the mythologies of other cultures for poetic as well as scientific purposes.

Chance, Love, and Logic in the Career of a Son of Odysseus

Chance played an important role in the formation of the mind and personality of Panos Bardis. Events of his childhood turned his energies back toward Greek mythology, the deepest level of culture of his ancestors, and toward escape to America from an unhappy present. He came to terms with his childhood by taking his stand on archaic Greek culture; he came to terms with the adult world and his career as a professor of sociology in the United States by acquiring technical competence in the positivistic methodology of social science. Chance played a basic role in his completion of his undergraduate and graduate studies outside the elite institutions and his taking up a professional role in the teaching institutions.

From the outset of his teaching career Bardis began to carry out research and to write poetry, activities that can be realized only with difficulty in the teaching and non-elite institutions. He has been amazingly productive, but forced to publish primarily in minor journals and newspapers. His substantive interests have primarily centered on the sphere of socialization (education, love, courtship, marriage, the personal aspects of religion, and death) and while problems of socialization have been central to both his scientific concerns and his poetic activity, it is not clear whether it has been his preoccupation with Greek mythology from childhood that tended to confine his adult interest to this sphere or whether his academic specialization and the heavy teaching demands of the non-elite and teaching institutions forced him to spend an inordinate amount of time on this area once he had been hired to teach in it or even whether the long delay in his achieving closure in his own problems of socialization that brought with it a life-long preoccupation with problems of socialization, particularly the family.

Bardis married Carol Kingery of South Bend, Indiana, in 1953. However, shortly after the marriage she developed nephritis and was severely ill from Bright's disease for the next nine years. Since she was always ill and the marriage was childless, these years were doubly tragic to Bardis who, from earliest childhood, had looked to the family as the last haven from the tempests of the outside world.

Contrasts in the role potentially played by their domestic fates appear between the careers of Sorokin and Bardis. Sorokin, who was born in 1889, met his wife-to-be for the first time in 1907 and they married soon after. She was a student at the Bestudjeff Women's University of Petersburg. The Sorokins locked their domestic lives into place early and throughout the rest of their long productive careers they were free to turn their attention to other spheres. Elina Sorokin was a scientist in her own right. She outlived her husband and her last act was to oversee the publication of a translated volume on the sociology of hunger that they had researched together shortly after Sorokin completed his Ph.D. and had taken up teaching duties at Petersburg under the Bolsheviks—a book that was a major component in the exile of the Sorokins from Russia.

Their twenties and thirties are their most creative periods for most scholars and scientists and though they frequently do much work thereafter it is usually in spheres well established by the age of 40. At a time when the Sorokins had permanently locked their domestic lives into place, permitting him to develop life-long concern with problems of power and civilization and her to raise her sons and establish a career in the biological sciences, Bardis was struggling to make-do with a tragically ill wife. She died in 1962 and only at the age of 38 was Bardis at long last in a position to look forward to a satisfactory family arrangement. And as if by some curious quirk of fate his father who had been plagued with asthma all his life died the same year as his first wife. I have never asked Bardis whether these two events—the death of his first wife and his father in the same year—were assimilated in his dreams and the shadow of illness took flight from the back of consciousness at this time. Bardis met his wife-to-be, Donna Jean Decker, as a fellow teacher at Toledo. Two years later, when he was nearly 40, they were married. Only then, for the first time, did Bardis enter upon the fulfilling domestic life for which he had always yearned. When asked what he was most preoccupied with while writing his poetry, Bardis replied:

> Loving and giving almost my entire existence to my family, especially creating two humanitarian, idealistic, creative, and beauty-loving beings out of my Byron Galen and Jason Dante. We are also a very health family, since my philosophy, which Donna, Byron, and Jason have adopted is *Mens sana in corpore sano.*

Thus at the age of 40—a time when most persons face the midlife crisis—Bardis finally was able to bring his private sphere of socialization under satisfactory control. This may be an important clue to the life-long interest of Sorokin in problems of power and civilization and of Bardis in socialization. However, the extent to which this is true can only be determined by Bardis himself or by the biographer who someday has access to his papers.

Quite apart from what was most important in bringing it about, the close linkage between Bardis's interest in problems of socialization and in archaic Greek culture is evident. And if one employs the term ''love'' as a general euphemism for an individual's aesthetic or expressive concerns and the term "logic" as a general euphemism for his scientific concern in increasing his knowledge and control of the world, it is clear that archaic culture and mythology are the matrixes of both Bardis's love and his logic. Moreover, there are precedents for his procedure in both aesthetics and science.

Nietzsche, who had a sound classical education, employed archetypes from Greek mythology for reorientation to the science of aesthetics. The opening words of *The Birth of Tragedy* could almost stand as an explicit formulation of Bardis's scientific procedure:

> We shall do a great deal for the science of aesthetics once we perceive not merely by logical inference, but with the immediate certainty of intuition, that the continuous development of art is bound up with the *Apollonian* and *Dionysian* duality: just as procreation depends on the duality of the sexes, involving perpetual strife with only periodically intervening reconciliations. The terms Dionysian and Apollonian we borrow from the Greeks, who disclose to the discerning mind the profound mysteries of their view of art, not, to be sure, in concepts, but in the impressively clear figures of their gods.[36]

Moreover, exploitation of mythology for insight into the problems of psychology and, particularly, the unconscious, has been dramatized in the works of Jung [37] and Freud.[38] And as illustrated by Freud's use of the Oedipus complex (the guilt of a man who violates the most serious of incest taboos, even though inadvertently, against sex with his mother) as a central clue in explaining problems that accompany attainment of psychological maturity and, at the same time, reasoning, in positivistic terms, that the human psyche can only possess a limited amount of energy which if not committed one way will find other outlets and which, once committed, is unavailable for alternative use—in short, in combining theoretical clues from mythology together amount of energy which if not committed one way will find other outlets and which, once committed, is unavailable for alternative use—in short, in combining theoretical clues from mythology together with presuppositions of positivistic science—Freud exemplifies a kind of scientific style which Bardis has also made his own. In his science, thus, Bardis belongs to a distinguished tradition.

In his poetry, however, Bardis is operating in a much older style that has not been fashionable recently. His most serious poetry consists in transforming events, predicaments, and powerful emotions in contemporary life into poetic reformulations of mythic material. And in his personal lifestyle in seeking to achieve equivalent levels of excellence in both his scientific research and his poetic creativity, Bardis is pursuing an older tradition still, one, in fact, that finds its best illustrations in Renaissance Italy and classical Greece.

In this, once again, Panos Bardis is a son of Odysseus whose highest personal ideal is to achieve the generalized excellence his forefathers called *aretê*.

Notes

1. Thomas Gray (1716-1771) Elegy (Written in a Country Church Yard).

2. Shakespeare, Sonnet XXIX.

3. Machiavelli, Niccolo (1950). *The Prince and The Discourses.* With an introduction by Max Lerner. New York: Modern Library.

4. Gray's Elegy.

5. Weber, Max (1946), "Science As a Vocation," in Hans H. Gerth and C. Wright Mills, *From Max Weber.* New York: Oxford University Press, pp. 136, 137.

6. Sorokin, Pitirim A. (1963). *A Long Journey.* New Haven, CT: College and University Press, pp. 275, 276, 277.

7. In the letter from Act II, Scene V of *Twelfth Night* is a letter intended as a practical joke poking fun at Malvolio's pomposity. The letter as a whole is interesting as an example of how much change, luck, fate, and fortune were on the minds of Shakespeare and his contemporaries: "If this fall into thy hand, resolve in my stars I am above thee; but be not afraid of greatness. Some are born great, some achieve greatness, and some have greatness thrust upon 'em. Thy Fates open their hands; let thy blood and spirit embrace them; and to inure thyself to what thou art like to be, cast thy humble slough and appear fresh. Be opposite with a kinsman, surly with servants. Let thy tongue tang arguments of state; put thyself into the trick of singularity. She thus advises thee with sighs for thee. Remember who commended thy yellow stockings and wish'd to see thee ever cross-garter'd. I say, remember. Go to, thou art made, if thou desir'st to be so. If not, let me see thee a steward still, the fellow of servants, and not worthy to touch Fortune's fingers."

8. For a study of the limited role played by merit in academic careers, see Lionel S. Lewis, *Scaling the Ivory Tower: Merit and Its Limits in Academic Careers.* Baltimore: Johns Hopkins University Press, 1975.

9. Gray's Elegy.

10. Kuhn, Thomas S. (1962). *The Structure of Scientific Revolutions.* Chicago: University of Chicago Press.

11. American Sociological Association. *Guide to Graduate Departments of Sociology 1980,* p. 196.

12. Bardis observes that men often hug and kiss each other in Greece. All material for this section was obtained by correspondence with Panos Bardis.

13. Martindale, Don (1975). *Prominent Sociologists Since World War II.* Columbus, OH: Charles E. Merrill, pp. 105ff.

14. Kitto, D.F. (1951). *The Greeks.* Edinburgh: R. & R. Clark, p. 172.

15. Nisbet, Robert A. (1976). *Sociology As an Art Form.* New York: Oxford University Press, pp. 8, 9, 10, 20.

16. Bardis, Panos D. (1978), "The Measurement of Love: The Orpheus-Eurydice, Zeus, and Penelope Types," *Social Science,* vol. 53, no.1, Winter, pp. 33-37.

17. Bardis, Panos D. (1981). *History of Thanatology.* Washington, DC: University Press of America, pp. 77, 78, 79.

18. "In the Library," *American Library Association Bulletin,* 52, no.5, May, 1958, p. 297.

19. "English Composition," *Science Education,* vol. 52, no. 1, February, 1968, p. 47.

20. "Eternal Tests," *Association of American Colleges Bulletin: Liberal Education,* vol. 45, no.2, May, 1959, p. 284.

21. "Sophopolis University," *Social Science,* vol. 36, no. 4, October, 1961, pp. 254-555.

22. "Protesting Protests," *National Tribune,* September 30, 1971, p. 4.

23. "The Cyprus Affair," *National Tribune,* September 5, 1974, p. 3.

24. "Nixon Diction," *Social Science,* 49, no.4, Autumn, 1974, p. 249.

25. "Polonaise," unpublished poem.

26. "First Kiss," *Poet,* 22,no.8, August 1981, pp. 38-39.

27. "Trilliums," *The News World,* July 1, 1978, p. 9A.

28. "Two Scarlet Poppies," *HELLENIC Times,* Jan. 11,1979, p. 12.

29. "The Pyrrhic of the Neutrino," *American Journal of Physics,* vol. 33, no. 8, August 1965, p. 661.

30. "Separation on the Acropolis," *Hellenic Times,* June 29, 1978, p. 9.

31. "The Lost Seraph," *Abira Digest,* 3, no.4, Spring-Summer,1981, p. 6.

32. "Peleus and Thetis," unpublished poem, 1981.

33. "Aegean Dream," *Hellenic Times,* July 8, 1976, p. 11.

34. "The Second Golden Age," unpublished poem.

35. "Boze Narodzenie," *The Poet,* March, 1981.

36. Nietzsche, Friedrich (no date). *The Birth of Tragedy* in *The Philosophy of Nietzsche.* New York: Modern Library, p. 951.

37. Jung, Carl Gustav (1902-1959). *Collected Works.* New York: Pantheon.

38. Freud, Sigmund (1953-1964). *The Standard Edition of the Complete Psychological Works of Sigmund Freud.* 24 vols. New York: Macmillan.

Chronology :
Panos Demetrios Bardis

1897 Demetrios George Bardis, father of Panos Bardis, born in August.

1903 Kalis Christopoulos, mother of Panos Bardis, born August 6.

1924 Panos Demetrios Bardis born at Lefcohorion, Arcadia, Greece, the eldest son of Demetrios George and Kali (Christopoulos) Bardis.

1926 Yannoula, sister of Panos, born in June.

1927 Panos, aged three, expected to help out in the fields and vineyards. Continues to work part-time in the fields and vineyards and later as a peddler throughout his youth and young manhood.

1928 Yannoula dies of pneumonia. A brother, John, born prematurely in the same year dies at birth.

1930 Panos enters Demotic (elementary) school at Lefcohorion.

1936 Graduates with diploma from Demotic School; enters the Lyceum (high school) at Langadia, Greece.

1937 Birth of Sarantia, sister of Panos.

1939 Sarantia dies of measles.

1942 Panos graduates with diploma from Lyceum.

1942- During troubled period of World War II Panos becomes a peddler in
1945 the Peloponnesis. Is repeatedly under suspicion by the authorities—the Greek Communists, Italian Fascists, and Greek Fascists as they succeed one another in power.

1943 Panos spends time in Spartan prison under Italian Fascists.

1945 Panos becomes student at the Panteios Supreme School of Athens. Supports himself as a peddler in Athens from June, 1945 to April, 1948.

1947 Panos arrested by Greek Fascists, spending 29 days in an Icarian Cave.

1948 Panos receives scholarship to study in the United States.
    Takes up undergraduate studies at Bethany College, West Virginia.

1950 Panos graduates Magna Cum Laude with B.A., Bethany College.
    Begins graduate studies at Notre Dame University.

1953 Granted M.A. at Notre Dame.
    Marries Carol Kingery of South Bend, Indiana.
    Takes up graduate work at Purdue University.

1955 Granted Ph.D. at Purdue University.
    Joins the faculty at Albion College.

1957 Publishes *Ivan and Artemis,* a novel.

1958 Becomes naturalized American citizen.

1959 Joins the faculty of the University of Toledo, Toledo, Ohio.
    Takes up duties as editor of *Social Science.*

1962 Demetrios George Bardis, father of Panos, dies, February 27.
    Carol Kingery Bardis who developed nephritis soon after her marriage to

Panos in 1953 dies childless.

1963 Promoted to full professor at the University of Toledo.

1964 Marries Donna Jean Decker, December 26.

1967 Son of Panos and Donna Jean Bardis, Byron Galen Bardis, born January 21.

Publishes *The Family in Changing Civilizations*.

1970 Son of Panos and Donna Jean Bardis, Jason Dante Bardis, born December 15.

1971 Publishes *The Encyclopedia of Campus Unrest*.

1975 Publishes *History of the Family* and *Studies in Marriage and the Family*.

1976 Publishes *Future of the Greek Language in the United States*.

1977 Co-editor with Man Das of *The Family in Asia*.

1981 Publishes *History of Thanatology*.

Appointed to editorial board of "Poetry Americas."

Appointed associate editor and book review editor of *Sociological Perspectives*.

Selected Bibliography

Panos D. Bardis

Books:

1957 *Ivan and Artemis* (novel). New York: Pageant Press.
1967 *The Family in changing Civilization.* New York: Associated Educational
Services Corporation, Simon & Schuster.
1969 Second enlarged edition, *ibid.*
1971 *Encyclopedia of Campus Unrest.* New York: Exposition Press.
1975 *History of the Family.* Lexington, MA: Xerox.
Studies in Marriage and the Family. Lexington, MA: Xerox.
1976 *The Future of the Greek Language in the United States.* San Francisco:
R. & E. Research Associates.
1978 *The Family in Asia,* edited with Man Singh Das. New Delhi: Vikas.
Second enlarged edition of *Studies in Marriage and the Family.*
Lexington, MA: Ginn.
1981 *History of Thanatology: Philosophical, Religious, Psychological and
Sociological Ideas Concerning Death from Primitive Times to the
Present.* Lanham, MD: University Press of America.

Selected Essays and Attitude Scales:

1959 "A Familism Scale," *Marriage and Family Living,* vol. 21, 4 (November):340-341.
1961 "A Religion Scale," *Social Science,* 36,2 (April):12o-123.
1967 "A Dating Scale: Exhibit 3-22," in Marvin Shaw and Jack Wright,
Scales for the Measurement of Attitudes. New York: McGraw-Hill,
pp. 101-103.
1969 "A Pill Scale: A Technique for the Measurement of Attitudes Toward
Oral Contraception," *Social Science,* 44,1 (January):47-51.
"Dating Liberalism Schedule," in Murray A. Straus, *Family
Measurement Techniques.* Minneapolis: University of Minnesota
Press, pp. 26-27.
1971 "Erotometer: A Technique for the Measurement of Heterosexual
Love," *International Review of Sociology,* 1, no. 1 (March):71-77.
"A Technique for the Measurement of Attitudes Toward Morality: A
Partial Index to Modernization," in Carole Carroll and Frederick
Carroll, *Methods of Sociological Research.* Meerut, India: Sadhna
Prakashan, pp. 109-110.
1972 "A Technique for the Measurement of Attitudes Toward Abortion,"
International Journal of Sociology of the Family. 2. 1 (March):1-7.
"Infometer: An International Technique for the Measurement of
Political Information," *Revista del Instituto de Ciencias Sociales,*

No. 20, pp. 376-377.

1973 "Sexometer," in National Council on Family relations, *1973 Annual Meeting Proceedings.* Toronto, Canada, p. 13.

1974 "Vasectomy Scale: Attitudes," National Council on Family Relations, *1974 annual Meeting Proceedings.* Minneapolis, p. 105.

"Gravidometer," *ibid.*, p. 22.

1978 "The Measurement of Love: The Orpheus-Eurydice, Zeus, and Penelope Types," *Social Science,* 53, 1 (Winter):33-47.

"Coitometer," in Robert Kaplan, *et al., Group Strategies in Understanding Human Sexuality.* Dubuque, IA: Brown, pp. 144-146.

1979 "The Kinetic-Potential theory of Love," in Mark Cook and Glenn Wilson, editors, *Love and Attraction.* Oxford: Pergamon Press, pp. 229-235.

1980 "Violence: Theory and Quantification," in George Kourvetaris and Betty Dobratz, *Political Sociology: Readings in Research and Theory.* New Brunswick, NJ: Transaction Books, pp. 221-224.

1981 "The Alcestis Complex: A Thanatological Innovation," paper read at an international conference on the sociology of religions, August 29-September 3, at Lausanne, Switzerland.

INDEX

(Page numbers set in **boldface** type indicate passages where that person is the major topic involved or encompassed.)